12th

THE DEVELOPMENT OF POSITIVE OBLIGATIONS UNDER THE EUROPEAN CONVENTION ON HUMAN RIGHTS BY THE EUROPEAN COURT OF HUMAN RIGHTS

During the last thirty years the European Court of Human Rights has been developing, at an expanding pace, positive obligations under the European Convention. This monograph seeks to provide a critical analysis of the burgeoning case law concerning positive obligations, a topic which is relatively uncharted in the existing literature. Positive obligations require many different forms of action by member states, ranging from effectively investigating killings through to protecting peaceful demonstrators from violent attacks by their opponents. The contemporary significance of these obligations is graphically illustrated by the fact that it is the obligation upon states to provide fair trials to determine civil and criminal proceedings within a reasonable time that is the source of the overwhelming majority of complaints to the European Court in recent years. The study examines the legal bases and content of key positive obligations. Conclusions are then drawn concerning the reasons for the development of these obligations and areas of potential expansion are identified.

Volume 2 in the series, Human Rights Law in Perspective

Human Rights Law in Perspective

Serial General Editor: Colin Harvey

The language of human rights figures prominently in legal and political debates at the national, regional and international levels. In the UK the Human Rights Act 1998 has generated considerable interest in the law of human rights. It will continue to provoke much debate in the legal community and the search for original insights and new materials will intensify.

The aim of this series is to provide a forum for scholarly reflection on all aspects of the law of human rights. The series will encourage work which engages with the theoretical, comparative and international dimensions of human rights law. The primary aim is to publish over time books which offer an insight into human rights law in its contextual setting. The objective is to promote an understanding of the nature and impact of human rights law. The series is inclusive, in the sense that all perspectives in legal scholarship are welcome. It will incorporate the work of new and established scholars.

Human Rights Law in Perspective is not confined to consideration of the UK. It will strive to reflect comparative, regional and international perspectives. Work which focuses on human rights law in other states will therefore be included in this series. The intention is to offer an inclusive intellectual home for significant scholarly contributions to human rights law.

Volume 1 Importing the Law in Post-Communist Transitions

Catherine Dupré

Volume 2 The Development of the Positive Obligations Under the European Convention on Human Rights by the European Court of Human Rights

Alastair Mowbray

The Development of Positive Obligations under the European Convention on Human Rights by the European Court of Human Rights

A.R. MOWBRAY LLB (Warw), PhD (Edin)
Professor of Public Law, University of Nottingham

·HART·
PUBLISHING

OXFORD – PORTLAND OREGON
2004

Hart Publishing
Oxford and Portland, Oregon

Published in North America (US and Canada) by
Hart Publishing c/o
International Specialized Book Services
5804 NE Hassalo Street
Portland, Oregon
97213-3644
USA

Hart Publishing is a specialist legal publisher based in Oxford, England.
To order further copies of this book or to request a list of other
publications please write to:

Hart Publishing, Salter's Boatyard, Folly Bridge,
Abingdon Road, Oxford OX1 4LB
Telephone: +44 (0)1865 245533 or Fax: +44 (0)1865 794882
e-mail: mail@hartpub.co.uk
WEBSITE: http//www.hartpub.co.uk

British Library Cataloguing in Publication Data
Data Available
ISBN 1–84113–261–6 (hardback)

Typeset by Hope Services (Abingdon) Ltd.
Printed and bound in Great Britain on acid-free paper by
Biddles Ltd, www.biddles.co.uk

Contents

Preface

'. . . *taking rights seriously means taking duties seriously.*' *Professor Henry Shue*[1]

During the last thirty years the European Court of Human Rights has been developing, at an expanding pace, positive obligations under the European Convention. My study seeks to analyse this important, but relatively uncharted, area of the Court's jurisprudence. As we shall discover, positive obligations require many different forms of action by governmental authorities (from providing appropriate medical care to injured/sick detainees through to ensuring the ability of employees to join and use trade unions to represent their interests). The contemporary significance of these obligations is graphically illustrated by the fact that it is the obligation upon member states to provide fair trials which determine civil and criminal proceedings within a reasonable time that is the source of the overwhelming majority of complaints to the European Court in recent times.

Throughout the gestation of this book I have received valuable help from my colleague Professor David Harris and publisher Richard Hart. Over many years I have also benefited immensely from the academic guidance and friendship of Professor Keith Ewing. The School of Law at Nottingham University has provided a supportive environment, including a period of study leave, in which to undertake this piece of research. Lorna Kennedy, a post-graduate student in the School, ably produced the table of cases.

The book is dedicated to my parents, Andrew and Patricia Mowbray.

I have sought to state the law as it stood at 1 January 2003.

Alastair Mowbray
Nottingham, Easter 2003

---

[1] H Shue, *Basic Rights: Subsistence, Affluence, and U.S. Foreign Policy*, 2nd edn (Princeton, NJ, Princeton University Press, 1996) 167.

Table of Cases

1

Introduction

————◆————

I N ACCORDANCE WITH the title, the basic objective of this study is to examine the development of significant positive obligations upon state parties to the European Convention on Human Rights[1] by the European Court of Human Rights.[2] Consequently, we shall be concentrating upon the jurisprudence, *i.e.* case law, of both the original Court[3] and the current Court[4] as the judicial organ of the Convention.[5] To delimit the work within a reasonable length we shall focus upon the case law regarding the major substantive rights enshrined in the Convention.[6] Others have written on the institutional obligations, such as respondent states furnishing all necessary facilities for fact-finding missions conducted by the Court under Article 38(1)(a),[7] of member states.[8] I have evaluated the potential obligation of states found to have breached Convention rights to pay financial compensation as 'just satisfaction', under Article 41 of the Convention,[9] to successful complainants elsewhere.[10]

---

[1] Convention for the Protection of Human Rights and Fundamental Freedoms, European Treaty Series No 5 (Rome, 4 November 1950). Hereafter generally referred to as the Convention or the ECHR for the sake of brevity.

[2] Hereafter commonly referred to as the Court or the European Court for the sake of brevity.

[3] It came into existence in January 1959 and operated on a part-time basis until its dissolution at the end of October 1998.

[4] A full-time body created under Protocol 11 to the Convention for the Protection of Human Rights and Fundamental Freedoms, Restructuring the Control Machinery Established Thereby, European Treaty Series No 155 (Strasbourg, 11 November 1994). The current Court began to operate officially on 1 November 1998. See further, A Mowbray, 'A New European Court of Human Rights' [1994] *Public Law* 540 and A Mowbray, 'The Composition and Operation of the New European Court of Human Rights' [1999] *Public Law* 219.

[5] On the functions performed by the former European Commission of Human Rights and the Committee of Ministers see A Mowbray, *Cases & Materials on the European Convention on Human Rights* (London, Butterworths, 2001) ch 1.

[6] On the protection of property (art 1), right to education (art 2) and right to free elections (art 3) contained in Protocol 1 to the Convention, European Treaty Series No 9 (Paris, 20 March 1952) see A Mowbray, n 5 above, chs 16–18.

[7] Note, unless otherwise stated all references to articles refer to articles of the Convention.

[8] See eg JG Merrills and AH Robertson, *Human Rights in Europe*, 4th edn (Manchester, Juris Publishing/MUP, 2001) 317.

[9] Originally art 50 of the Convention prior to the amendments introduced by Protocol 11.

[10] A Mowbray, 'The European Court of Human Rights' Approach to Just Satisfaction' [1997] *Public Law* 647.

The Court has not provided an authoritative definition of positive obligations. However, Judge Martens defined them as 'requiring member states to . . . take action.'[11] This simple definition captures the essence of the varied obligations that we will be scrutinising below as it emphasises that their key characteristic is the duty upon states to undertake specific affirmative tasks: examples include to investigate a killing,[12] to protect vulnerable persons from serious ill-treatment inflicted by others,[13] to provide arrested persons with a prompt explanation of the reasons for their arrest,[14] to provide free legal assistance for impecunious criminal defendants,[15] to provide legal recognition of the new gender acquired by transsexuals who have successfully completed gender re-assignment treatment[16] and to deploy reasonable police resources to protect media organisations from unlawful violence directed at curbing the legitimate exercise of free expression.[17]

In the ensuing chapters we shall consider the legal bases of the major positive obligations within the dominant Convention rights. Are they derived from express textual requirements of the Convention or implied judicial creations? Where they are of the latter type what justifications have been articulated by the Court to explain their recognition and imposition on member states? Also, what methodology has been adopted by the Court to determine the existence, scope and breach of implied positive obligations? It will also be crucial to ascertain what are the precise contents of these key positive obligations, both express and implied: *i.e.* the forms of action required of states such as enacting new criminal offences,[18] re-organising their judicial systems to ensure their capacity to determine cases within a reasonable timeframe[19] and according different treatment to persons' Convention rights depending on their distinct circumstances.[20] In analysing these issues we shall, hopefully, be contributing, albeit modestly, to the wider study of the nature of the rights and corresponding obligations arising under human rights treaties. As Professors Steiner and Alston note in respect of United Nations conventions:

> To understand the significance and implications of the rights stated in the ICCPR,[21] CEDAW[22] and other human rights treaties, it is helpful to examine the related duties/obligations of states—even though human rights conventions rarely talk of duties. Attention to such duties both clarifies the significance of the related rights and

[11] Dissenting Opinion of Judge Martens in *Gul v Switzerland* 1996-I 165.
[12] For example, *Kelly v UK* (4 May 2001) below ch 2 n 45.
[13] For example, *Z v UK* (10 May 2001) below ch 3 n 2.
[14] For example, *Fox, Campbell & Hartley v UK* A.182 (1990) below ch 4 n 16.
[15] For example, *Artico v Italy* A.37 (1980) below ch 5 n 57.
[16] For example, *Christine Goodwin v UK* (11 July 2002) below ch 6 n 15.
[17] For example, *Ozgur Gundem v Turkey* (16 March 2000) below ch 7 n 18.
[18] For example, *X & Y v Netherlands* A.91 (1985) below ch 6 n 2.
[19] For example, *Buchholz v Germany* A.42 (1981) below ch 5 n 26.
[20] For example, *Thlimmenos v Greece* (6 April 2000) below ch 7 n 41.
[21] International Covenant on Civil and Political Rights (1966) 999 UNTS 171.
[22] Convention on the Elimination of All Forms of Discrimination Against Women (1979) UN Doc A/34/46.

thus helps to sort out ideas, and points to strategies of change. The effort, then, is to decompose a right into its related state duties, and thereby gain a clearer notion of the content or proposed content of the right itself.[23]

The topic of positive obligations under the ECHR has been subject to limited commentary in the existing literature. One of the earliest discussions was provided by Professor Merrills. He observed that there were several 'exceptional' Articles of the Convention which required states 'to do something', an example being Article 6(3) which obliges states to provide free legal assistance to defendants in certain criminal cases.[24] However;

> . . . the Convention is mainly concerned not with what a State must do, but with what it must not do; that is, with its obligation to refrain from interfering with the individual's rights. Nevertheless, utilising the principle of effectiveness, the Court has held that even in respect of provisions which do not expressly create a positive obligation, there may sometimes be a duty to act in a particular way.[25]

Merrills considered that the case law concerning Article 8 revealed some examples of the Court placing states under positive obligations, for example to legally recognise the family relationship between a mother and her illegitimate child.[26] He identified the principle of effectiveness, defined as 'a means of giving the provisions of a treaty the fullest weight and effect consistent with the language used and with the rest of the text and in such a way that every part of it can be given meaning,'[27] as the crucial jurisprudential tool for the development of positive obligations under the Convention. But he believed that:

> Every government is aware that by subscribing to the Convention, it places itself in a position in which domestic laws and practices may have to be modified to avoid impinging on the various liberties the Convention was brought into being to protect. What a government may not bargain for is to find itself put to considerable trouble and expense as a result of an obligation to advance particular social or economic policies which it may not wholly support. While this is not a conclusive objection to the Court's employing the principle of effectiveness to develop the law and identify positive obligations in the Convention, it unquestionably argues for caution in so doing.[28]

We shall, therefore, have to evaluate the role of this principle in the subsequent case law on positive obligations and determine whether the contemporary Court has been cautious in developing and applying these obligations.

---

[23] HJ Steiner and P Alston, *International Human Rights In Context,* 2nd edn (Oxford, OUP, 2000) 180–81.

[24] JG Merrills, *The Development of International Law by the European Court of Human Rights* (Manchester, MUP, 1993) 102–3.

[25] *Ibid* p 103.

[26] As in *Marckx v Belgium* A.31 (1979).

[27] Above n 24 p 98.

[28] *Ibid* p 106.

Several commentators have emphasised the importance of states being obliged in certain circumstances to take preventive or protective action to safeguard Convention rights. Andrew Clapham concluded:

> . . . there is now no doubt that, according to the European Court of Human Rights, the Convention creates obligations for States which may involve the adoption of measures 'even in the sphere of the relations of individuals between themselves' (*X. and Y. v Netherlands*, para. 23).[29] These measures have to go beyond the mere availability of a remedy, and, in the context of Article 8, they must be 'designed to secure respect for private life' (*X. and Y. v Netherlands*, para. 23). In the context of Article 11 the Convention may require 'positive measures to be taken, even in the sphere of relations between individuals, if need be' (*Plattform Arzte*, para. 32[30]). Close examination of these phrases suggests that the state obligation is more than a duty to provide a forum for the resolution of the dispute. The obligation to 'secure respect' goes beyond providing reparation for damage suffered. And the obligation to take 'positive measures' may mean actual expenditure and the deployment of resources to ensure that the right can be freely exercised 'without interference from private individuals.'[31]

Hence member states can be under duties to protect persons from the violation of their Convention rights from both other private individuals and public officials. Rabinder Singh QC has expressed the view that: '[t]o be effective, even civil and political rights have to be protected—and protection has a price. The right of access to the courts would be meaningless if there were no courts, or if they were not properly financed, or if only a few people could get to them owing to lack of money.'[32] He cited *Airey v Ireland*,[33] as an example of the Court imposing a 'positive duty' upon states, to provide civil legal aid for complex cases, to demonstrate how states may be obliged to protect fundamental rights. Later, Jeremy McBride's analysis of Article 2, right to life, cases determine that:

> There can be no question that there is some obligation to help those at risk of death. Furthermore, although there will always be scope for argument about whether such a risk really exists and whether enough is being done to tackle it, the developing case law precludes these issues from being treated lightly. Protection is a key rationale for the State's existence and a remedy for failure to discharge this responsibility can be found in Strasbourg.[34]

The writings of the above commentators reveal that the Court may demand that states take protective action to safeguard a variety of Convention rights. Consequently, our study must examine the types of protective measures required by the major positive obligations found within the Convention.

[29] Above n 18.

[30] *Plattform "Arzte fur das Leben" v Austria*, A.139 (1988).

[31] A Clapham, *Human Rights in the Private Sphere* (Oxford, Clarendon Press, 1993) 345.

[32] R Singh, *The Future of Human Rights in the United Kingdom: Essays on Law and Practice* (Oxford, Hart Publishing, 1997) 54.

[33] A.32 (1979).

[34] J McBride, 'Protecting Life: a Positive Obligation to Help' 24 (1999) *European Law Review Human Rights Survey* HR/43, at p HR/54.

An important exponent of Convention positive obligations has been Keir Starmer QC. He devoted a chapter of his practitioners' textbook to them.[35] In his opinion the theoretical basis for such obligations is a combination of three inter-related principles. First, the requirement under Article 1 that states should secure Convention rights to all persons within their jurisdiction. Secondly, the principle that Convention rights must be practical and effective. Thirdly, the principle, derived from Article 13, that effective domestic remedies should be provided for arguable breaches of Convention rights. Starmer identifies five categories of duties placed upon states by Convention positive obligations. A basic duty to create a national legal framework which provides effective protection for Convention rights.[36] A duty to prevent breaches of Convention rights. Starmer considers that the preventive duty arises in at least three situations: (a) where fundamental rights, such as the right to life (Article 2), are at stake,[37] (b) where intimate interests, such as family life (Article 8) are at issue[38] and (c) where Convention rights cannot be effectively protected by the legal framework.[39] The third duty identified by Starmer is that of states providing information and advice relevant to the breach of Convention rights.[40] Fourthly, the duty to respond to breaches of Convention rights, *e.g.* by conducting an investigation.[41] Fifthly, the duty to provide resources to individuals to prevent breaches of their Convention rights.[42] In a subsequent publication Starmer perceptively observed that, '[i]n many respects positive obligations are the hallmark of the European Convention on Human Rights, and mark it out from other human rights instruments; particularly those drafted before the Second World War.'[43]

Professor Feldman, like Professor Merills, has expressed the view that: '[m]ost of the rights under the Convention are negative rights, or rights to freedom from interference. However, a few rights impose obligations on the state to take positive action to protect people.'[44] He noted that some of the positive obligations are imposed expressly by the language of the Convention,[45] but '[a] more extensive and less clearly defined set of positive obligations . . .'[46] have been implied by the Court. In his assessment the impetus behind the development of implied obligations has been, '. . . the dynamic interpretation of the

---

[35] K Starmer, *European Human Rights Law* (London, Legal Action Group, 1999) ch 5.
[36] A breach of this duty was found to have occurred in *X & Y v Netherlands*, above n 18.
[37] For example, *Osman v UK* 1998-VIII below ch 2 n 12.
[38] For example, *Marckx*, above n 26.
[39] For example, *Plattform*, above n 30.
[40] For example, *Guerra v Italy* 1998-I below ch 6 n 23.
[41] For example, *Aydin v Turkey* 1997-VI below ch 3 n 30.
[42] For example, *Airey*, above n 33.
[43] K Starmer, 'Positive Obligations Under the Convention' in J Jowell and J Cooper (eds) *Understanding Human Rights Principles* (Oxford, Hart Publishing, 2001) 159.
[44] D Feldman, *Civil Liberties and Human Rights in England and Wales*, 2nd edn (Oxford, OUP, 2002) 53.
[45] For example, the obligation to provide fair trials contained in art 6(1) below ch 5.
[46] Above n 44.

Convention in the light of changing social and moral assumptions . . .'[47] This has resulted in there being, '. . . more extensive obligations on states than are immediately obvious from a superficial perusal of the text.'[48] As has already been explained, the current study will aim to provide a systematic examination of the scope of important positive obligations thereby enabling a fuller understanding of the Convention duties of member states.

In the following seven chapters we shall analyse the development of significant positive obligations under Articles 2, 3, 5, 6, 8, 9, 10, 11, 13 and 14. Each chapter will focus on one Article (with the exception of Chapter 7 which encompasses Articles 9, 10, 11 and 14 because they share many similarities) as this structure replicates the division of rights in the Convention. By examining each of these Articles separately it will be possible to discover the range of express and implied positive obligations found within the major substantive provisions and the factors underpinning their development. Furthermore, parties to proceedings before the Court and the judgments of the latter body address positive obligations in terms of the requirements of the substantive Articles. Of course, where there are links between positive obligations arising under different Articles, such as the duties to conduct effective investigations into allegations of killings or serious ill-treatment under Articles 2 and 3,[49] we shall seek to identify and elaborate them. Chapter 9 completes the study by drawing conclusions about the nature of the positive obligations analysed in the previous chapters, the history of the Court's development of these obligations and the potential for future expansion of such obligations.

---

[47] Above n 44 p 55.
[48] *Ibid.*
[49] Below chs 2–3.

2

Article 2: Right to life

The text of this fundamental provision demands that:

(1) Everyone's right to life shall be protected by law. No one shall be deprived of his life intentionally save in the execution of a sentence of a court following his conviction of a crime for which this penalty is provided by law.

(2) Deprivation of life shall not be regarded as inflicted in contravention of this Article when it results from the use of force which is no more than absolutely necessary:

    (a) in defence of any person from unlawful violence;

    (b) in order to effect a lawful arrest or to prevent the escape of a person lawfully detained;

    (c) in action lawfully taken for the purpose of quelling a riot or insurrection.

PLANNING AND CONTROL OF SECURITY FORCES' OPERATIONS

In *McCann and Others v United Kingdom*,[1] the first case before the Court involving Article 2, the applicants contended that paragraph one of this provision imposed a positive duty on states to 'protect' life. They argued that this required states to, *inter alia*, provide adequate training and exercise strict control over their security forces' operations which might involve the use of lethal force. From their perspective the security operation which ended with the lethal shootings of their three relatives by British SAS (Special Air Service) soldiers did not satisfy these Convention obligations. The Court held that, in the context of this case, the applicants' arguments should be assessed under Article 2(2) in terms of the proportionality of the official response to the perceived threat of a terrorist attack. A bare majority of the Grand Chamber (ten votes to nine) concluded that the control and organisation of the British led anti-terrorist operation in Gibraltar during early 1988 did not comply with Article 2.

> 212. Although detailed investigation at the inquest into the training received by the soldiers was prevented by the public interest certificates which had been issued . . . it is not clear whether they had been trained or instructed to assess whether the use of firearms to wound their targets may have been warranted by the specific circumstances that confronted them at the moment of arrest.

[1] A.324 (1995).

Their reflex action in this vital respect lacks the degree of caution in the use of firearms to be expected from law enforcement personnel in a democratic society, even when dealing with dangerous terrorist suspects, and stands in marked contrast to the standard of care reflected in the instructions in the use of firearms by the police which had been drawn to their attention and which emphasised the legal responsibilities of the individual officer in the light of conditions prevailing at the moment of engagement . . .

This failure by the authorities also suggests a lack of appropriate care in the control and organisation of the arrest operation.

213. In sum, having regard to the decision not to prevent the suspects from travelling into Gibraltar, to the failure of the authorities to make sufficient allowances for the possibility that their intelligence assessments might, in some respects at least, be erroneous and to the automatic recourse to lethal force when the soldiers opened fire, the Court is not persuaded that the killing of the three terrorists constituted the use of force which was no more than absolutely necessary in defence of persons from unlawful violence within the meaning of Article 2 para. 2 (a) (art. 2-2-a) of the Convention.

214. Accordingly, the Court finds that there has been a breach of Article 2 (art. 2) of the Convention.

The nine dissenting judges, including President Ryssdal and the three most senior members of the Court, issued a joint opinion in which they fundamentally disagreed with the majority's evaluation of the control and organisation of the Gibraltar anti-terrorist operation. They considered that it was essential for the Court to (1) 'resist the temptations offered by the benefit of hindsight,'[2] (2) not allow the deceased the tactical advantage of regarding members of the security forces as legitimate targets and the death or injury of civilians as of little consequence whilst the authorities needed to act within the constraints of the law and (3) take full account of the prior information received by the authorities that the IRA (Irish Republican Army) intended to mount a major terrorist attack in Gibraltar. In their view:

25. The accusation of a breach by a State of its obligation under Article 2 (art. 2) of the Convention to protect the right to life is of the utmost seriousness. For the reasons given above, the evaluation in paragraphs 203 to 213 of the judgment seems to us to fall well short of substantiating the finding that there has been a breach of the Article (art. 2) in this case. We would ourselves follow the reasoning and conclusion of the Commission in its comprehensive, painstaking and notably realistic report.[3] Like the Commission, we are satisfied that no failings have been shown in the organisation and control of the operation by the authorities which could justify a conclusion that force was used against the suspects disproportionately to the purpose of defending innocent persons from unlawful violence. We consider that the use of lethal force in this case, however regrettable the need to resort to such force may be, did not exceed what was, in the circumstances as known at the time, 'absolutely necessary' for that purpose and

---

[2] A.324 (1995), Joint Dissenting Opinion para 8.
[3] Issued on 4 March 1994. By eleven votes to six the Commission was of the opinion that there had been no violation of art 2.

So the UK did not exactly use the language of 'a positive obligation'!

Article 2: Right to life 9

did not amount to a breach by the United Kingdom of its obligations under the Convention.

Whilst not expressly adopting the applicants' language of a positive duty both the majority and minority of the Court in *McCann* scrutinised the authorities' organisation and control of the challenged anti-terrorist operation as a fundamental element in assessing whether Article 2 had been complied with. Therefore, this case represents the foundation of the Court's willingness to scrutinise the care taken by member states' relevant authorities in implementing security forces' operations.

The Court's evaluation of the adequacy of the planning and control of security forces' operations has subsequently been extended into violent situations not involving terrorists. In *Andronicou and Constantinou v Cyprus*,[4] the Court was faced with the aftermath of a domestic dispute in which the first applicants' son had held his fiancee, the second applicants' daughter, hostage in his flat. After some hours of fruitless police negotiations with Lefteris Andronicou (the hostage taker) the chief of police authorised the deployment of Police Special Forces (MMAD). The MMAD officers were briefed, by their head, that Lefteris was armed with a double-barrelled hunting gun and they should only fire (the officers were armed with machine guns and pistols) if Elsie Constantinou's (the hostage) life or their own lives were in danger. A few hours later a rescue operation was launched. Several MMAD officers fired tear gas into the flat (one officer inadvertently fired real bullets). When MMAD officers entered the flat Lefteris shot the first officer, in the shoulder, and then shot Elsie. Other MMAD officers opened fire on Lefteris and he was killed (at least 25 bullets hit him). Elsie was also hit by two police bullets. She was taken to hospital by police car (no ambulance having been on standby during the police operation) and died after emergency surgery.

The applicants complained that, *inter alia*, the Cypriot authorities had failed to minimise recourse to lethal force in the planning and control phases of the rescue operation in breach of Article 2. The Commission, by fifteen votes to three, found a violation of that Article in part due to the authorities' planning decision to utilise the MMAD (who were trained to shoot to kill when they perceived themselves to be in danger) to end a domestic dispute.[5] However, a bare majority of the Court (five votes to four) found no breach of Article 2.

183. As to the context, the authorities clearly understood that they were dealing with a young couple and not with hardened criminals or terrorists. The negotiations and the resolve to negotiate up until the last possible moment clearly indicate that the authorities never lost sight of the fact that the incident had its origins in a 'lovers' quarrel' and that this factor had to be taken into account if, in the final analysis, it transpired that force had to be used to free Elsie Constantinou. . . .

[4] 1997-VI.
[5] Report of 23 May 1996.

While there may have been shortcomings as regards, for example, the lack of crowd control or the absence of a dedicated telephone line between the police negotiator and Lefteris Andronicou, the Court considers nevertheless that the negotiations were in general conducted in a manner which can be said to be reasonable in the circumstances. . . .

185. In the Court's view the authorities' decision to use the *MMAD* officers in the circumstances as they were known at the time was justified. Recourse to the skills of a highly professionally trained unit like the *MMAD* would appear to be quite natural given the nature of the operation which was contemplated. The decision to use the *MMAD* officers was a considered one of last resort. It was discussed both at the highest possible level in the police chain of command and at ministerial level . . . and only implemented when the negotiations failed and, as noted above, in view of a reasonably held belief that the young woman's life was in imminent danger. While it is true that the officers deployed were trained to shoot to kill if fired at, it is to be noted that they were issued with clear instructions as to when to use their weapons. They were told to use only proportionate force and to fire only if Elsie Constantinou's life or their own lives were in danger. . . .

As to the decision to arm the officers with machine guns, it must be emphasised once again that the use of any firearm was never intended in the execution of the plan. However, given that Lefteris Andronicou was armed with a double-barrelled shotgun and it was not to be excluded that he had other weapons, the authorities had to anticipate all possible eventualities. It might be added that the machine guns had the advantage that they were fitted with flashlights which would enable the officers to overcome any difficulties encountered in identifying the precise location of the young woman in a dark room filled with tear gas and at the same time leave their hands free to control their weapons in the event of coming under fire. Furthermore, the use by the officers of their machine guns was subject to the same clear instructions as applied to the use of their pistols. . . .

186. Having regard to the above considerations the Court is of the view that it has not been shown that the rescue operation was not planned and organised in a way which minimised to the greatest extent possible any risk to the lives of the couple.

The four dissenting judges issued separate opinions in which they expressed the common view that they deployment of the heavily armed MMAD officers to deal with a domestic hostage situation was not a sufficiently careful or proportionate plan of action. In the opinion of Judge Palm:

> . . . I find it wholly out of proportion under the circumstances to implement a plan using *MMAD* officers who were equipped with machine guns and trained to shoot to kill when they perceived themselves to be in danger and send them into a small, badly lit room where the young couple were. It is evident that this plan and use of force exposed Elsie Constantinou and Lefteris Andronicou to a foreseeable risk of being killed. This could have been avoided had the operation been carried out with more caution and in greater conformity with the requirements of Article 2.

Similarly, Judge Jungwiert considered that:

> . . . In the rescue plan and the armed intervention there was a serious and unnecessary disproportion between the means used and the situation that had to be faced.

It is regrettable that the operation, whose only objective aim was to save Elsie Constantinou's life and arrest Lefteris Andronicou, was carried out without the necessary care and appropriate consideration for the person concerned.

Having considered the behaviour of the police special forces (*MMAD*) and especially the way in which they were commanded, for which the Government of the respondent State are fully responsible, I continue to believe that the operation was marked by a lack of organisation and appropriate equipment.

Lefteris Andronicou was hit by at least twenty-five bullets fired by automatic weapons. He collapsed after the first few shots but the officers of the *MMAD* continued to fire.

Using machine guns in a small confined space without proper lighting and knowing that the very person to be rescued was next to or in front of the person being aimed at, Lefteris Andronicou, seems to me more than irresponsible.

In order to achieve the desired objective, there were other readily available means. The manifest shortcomings of the organisation and management of the rescue operation in actual fact brought about the opposite of what was sought to be achieved. In my opinion, it was difficult to imagine a worse outcome of the operation . . .

The great divergence between the majority and minority views of the legality of the MMAD operation, assessed against the standards of Article 2, echo the divisions in the earlier Grand Chamber determination of *McCann*. The majority in *Andronicou* appear to have been willing to discount a number of significant defects in the planning and implementation of the rescue mission. Surely, for example, it would have been an obvious precaution to have an emergency medical team (comprising doctors and/or para-medics) and equipment (including an ambulance) in attendance to provide immediate treatment for any person injured in the security operation?

The Court was, however, unanimous in finding the planning and conduct of an anti-terrorist ambush by gendarmes which resulted in the death of the applicant's sister (Havva) breached Article 2 in *Ergi v Turkey*.[6] The security forces set up an ambush outside the applicant's village in south east Turkey on 29 September 1993 to capture members of the PKK (Workers Party of Kurdistan). Firing of weapons ensued and Havva was killed by a bullet when she went out onto the veranda of the family house. The Commission issued a report in which it, unanimously, found a violation of Article 2 on account of the planning and conduct of the ambush operation.[7] Subsequently, the Court reached a similar conclusion.

> 79. At the outset, the Court notes that, on the Government's own account, the security forces had carried out an ambush operation and had engaged in an armed clash with the PKK in the vicinity of the village. . . . As mentioned above, they disputed, and the Court has not found it established, that the bullet which killed Havva Ergi was fired by the security forces. However, the Court is not convinced by the Government's submission that it is inappropriate for the Court to review whether the planning and conduct of the operation was consistent with Article 2 of the Convention.

[6] 1998-IV. More generally see, C Buckley, 'The European Convention on Human Rights and the Right to Life in Turkey' (2001) 1 *Human Rights Law Review* 35.
[7] 20 May 1997.

. . . In keeping with the importance of this provision in a democratic society, the Court must, in making its assessment, subject deprivations of life to the most careful scrutiny, particularly where deliberate lethal force is used, taking into consideration not only the actions of the agents of the State who actually administer the force but also all the surrounding circumstances, including such matters as the planning and control of the actions under examination (see the above-mentioned *McCann and Others* judgment, p. 46, §§ 148–50).

Furthermore, under Article 2 of the Convention, read in conjunction with Article 1, the State may be required to take certain measures in order to 'secure' an effective enjoyment of the right to life.

In the light of the above considerations, the Court agrees with the Commission that the responsibility of the State is not confined to circumstances where there is significant evidence that misdirected fire from agents of the State has killed a civilian. It may also be engaged where they fail to take all feasible precautions in the choice of means and methods of a security operation mounted against an opposing group with a view to avoiding and, in any event, to minimising, incidental loss of civilian life.

Thus, even though it has not been established beyond reasonable doubt that the bullet which killed Havva Ergi had been fired by the security forces, the Court must consider whether the security forces' operation had been planned and conducted in such a way as to avoid or minimise, to the greatest extent possible, any risk to the lives of the villagers, including from the fire-power of the PKK members caught in the ambush.

80. . . .The Commission found on the evidence that security forces had been present in the south [of the applicant's village]. In these circumstances, the villagers had been placed at considerable risk of being caught in cross-fire between security forces and any PKK terrorists who had approached from the north or north-east. Even if it might be assumed that the security forces would have responded with due care for the civilian population in returning fire against terrorists caught in the approaches to the village, it could not be assumed that the terrorists would have responded with such restraint. There was no information to indicate that any steps or precautions had been taken to protect the villagers from being caught up in the conflict.

Accordingly, in the absence of evidence from gendarmes involved in the planning and conduct of the operation, the Commission was not satisfied that the ambush operation carried out close to Kesentas village had been implemented with the requisite care for the lives of the civilian population.

81. The Court, having regard to the Commission's findings . . . and to its own assessment, considers that it was probable that the bullet which killed Havva Ergi had been fired from the south or south-east, that the security forces had been present in the south and that there had been a real risk to the lives of the civilian population through being exposed to cross-fire between the security forces and the PKK. In the light of the failure of the authorities of the respondent State to adduce direct evidence on the planning and conduct of the ambush operation, the Court, in agreement with the Commission, finds that it can reasonably be inferred that insufficient precautions had been taken to protect the lives of the civilian population. . . .

86. Having regard to the above considerations, the Court finds that the Turkish authorities failed to protect Havva Ergi's right to life on account of the defects in the planning and conduct of the security forces' operation. . .

The analysis of the Court in *Ergi* is of great importance in the evolution of the positive obligation on states to exercise appropriate care in the planning and control of operations by their security forces. The judgment clearly elaborates the need for domestic authorities, when planning these operations, to have regard to the dangers posed to innocent bystanders from both security personnel and the suspected terrorists/criminals against whom the operation is directed. The authorities must develop and implement plans which 'take all feasible precautions . . . with a view to avoiding and , in any event, to minimising, incidental loss of civilian life.'[8] These are stringent requirements but given the importance of the right to life and the professionalism which can rightly be expected of security forces operating in democratic European states they are essential attributes of this positive obligation.

The Court has also found a member state liable for the actions of civilian volunteers acting in association with the full-time security forces in *Avsar v Turkey*.[9] The case primarily concerned the actions of village guards who are civilians appointed by the Council of Elders in particular villages or civilians who volunteer themselves and are appointed by provincial governors. Village guards are armed and have the duties of protecting the life, honour and property of persons within the boundaries of their villages. They have also been used for a wider range of security activities, such as reporting on strangers visiting their villages, identifying villagers disseminating separatist propaganda and preventing attacks on the national infrastructure (roads, bridges and dams *etc.*). The district gendarme commander is responsible for the training and supervision of the village guards in his area.

The Avsar family lived in south east Turkey and they were regarded by the authorities as having a history of involvement with the PKK. In April 1994 Abdulkerim Avsar was in prison awaiting trial on charges of terrorism. On 22 of April five village guards accompanied by a former PKK member (a 'confessor') and another unidentified man (who acted with authority as a member of the security forces) entered the Avsar family shop. They insisted that one of the Avsar brothers go with them to make a statement for Abdulkerim. After some resistance Mehmet Avsar agreed to accompany them. He was taken to a gendarmerie. Later he was removed by two of the village guards, the confessor and the unidentified person. On the 7 May the body of Mehmet, he had been shot, was found outside the city of Diyarbakir. Nearly six years later one of the village guards was convicted of murdering Mehmet whilst the other four guards and the confessor were convicted of abduction.

The brother of Mehmet complained to Strasbourg alleging, *inter alia*, a breach of Article 2 as Mehmet was in the custody of security officials and killed in circumstances that fell outside Article2(2). The Court, by six votes to one, upheld this claim.

---

[8] *Ibid* para 79.
[9] Judgment of 10 July 2001.

412. The Court is satisfied that Mehmet Şerif Avşar may be regarded as having died after having been taken into custody by agents of the State. It does not accept the Government's submission that the crime was committed by persons acting in their private capacity without the knowledge of the authorities and thereby beyond the scope of the State's responsibility.

413. The village guards enjoyed an official position, with duties and responsibilities. They had been sent to Diyarbakır to participate in the apprehension of suspects and they held themselves out to the Avsar family as acting on authority. The seventh person, a security officer, also held himself out as acting officially. The participants were, and purported to act as, agents of the State, and made use of their position in forcing Mehmet Serif Avsar to go with them. In these circumstances, the Government is answerable for their conduct.

414. In that context, the Court has already found that there was a lack of accountability as regarded the security forces in south-east Turkey in or about 1993 (see [*Mahmut Kaya v Turkey*][10] . . .). This case additionally highlights the risks attaching to the use of civilian volunteers in a quasi-police function. Notwithstanding the official denials that guards were used outside their own villages, it has been established in this case that guards were used regularly on a variety of official operations, including the apprehension of suspects. According to the regulations provided by the Government, village guards were hierarchically subordinate to the district gendarme commander. However, it is not apparent what supervision was, or could be exerted over guards who were engaged in duties outside the jurisdiction of the district gendarme commander. Nor, as the village guards were outside the normal structure of discipline and training applicable to gendarmes and police officers, is it apparent what safeguards there were against wilful or unintentional abuses of position carried out by the village guards either on their own initiative or under the instructions of security officers who themselves were acting outside the law. . . .

416. No justification for the killing of Mehmet Serif Avsar being provided, the Court concludes that the Government are liable for his death.

There has accordingly been a breach of Article 2 in this respect.

This ruling is to be welcomed as it seeks to ensure that states are accountable for both the regular security forces and also civilian volunteers. Indeed, the judgment highlights the potential dangers to respect for human rights posed by the latter category of persons. This is increased where the civilian volunteers are armed, operate in areas where they have strong personal relationships with victims and suspects, and are subject to limited supervision. Clearly if states wish to use civilian volunteers they must provide them with rigorous training as to the proper use and limitations of their legal powers and subject them to effective supervision and discipline.

We have examined how the Court has been developing the positive obligation upon states to take appropriate care in the planning and control of security forces' operations to minimise the risk to the lives of affected persons (encompassing targeted persons, such as the terrorist suspects in *McCann*, and innocent

---

[10] Below n 13.

bystanders, like Havva Ergi). The jurisprudential justifications for the imposition of this obligation are twofold. First, under Article 2(1) states are required to 'protect' everyone's right to life. This requirement is not satisfied merely by enacting laws seeking to protect the right to life, it also demands affirmative action by officials. Secondly, the circumstances where the deprivation of life are permitted under Article 2(2) have been, rightly, narrowly construed by the Court. Consequently, states have to ensure that the use of force by their security personnel (regular and civilian) meets the standard of being 'no more than absolutely necessary' for dealing with the three categories of situations where deadly force may be justified. In other words security force operations must involve a proportionate response to the threat they are aimed at combating. This is not, however, always a straightforward assessment for either the domestic authorities or the Court (*e.g.* the deployment of the heavily armed MMAD unit in response to a domestic hostage crisis in *Andronicou*).

PROTECTIVE POLICING MEASURES

A related positive obligation is the duty on member states to provide individuals with suitable measures of protection against immediate threats to their lives from third parties. This obligation was first articulated by the Court[11] in *Osman v United Kingdom*.[12] The applicants (Mrs Osman and her son, Ahmet) complained, *inter alia*, that the police in London had failed to protect the lives of Mr Osman and Ahmet as required by Article 2. Mr Osman had been shot dead and the latter seriously wounded by a former teacher of Ahmet who had developed an obsession with him. The teacher, who a year earlier had changed his name by deed poll to imitate Ahmet's, also wounded the deputy headmaster (and killed his son) at Ahmet's school. Prior to the killings the police had been informed of the teacher's attachment but they decided that the matter should be dealt with by the school authorities, as there was no sexual element to the attachment. The teacher was seen by a psychiatrist and determined to be medically unfit to work. The Grand Chamber explained the protective obligation of states in the following terms:

> 115. The Court notes that the first sentence of Article 2 § 1 enjoins the State not only to refrain from the intentional and unlawful taking of life, but also to take appropriate steps to safeguard the lives of those within its jurisdiction (see the *L.C.B. v the United Kingdom* judgment of 9 June 1998, *Reports of Judgments and Decisions* 1998-III, p. 1403, § 36). It is common ground that the State's obligation in this respect extends beyond its primary duty to secure the right to life by putting in place effective criminal-law provisions to deter the commission of offences against the person backed up by law-enforcement machinery for the prevention, suppression and sanctioning of

---

[11] It was one of the last judgments delivered by the original Court.
[12] 1998-VIII.

breaches of such provisions. It is thus accepted by those appearing before the Court that Article 2 of the Convention may also imply in certain well-defined circumstances a positive obligation on the authorities to take preventive operational measures to protect an individual whose life is at risk from the criminal acts of another individual. The scope of this obligation is a matter of dispute between the parties.

116. For the Court, and bearing in mind the difficulties involved in policing modern societies, the unpredictability of human conduct and the operational choices which must be made in terms of priorities and resources, such an obligation must be interpreted in a way which does not impose an impossible or disproportionate burden on the authorities. Accordingly, not every claimed risk to life can entail for the authorities a Convention requirement to take operational measures to prevent that risk from materialising. Another relevant consideration is the need to ensure that the police exercise their powers to control and prevent crime in a manner which fully respects the due process and other guarantees which legitimately place restraints on the scope of their action to investigate crime and bring offenders to justice, including the guarantees contained in Articles 5 and 8 of the Convention.

In the opinion of the Court where there is an allegation that the authorities have violated their positive obligation to protect the right to life in the context of their above-mentioned duty to prevent and suppress offences against the person (see paragraph 115 above), it must be established to its satisfaction that the authorities knew or ought to have known at the time of the existence of a real and immediate risk to the life of an identified individual or individuals from the criminal acts of a third party and that they failed to take measures within the scope of their powers which, judged reasonably, might have been expected to avoid that risk. The Court does not accept the Government's view that the failure to perceive the risk to life in the circumstances known at the time or to take preventive measures to avoid that risk must be tantamount to gross negligence or wilful disregard of the duty to protect life. . . . Such a rigid standard must be considered to be incompatible with the requirements of Article 1 of the Convention and the obligations of Contracting States under that Article to secure the practical and effective protection of the rights and freedoms laid down therein, including Article 2 (see, *mutatis mutandis*, the above-mentioned *McCann and Others* judgment, p. 45, § 146). For the Court, and having regard to the nature of the right protected by Article 2, a right fundamental in the scheme of the Convention, it is sufficient for an applicant to show that the authorities did not do all that could be reasonably expected of them to avoid a real and immediate risk to life of which they have or ought to have knowledge. This is a question which can only be answered in the light of all the circumstances of any particular case.

A large majority, seventeen votes to three, went on to conclude that the applicants had not been able to satisfy this test as they were unable to establish any stage in the events prior to the shootings when the London police knew or ought to have known that the Osman family were at such a risk from the former teacher. Therefore, no breach of Article 2 had occurred.

The Court's interpretation of Article 2(1) to require not only the basic rule of law responsibilities of states to enact and implement criminal law prohibition of murder and other serious offences against the person, but also to mandate the taking of reasonable 'preventive operational measures' to safeguard individuals known to be at 'immediate risk to life' from the actions of others is another example of the Court seeking to make the Convention guarantees of practical value. Nevertheless, the majority's assessment that the above test of state liability had not been satisfied by the facts of the, tragic, Osman case also indicated that the Court would be cautious in finding that domestic police and associated authorities had failed to provide adequate measures of individual protection. Governments will be able to invoke the need to prioritise the allocation of finite police resources and the avoidance of infringements of the Convention rights of suspects as countervailing factors when challenged as to whether they provided adequate protection for specific persons.

The extreme circumstances necessary before the Court will find a breach of this positive obligation were revealed in *Mahmut Kaya v Turkey*.[13] The applicant's brother, Hasan, had been a medical doctor who practised in south-east Turkey. In 1992 Hasan told the applicant that he believed his life was in danger as he had treated persons opposed to the government. In February 1993 Hasan went, with a friend, to secretly treat a wounded member of the PKK. Several days later the bodies of Hasan and his friend were found over 130 km away. Both victims had been tied up and shot in the head. The applicant, relying upon *Osman*, asserted that, *inter alia*, the Turkish authorities had failed to protect the life of his brother from contra-guerrilla entities operating in the region.[14] The Court applied the *Osman* test to determine whether Turkey was in breach of its protective obligation. A large majority, six votes to one, held that it was.

87. In the present case, the Court recalls that it has not been established beyond reasonable doubt that any State agent was involved in the killing of Hasan Kaya. There are however strong inferences that can be drawn on the facts of this case that the perpetrators of the murder were known to the authorities. The Court refers to the circumstance that Metin Can and Hasan Kaya were transported by their kidnappers from Elazığ to Tunceli over 130 kilometres through a series of official checkpoints.
. . .

The question to be determined by the Court is whether in the circumstances the authorities failed in a positive obligation to protect Hasan Kaya from a risk to his life.
. . .

89. The Government have claimed that Hasan Kaya was not at more risk than any other person, or doctor, in the south-east region. The Court notes the tragic number of victims to the conflict in that region. It recalls however that in 1993 there were rumours current alleging that contra-guerrilla elements were involved in targeting persons suspected of supporting the PKK. It is undisputed that there were a significant number of killings which became known as the 'unknown perpetrator killing' phenomenon and which included prominent Kurdish figures such as Mr Musa Anter as well as other journalists. . . . The Court is satisfied that Hasan Kaya as a doctor suspected of aiding and abetting the PKK was at this time at particular risk of falling

---

[13] Judgment of 28 March 2000.
[14] The Susurluk Report (1998) informed the Prime Minister's Office that the authorities were aware of killings being carried out by such groupings and unlawful dealings between political figures, government agencies and clandestine groups.

victim to an unlawful attack. Moreover, this risk could in the circumstances be regarded as real and immediate.

90. The Court is equally satisfied that the authorities must be regarded as being aware of this risk. It has accepted the Commission's assessment of the evidence of Bira Zordağ, who recounted that the police at Elaziğ questioned him about Hasan Kaya and Metin Can and made threats that they would be punished. . . .

The majority considered that ordinary criminal law protection was not effective in the south-east region at the time of Hasan's killing, because of basic defects in the rule of law including the removal of public prosecutors' jurisdiction over certain offences allegedly committed by officials, the repeated failure of official investigations into killings to comply with the minimum requirements of Article 2[15] and the utilisation of special courts whose composition did not satisfy Article 6(1). The government's assertion that it could not have done more to protect Hasan was also rejected.

99. . . . A wide range of preventive measures would have been available to the authorities regarding the activities of their own security forces and those groups allegedly acting under their auspices or with their knowledge. The Government have not provided any information concerning steps taken by them prior to the *Susurluk* report to investigate the existence of contra-guerrilla groups and the extent to which State officials were implicated in unlawful killings carried out during this period, with a view to instituting any appropriate measures of protection.

The Court concludes that in the circumstances of this case the authorities failed to take reasonable measures available to them to prevent a real and immediate risk to the life of Hasan Kaya. There has, accordingly, been a violation of Article 2 of the Convention.

Judge Golcuklu[16] placed primary responsibility upon Hasan for safeguarding his own well-being:

. . . surely it is for people living in the region who feel threatened to exercise greater care than others and to take their own safety precautions, rather than wait for the Government to protect them against those dangers?

Surely it was unwise and foolhardy of the deceased to leave with strangers for an unknown destination when, as the Commission found, he was aware of the risk he was running?

Unfortunately, no government is able to make security agents available to accompany persons who feel threatened or to provide them with personal protection in a high-risk area where perhaps hundreds or even thousands of people are in a like situation. Indeed, Hasan Kaya at no stage requested protection. . . .

The judgment of the Court in *Mahmut Kaya* exposed major deficiencies in the practical effectiveness of the criminal justice process in south-east Turkey combined with strong indications of illicit links between officials and nationalistic death squads. Therefore, against this horrendous factual backdrop, it is

[15] Analysed below n 37.
[16] Sitting as an ad hoc judge of Turkish nationality.

understandable that the majority considered that the authorities had not taken adequate measures to protect Hasan's life despite his dangerous (albeit presumably well intentioned) behaviour.

A similar breach of this positive obligation was found in *Akkoc v Turkey*.[17] The applicant was a former teacher and trade union activist in south-east Turkey. She and her husband (Zubeyir), also a teacher and union activist of Kurdish origin, received several threatening telephone calls. They reported the threats to the public prosecutor but no action was taken. A few weeks later Zubeyir was shot dead by an unknown person. The applicant alleged, *inter alia*, that the Turkish authorities had failed in their positive obligation to protect Zubeyir's right to life. Applying the *Osman* test a majority of the Chamber, six votes to one, determined:

> 81. . . . The Court is satisfied that Zübeyir Akkoç as a Kurdish teacher involved in activities perceived by the authorities as being unlawful and in opposition to their policies in the south-east was at this time at particular risk of falling victim to an unlawful attack. Moreover, this risk could in the circumstances be regarded as real and immediate.

> 82. The Court is equally satisfied that the authorities must be regarded as being aware of this risk. Though the Government disputed the seriousness of the threatening telephone calls, the Court finds it rather significant that the public prosecutor took no steps in response to the petitions lodged by the applicant and her husband.

The Chamber repeated the criticisms, delivered in *Mahmut Kaya*, of the effectiveness of the criminal justice system operating in south-eastern Turkey at that time and noting the public prosecutor's failure to act on the applicant's complaints regarding the death threats concluded that there had been a breach of the duty to take reasonable measures to protect the life of a person subject to immediate risk from the criminal acts of others. Judge Golcuklu was again the dissentient. He observed that:

> 1. . . . In the south-east of the country, ten times as many members of the security forces have been assigned to combat terrorism as elsewhere. Surely, under the Court's case law, the positive obligation on the State is to use best endeavours in the circumstances and is not an absolute obligation?

Unfortunately, in numerous cases[18] the Court has found that those personnel have themselves committed serious violations of Convention rights.

Another Chamber was unanimous in concluding that Cyprus was not in beach of its duty under Article 2 to protect the life of a Turkish-Cypriot who was lethally shot. In *Denizci and Others v Cyprus*,[19] the Court found that:

---

[17] Judgment of 10 October 2000. Note the Chamber was drawn from the same Section (First) as the Chamber which gave judgment in *Mahmut Kaya*.

[18] For example, in *Akkoc* the Court was unanimous in determining that the applicant had been tortured, in breach of art 3, whilst being detained by the Diyarbakir Security Directorate.

[19] Judgment of 23 May 2001.

376. . . . there is nothing to suggest that, even supposing that Ilker Tufansoy feared that his life was at real and immediate risk, he had ever reported these fears to the Cypriot police. Nor is there anything to indicate that the Cypriot authorities ought to have known that Ilker Tufansoy was at risk of attack from the criminal acts of a third party and failed to take steps to protect him.

We can conclude that outside of the extra-ordinary security situation in south-east Turkey the Court has been reluctant to determine that member states have failed to provide adequate police protection to vulnerable individuals living in the community. This is because the Court appreciates the difficult operational challenges facing domestic police forces and has been careful not to second-guess their *bona fide* practical actions. Even in a normal policing context successful applicants will need to be able to establish that the authorities knew, or ought to have known, of the immediate risk to the life of an identified individual (*e.g.* by potential victims and/or their families informing the police of the threats) and that the police (or other state agents) failed to take reasonable protective measures. These are clearly difficult burdens to satisfy.

A unanimous Chamber applied a variant of this positive obligation to evaluate the conduct of several public authorities responsible for the welfare of a prisoner in *Paul and Audrey Edwards v United Kingdom*.[20] The applicants' thirty year old son had been remanded in custody by magistrates for making inappropriate comments to women in the street (he had a history of mental illness). He was later transferred to Chelmsford Prison and placed in a cell. Another remand prisoner (Linford), who had previously been diagnosed as suffering from schizophrenia, was also placed in the same cell (because of a shortage of cells). A few hours later Linford killed the applicants' son in a violent attack. Subsequently, Linford was convicted of manslaughter by reason of diminished responsibility and placed in a secure special hospital. The applicants' contended, *inter alia*, that the relevant authorities had failed to protect the life of their son in breach of their obligations under Article 2. After citing *Osman* the Court held that; '[i]n the context of prisoners, the Court has had previous occasion to emphasise that persons in custody are in a vulnerable position and that the authorities are under a duty to protect them.'[21] The judges went on to find that many public agencies (including doctors, the police, the Crown Prosecution Service and the courts) had failed to pass on information about the health and background of Linford to the prison authorities and the latter had undertaken an inadequate screening of him when he arrived at Chelmsford Prison. Cumulatively, these failures amounted to a breach of the state's obligation to protect the life of the applicants' son under Article 2.

The tragic facts of *Edwards* demonstrate that it is not only the police who may be liable to provide protection to persons from the known (or constructively known) real threats posed by others. Where persons are imprisoned the

---

[20] Judgment of 14 March 2002.
[21] *Ibid* para 56.

public authorities (widely drawn in *Edwards*) having responsibility for the care of detainees are under a similar obligation. This is a highly desirable extension of *Osman* as prisoners obviously have limited abilities to protect themselves (*e.g.* they normally have no choice of whom they live with).

A Grand Chamber further developed this obligation of protection to encompass prisoner release schemes in *Mastromatteo v Italy*.[22] The applicant's son had been shot dead by a bank robber, as the robber tried to escape from the crime scene. The robber and two of his accomplices were serving prison sentences, for violent crimes, at the time of the robbery. However, they had been granted either prison leave or discharge to a semi-custodial regime by the judiciary. The applicant contended that the state had failed to protect the life of his son in breach of its positive obligations under Article 2. After referring to *Osman* and *Edwards* the Court held that:

> 69. . . . The instant case differs from those cases in that it is not a question here of determining whether the responsibility of the authorities is engaged for failing to provide personal protection to [the applicant's son]; what is at issue is the obligation to afford general protection to society against the potential acts of one or of several persons serving a prison sentence for a violent crime and the determination of the scope of that protection.

The judgment also acknowledged that whilst one of the basic purposes of imprisonment was to protect society, 'at the same time the Court recognises the legitimate aim of a policy of progressive social reintegration of persons sentenced to imprisonment.'[23] Taking account of the key features of the Italian prisoner release scheme (including the need for eligible prisoners to have served a minimum period of imprisonment, to have a record of good behaviour whilst in prison and for a judge to assess the danger to society if a particular prisoner was to be released), together with statistical evidence on the criminal behaviour of prisoners given early release (showing *e.g.* that the percentage of prisoners on leave who absconded was about 1%) the Court, unanimously, concluded that the Italian scheme was compatible with the state's obligations under Article 2. Also the individual judicial decisions to grant leave to the prisoners involved in the robbery and subsequent killing of the applicant's son were found to be in conformity with Article 2 because:

> 76. The Court considers that there was nothing in the material before the national authorities to alert them to the fact that the release of M.R. or G.M. would pose a real and immediate threat to life, still less that it would lead to the tragic death of A. Mastromatteo as a result of the chance sequence of events which occurred in the present case. Nor was there anything to alert them to the need to take additional measures to ensure that, once released, the two did not represent a danger to society.

[22] Judgment of 24 October 2002.
[23] *Ibid* para 72.

So Mastromatteo was an extension to the obligation of protection – No violation of Art 2

The judgment in *Mastromatteo* sought to achieve a delicate balance between the desirability of promoting social reintegration amongst prisoners and the need to protect the general public from the foreseeable risks of violent crimes being committed by prisoners given early release or home leave. The Court subjected the Italian scheme's criteria and operation to a thorough scrutiny for their conformity with the obligation upon states to protect life under Article 2. Statistically the scheme generated only a very small risk to the public. Furthermore, the Court was careful not to apply the benefit of hindsight when evaluating the release decisions taken by the Italian judiciary. Consequently, this case demonstrated the Court's sensitive expansion of the scope of states' positive obligations under Article 2.

PROVISION OF MEDICAL SERVICES

There is developing jurisprudence that the Court considers Article 2 as being capable of encompassing the obligation on Sates to provide a limited range of medical facilities and services. This possibility was explored by a Chamber of the old Court in *L.C.B. v United Kingdom*.[24] The applicant's father had been present, as a member of the Royal Air Force, at four atmospheric nuclear weapons tests conducted by the UK in 1957 and 1958. The applicant was born in 1966 and in 1970 she was diagnosed as having leukaemia. She underwent chemotherapy for several years and this had a serious effects upon her childhood and education. She continues to receive medical check-ups and is afraid to have children in case they are born with a genetic predisposition to cancer. In 1992 she became aware of a report, from the British Nuclear Tests Veterans' Association, indicating a high incidence of cancers amongst the children of personnel involved in the British nuclear tests programme. She complained to Strasbourg arguing, *inter alia*, that the respondent state's failure to warn her parents of the health/cancer risks to any children they might have as a consequence of her father's radiation exposure from the nuclear tests or to monitor her health (for such illnesses) prior to her diagnosis in 1970 amounted to a violation of Article 2. The Court was unanimous in holding that:

> 36. . . . In this connection, the Court considers that the first sentence of Article 2 § 1 enjoins the State not only to refrain from the intentional and unlawful taking of life, but also to take appropriate steps to safeguard the lives of those within its jurisdiction (cf. the Court's reasoning in respect of Article 8 in the *Guerra and Others v Italy* judgment of 19 February 1998, *Reports* 1998-I, p. 227, § 58, and see also the decision of the Commission on the admissibility of application no. 7154/75 of 12 July 1978, Decisions and Reports 14, p. 31). It has not been suggested that the respondent State intentionally sought to deprive the applicant of her life. The Court's task is, therefore, to determine whether, given the circumstances of the case, the State did all that could have been required of it to prevent the applicant's life from being avoidably put at risk. . . .

[24] 1998-III.

37. ... It notes in particular that records of contemporaneous measurements of radiation on Christmas Island[25] indicate that radiation did not reach dangerous levels in the areas in which ordinary servicemen were stationed. Perhaps more importantly for the issues under Article 2, these records provide a basis to believe that the State authorities, during the period between the United Kingdom's recognition of the competence of the Commission to receive applications on 14 January 1966 and the applicant's diagnosis with leukaemia in October 1970, could reasonably have been confident that her father had not been dangerously irradiated.

38. Nonetheless, in view of the lack of certainty on this point, the Court will also examine the question whether, in the event that there was information available to the authorities which should have given them cause to fear that the applicant's father had been exposed to radiation, they could reasonably have been expected, during the period in question, to provide advice to her parents and to monitor her health.

The Court considers that the State could only have been required of its own motion to take these steps in relation to the applicant if it had appeared likely at that time that any such exposure of her father to radiation might have engendered a real risk to her health.

39. Having examined the expert evidence submitted to it, the Court is not satisfied that it has been established that there is a causal link between the exposure of a father to radiation and leukaemia in a child subsequently conceived. As recently as 1993, the High Court judge sitting in the cases of *Reay* and *Hope v British Nuclear Fuels PLC*,[26] having examined a considerable amount of expert evidence, found that 'the scales tilt[ed] decisively' in favour of a finding that there was no such causal link. . . . The Court could not reasonably hold, therefore, that, in the late 1960s, the United Kingdom authorities could or should, on the basis of this unsubstantiated link, have taken action in respect of the applicant.

41. In conclusion, the Court does not find it established that, given the information available to the State at the relevant time (see paragraph 37 above) concerning the likelihood of the applicant's father having been exposed to dangerous levels of radiation and of this having created a risk to her health, it could have been expected to act of its own motion to notify her parents of these matters or to take any other special action in relation to her.

It follows that there has been no violation of Article 2.

Although the above judgment did not find the UK had failed to provide the applicant or her parents with an adequate level of medical advice and monitoring, the Court's analysis of Article 2(1) revealed that these types of claims could be brought as an aspect of a member state's inchoate obligation to 'take appropriate steps to safeguard the lives of those within its jurisdiction.' Arguably, the greater the scientifically verifiable risk to the life of a specific individual the more pressing the corresponding duty upon the relevant state to provide appropriate health care.

A Chamber of the full-time Court, unanimously, found the failure of the authorities to provide adequate medical treatment for a seriously injured

[25] The South Pacific island where the tests were conducted
[26] [1994] Env LR 320.

detainee was a contributory factor in concluding that a breach of Article 2 had occurred in *Velikova v Bulgaria*.[27] The applicant's partner (Mr Tsonchev) had been arrested on suspicion of cattle theft. After a few hours in police detention Tsonchev complained that he did not feel well. According to the police officers in charge of his custody they telephoned for an ambulance and a doctor and para-medic arrived soon after to examine Tsonchev. The officers claimed that the doctor stated that Tsonchev was too drunk to be examined at that time and the doctor would return when Tsonchev had sobered up. Several hours later the senior officer noticed that Tsonchev was sick and again called for medical help. The same doctor and para-medic returned and the former found Tsonchev to be dead. Subsequent test disclosed that the cause of death was acute blood loss resulting from numerous impacts upon his body. Before the Court, the government was not able to produce any documentary records concerning the medical care given to Tsonchev during his detention.

> 74. The Court finds, therefore, that there is sufficient evidence on which it may be concluded beyond reasonable doubt that Mr Tsonchev died as a result of injuries inflicted while he was in the hands of the police. The responsibility of the respondent State is thus engaged.
>
> 75. The Court also finds that there is no evidence of Mr Tsonchev having been examined, with the proper care due by a medical professional, at any time when he was in custody suffering from grave injuries.
>
> 76. The Court concludes, therefore, that there has been a violation of Article 2 of the Convention in respect of the death of Mr Tsonchev.

The seriousness of the deceased's injuries and consequent life-threatening condition obviously demanded a more thorough medical examination and treatment than the cursory appraisal he (allegedly) received. Surely states ought to be under a clear Convention obligation to provide adequate medical care for detainees as such persons are in a vulnerable position and cannot seek health care of their own volition?[28]

Indeed, during the subsequent case of *Anguelova v Bulgaria*,[29] the Court, unanimously, found a separate breach of Article 2 due to the failure of the authorities to provide timely medical care to another seriously injured detainee. The applicant's seventeen year old son had been arrested by the police on suspicion of theft. After a few hours in police detention it became apparent that his health had greatly deteriorated (he had injuries on his forehead and was breathing deeply). The officers at the police station did not call for an ambulance but recalled from patrol those officers who had arrested the detainee. Then the arresting officers went to the hospital and escorted an ambulance back to the

---

[27] Judgment of 18 May 2000. Note, a few weeks later in *Ilhan v Turky* (27 June 2000), a Grand Chamber, by twelve votes to five, held that generally non-lethal maltreatment of detainees should be examined under art 3.

[28] We shall examine this issue further in respect of the positive obligations upon states under art 3, see below ch 3 n 20.

[29] Judgment of 13 June 2002.

police station to collect the detainee. The detainee was found to be dead by the time he arrived at the hospital. The Court found that the behaviour of the police officers and the absence of action taken against those officers by the authorities constituted a violation of 'the State's obligation to protect the lives of persons in custody'[30] The behaviour of the police officers was both suspicious and obviously well below the standard of reasonable care for a seriously ill detainee. Therefore, we should welcome the Court's maturation of the positive obligations upon states to include a duty to provide timely medical care to detainees.

The Grand Chamber in the historically rare[31] inter-state case of *Cyprus v Turkey*[32] made some interesting comments regarding the health care liabilities of states under Article 2. One of the, many, complaints lodged by Cyprus was the contention that the authorities in northern Cyprus had failed to provide (or allowed the receipt of) adequate medical services to the several hundred Greek Cypriots and Maronites still living in the northern region thereby breaching Article 2. The Court, by sixteen votes to one, held that:

> 219. The Court observes that an issue may arise under Article 2 of the Convention where it is shown that the authorities of a Contracting State put an individual's life at risk through the denial of health care which they have undertaken to make available to the population generally. It notes in this connection that Article 2 § 1 of the Convention enjoins the State not only to refrain from the intentional and unlawful taking of life, but also to take appropriate steps to safeguard the lives of those within its jurisdiction (see the *L.C.B. v the United Kingdom* judgment of 9 June 1998, *Reports* 1998-III, p. 1403, § 36). It notes, however, that the Commission was unable to establish on the evidence that the 'TRNC'[33] authorities deliberately withheld medical treatment from the population concerned or adopted a practice of delaying the processing of requests of patients to receive medical treatment in the south. It observes that during the period under consideration medical visits were indeed hampered on account of restrictions imposed by the 'TRNC' authorities on the movement of the populations concerned and that in certain cases delays did occur. However, it has not been established that the lives of any patients were put in danger on account of delay in individual cases. It is also to be observed that neither the Greek-Cypriot nor Maronite populations were prevented from availing themselves of medical services including hospitals in the north. The applicant Government are critical of the level of health care available in the north. However, the Court does not consider it necessary to examine in this case the extent to which Article 2 of the Convention may impose an obligation on a Contracting State to make available a certain standard of health care.
> . . .

---

[30] *Ibid* para 130.

[31] This was only the second inter-State case to reach the Court for determination. The first inter-State case judged by the Court was *Ireland v UK* A.25 (1978).

[32] Judgment of 10 May 2001. For a commentary by Judge Loucaides (who did not participate in the case) see, Loukis G Loucaides, 'The Judgment of the European Court of Human Rights in the Case of Cyprus v Turkey' (2002) 15 *Leiden Journal of International Law* 225.

[33] The 'Turkish Republic of Northern Cyprus' a self-proclaimed entity, not recognised by the international community (except Turkey), exercising governmental powers over northern Cyprus.

221. The Court concludes that no violation of Article 2 of the Convention has been established by virtue of an alleged practice of denying access to medical services to Greek Cypriots and Maronites living in northern Cyprus.

Whilst the Court did not find a breach regarding the above health care complaints, the *Cyprus* judgment refined the earlier *L.C.B.* ruling to expressly provide that states may be liable under Article 2 for witholding from an individual life-saving medical care which they have promised to make generally available. The significance of this obligation is that it is left up to particular states to define their own level of health care provision. Only if a state fails to meet its own declared standard, in a life threatening case, could Article 2 be invoked. However, the Court went on tantalisingly to suggest that Article 2 may also require the provision of a minimum level of health care by member states. Such a development could be justified jurisprudentially through the protean nature of the overarching obligation upon states to protect everyone's right to life under Article 2(1). The Court is, nevertheless, being very cautious in mandating the provision of specific health care measures under this Article. No doubt the judges are highly sensitive to the expanding range of member states and the consequent diversity in health care provision due to wide differences in national economic resources.[34] Therefore, the positive obligation regarding the provision of medical care is at an early stage of development under Article 2.

Even when medical care is provided by the private sector states retain a regulatory role, as was confirmed by a Grand Chamber in *Calvelli and Ciglio v Italy*.[35] The applicants' baby had died two days after birth in a private clinic. Six years later the responsible doctor (and joint owner of the clinic) was found guilty of involuntary manslaughter. He successfully appealed against his conviction to the Court of Cassation and by the time his case was sent back for retrial it had become statute barred. The applicants, who had been civil parties to the criminal proceedings, settled their claims against the doctor/clinic when the latter's insurers agreed to pay them 95 million Lire compensation. The applicants claimed that, *inter alia*, the inability to prosecute the doctor, because of delays in the proceedings and the time-bar, constituted a violation of Article 2. After referring to *McCann* and *L.C.B.,* the Court stated that:

49. . . . . The aforementioned positive obligations therefore require States to make regulations compelling hospitals, whether public or private, to adopt appropriate measures for the protection of patients' lives. They also require an effective independent judicial system to be set up so that the cause of death of patients in the care of the medical profession, whether in the public or the private sector, can be determined and those responsible made accountable . . .

The Court then examined the Italian judicial response to the death of the applicants' baby:

[34] For example, in the late 1990s Denmark had a per capita average income of $14,090 whereas Georgia's was $1,060.
[35] Judgment of 17 January 2002.

51. . . . if the infringement of the right to life or to personal integrity is not caused intentionally, the positive obligation imposed by Article 2 to set up an effective judicial system does not necessarily require the provision of a criminal-law remedy in every case. In the specific sphere of medical negligence the obligation may for instance also be satisfied if the legal system affords victims a remedy in the civil courts, either alone or in conjunction with a remedy in the criminal courts, enabling any liability of the doctors concerned to be established and any appropriate civil redress, such as an order for damages and for the publication of the decision, to be obtained. Disciplinary measures may also be envisaged.

According to a large majority, fourteen votes to three, as the applicants had entered into a voluntary settlement of their civil proceedings against the doctor they had deprived themselves of the 'best means'[36] of a judicial determination of the doctor's responsibility and could no longer claim to be a 'victim' of a breach of the Convention.

The determination in *Calvelli and Ciglio* was rather lenient to the state as the delayed and eventually time-barred prosecution of the doctor was not considered to amount to a breach of Article 2. In their joint dissenting opinion Judges Rozakis and Bonello expressed the belief that, '. . . considering civil proceedings as a satisfactory means of recourse satisfying the requirements of Article 2 amounts to a debasement of the protection of the right to life provided for by this Article; it amounts to a "privatisation" of the protection of the right to life.' However, at least the Grand Chamber held states are under a general obligation to regulate the provision of medical services.

TO INVESTIGATE KILLINGS

This implied positive obligation was first articulated by a Grand Chamber of the original Court in *McCann v United Kingdom*.[37] The Court held that, '. . . there should be some form of effective official investigation when individuals have been killed as a result of the use of force by, *inter alios*, agents of the State.'[38] In subsequent cases the Court has gradually broadened the circumstances where the obligation arises. For example, three years later in *Ergi v Turkey*,[39] a unanimous Chamber found Turkey to be in breach of this obligation even though the Court was not satisfied beyond reasonable doubt that the victim had been shot by government security personnel during a counter-terrorist ambush. Developing the earlier Grand Chamber's elaboration of the preconditions necessary to trigger the state's duty to undertake such an inquiry the Court ruled that:

---

[36] *Ibid* para 55.

[37] Above n 1. This topic has also been examined in A Mowbray, 'Duties of Investigation Under the European Convention on Human Rights' (2002) 51 *International and Comparative Law Quarterly* 435.

[38] *Ibid* para 161.

[39] Above n 6.

82. . . . this obligation is not confined to cases where it has been established that the killing was caused by an agent of the State. Nor is it decisive whether members of the deceased's family or others have lodged a formal complaint about the killing with the relevant investigatory authority. In the case under consideration, the mere knowledge of the killing on the part of the authorities gave rise *ipso facto* to an obligation under Article 2 of the Convention to carry out an effective investigation into the circumstances surrounding the death.

Furthermore, a Grand Chamber of the full-time Court has held that the obligation can additionally exist in situations where it has not been conclusively established that a person has been unlawfully killed. In *Cyprus v Turkey*[40] the Court noted that the evidence before it did not establish that the alleged 1,485 missing persons detained or killed by the Turkish military forces, or their supporters, during the 1974 military occupation of the northern part of Cyprus had actually been unlawfully killed. Nevertheless, the procedural obligation to conduct an effective investigation, . . . also arises upon proof of an arguable claim that an individual who was last seen in the custody of the state, subsequently disappeared in a context which may be considered life-threatening.[41] The Court, by sixteen votes to one, concluded that Cyprus had satisfied this burden:

133. . . . the evidence bears out the applicant Government's claim that many persons now missing were detained either by Turkish or Turkish-Cypriot forces. Their detention occurred at a time when the conduct of military operations was accompanied by arrests and killings on a large scale. The Commission correctly described the situation as life-threatening. . . .

134. That the missing persons disappeared against this background cannot be denied. The Court cannot but note that the authorities of the respondent State have never undertaken any investigation into the claims made by the relatives of the missing persons that the latter had disappeared after being detained in circumstances in which there was real cause to fear for their welfare. . . . No attempt was made to identify the names of the persons who were reportedly released from Turkish custody into the hands of Turkish-Cypriot paramilitaries or to inquire into the whereabouts of the places where the bodies were disposed of. It does not appear either that any official inquiry was made into the claim that Greek-Cypriot prisoners were transferred to Turkey. . . .

136. Having regard to the above considerations, the Court concludes that there has been a continuing violation of Article 2 on account of the failure of the authorities of the respondent State to conduct an effective investigation aimed at clarifying the whereabouts and fate of Greek-Cypriot missing persons who disappeared in life-threatening circumstances.

Consequently, where public authorities of member states are aware that a person has been killed, either by a public official or another private person, or they are confronted with an arguable claim that a detainee has disappeared in

---

[40] Above n 32.
[41] *Ibid* para 132.

life-threatening circumstances they are now under a Convention positive obligation to diligently investigate the causes and circumstances of the death/disappearance.

The next questions we must address are why has the Court developed such an obligation and upon what jurisprudential foundations has it been constructed? In *McCann* the judgment stated that:

> 161. The Court confines itself to noting, like the Commission, that a general legal prohibition of arbitrary killing by the agents of the State would be ineffective, in practice, if there existed no procedure for reviewing the lawfulness of the use of lethal force by State authorities. The obligation to protect the right to life under this provision (art. 2), read in conjunction with the State's general duty under Article 1 (art. 2+1) of the Convention to 'secure to everyone within their jurisdiction the rights and freedoms defined in [the] Convention', requires by implication that there should be some form of effective official investigation when individuals have been killed as a result of the use of force by, *inter alios*, agents of the State.

Hence, the original justification for the creation of this positive obligation was to seek to ensure the practical effectiveness at the domestic level of Article 2's limitations on the use of lethal force by governmental agents. Although the language of Article 2 did not expressly provide for this correlative duty the Court was willing to read it in as a necessary element of the combined requirements of Articles 2 and 1.[42] A Grand Chamber of the full-time Court endorsed this approach in *Ilhan v Turkey*:[43]

> 91. Procedural obligations have been implied in varying contexts under the Convention, where this has been perceived as necessary to ensure that the rights guaranteed under the Convention are not theoretical or illusory but practical and effective. The obligation to provide an effective investigation into the death caused, *inter alios*, by the security forces of the State was for this reason implied under Article 2 which guarantees the right to life (*see McCann and Others v the United Kingdom . . .*). This provision does however include the requirement that the right to life be 'protected by law'. It also may concern situations where the initiative must rest on the State for the practical reason that the victim is deceased and the circumstances of the death may be largely confined within the knowledge of state officials.

The latter part of the above explanation also highlights the practical factor that such killings may frequently occur in circumstances, such as during purported arrests of suspected criminals or whilst such persons are being detained for questioning, where there are few, if any, independent witnesses to testify as to what occurred. Therefore, the Court was trying to ensure that state officials do not abuse their powers in these types of situations by obliging states to conduct effective investigations into all killings by their agents.

---

[42] Note, in *Bankovic v Belgium (and 16 other NATO member states)*, Admissibility Decision of 12 December 2001, the Grand Chamber (unanimously) interpreted art 1 as having an essentially territorial scope.

[43] Above n 27.

The case load crisis facing the Court in recent years appears to be another element in the creation of this type of positive obligation. In the report of the Evaluation Group, composed of Ambassador Harman, President Wildhaber and Deputy Secretary-General Kruger, examining the origins and solutions to the growing backlog of cases at Strasbourg, the Group identified one source of time-consuming and expensive activity of the Court as being fact-finding missions which had to be undertaken when national institutions failed to effectively investigate alleged breaches of Convention rights. The report noted that, [t]o some extent, the Court has itself avoided the need to embark on fact-finding missions with their attendant problems by holding in its case-law that procedural deficiencies, such as lack of investigation or of a remedy, may of themselves constitute a violation of the Convention.[44] This observation suggests that the imperative to maximize the use of the Court's limited financial and personnel resources has played a part in the jurisprudential development of investigation obligations.

During the subsequent judgment in *Kelly and Others v The United Kingdom*,[45] the unanimous Chamber pronounced a twofold justification for the duty to hold domestic inquiries; 'the essential purpose of such investigation is to secure the effective implementation of the domestic laws which protect the right to life and, in those cases involving state agents or bodies, to ensure their accountability for deaths occurring under their responsibility.'[46] This explanation reflects the widening of the scope of the investigation obligation to encompass killings by both private persons and state personnel.

As the case law on this positive obligation has grown it has become possible to ascertain the Court's basic requirements in regard to effective domestic investigations. However, we must recognise that there is not a precise standard form of inquiry mandated by Article 2, instead it depends upon the circumstances of the particular killing, the processes of the relevant domestic legal system and the Court's evaluation of the effectiveness of the specific investigation. In *Velikova v Bulgaria*,[47] the applicant alleged, *inter alia*, that there had not been a meaningful investigation into the death of her long-term partner whilst he was detained in police custody. The Court, unanimously, held that:

> 80. . . . the nature and degree of scrutiny which satisfies the minimum threshold of the investigation's effectiveness depends on the circumstances of the particular case. It must be assessed on the basis of all relevant facts and with regard to the practical realities of investigation work. It is not possible to reduce the variety of situations which might occur to a bare check list of acts of investigation or other simplified criteria . . .

---

[44] Report of the Evaluation Group to the Committee of Ministers on the European Court of Human Rights, 27 September 2001 (available from http://cm.coe.int), para 63. For an examination of the report see, A Mowbray, 'Proposals for Reform of the European Court of Human Rights' [2002] *Public Law* 252.

[45] Judgment of 4 May 2001.

[46] *Ibid* para 94.

[47] Above n 27.

The Court went on to find that there were a series of unexplained fundamental omissions, including the investigator failing to obtain the estimated time of death from the forensic expert called to the scene and the failure to interview several key witnesses, throughout the investigation. Consequently;

> 82. The Court considers that unexplained failure to undertake indispensable and obvious investigative steps is to be treated with particular vigilance. In such a case, failing a plausible explanation by the respondent Government as to the reasons why indispensable acts of investigation have not been performed, the State's responsibility is engaged for a particularly serious violation of its obligation under Article 2 of the Convention to protect the right to life.

Hence the Court found a breach of the effective domestic investigation obligation inherent within that Article.

In the later case of *Kelly and Others v The United Kingdom*,[48] the Court elaborated the fundamental institutional and procedural requirements of effective investigations into alleged unlawful killings by state agents.[49]

> 95. . . . it may generally be regarded as necessary for the persons responsible for and carrying out the investigation to be independent from those implicated in the events. . . . This means not only a lack of hierarchical or institutional connection but also a practical independence (see for example the case of *Ergi v Turkey* judgment of 28 July 1998, *Reports* 1998-IV, §§ 83–84 where the public prosecutor investigating the death of a girl during an alleged clash showed a lack of independence through his heavy reliance on the information provided by the gendarmes implicated in the incident).
>
> 96. The investigation must also be effective in the sense that it is capable of leading to a determination of whether the force used in such cases was or was not justified in the circumstances . . . and to the identification and punishment of those responsible. This is not an obligation of result, but of means. The authorities must have taken the reasonable steps available to them to secure the evidence concerning the incident, including *inter alia* eye witness testimony, forensic evidence and, where appropriate, an autopsy which provides a complete and accurate record of injury and an objective analysis of clinical findings, including the cause of death. . . . Any deficiency in the investigation which undermines its ability to establish the cause of death or the person responsible will risk falling foul of this standard.
>
> 97. A requirement of promptness and reasonable expedition is implicit in this context. . . . It must be accepted that there may be obstacles or difficulties which prevent progress in an investigation in a particular situation. However, a prompt response by the authorities in investigating a use of lethal force may generally be regarded as essential in maintaining public confidence in their adherence to the rule of law and in preventing any appearance of collusion in or tolerance of unlawful acts.
>
> 98. For the same reasons, there must be a sufficient element of public scrutiny of the investigation or its results to secure accountability in practice as well as in theory. The

---

[48] Above n 45.

[49] Note, the same Chamber pronounced identical requirements in the simultaneous cases of *Hugh Jordan v UK*, paras 105–9; *McKerr v UK*, paras 111–15 and *Shanaghan v UK*, paras 88–92: Judgments of 4 May 2001.

degree of public scrutiny required may well vary from case to case. In all cases, however, the next of kin of the victim must be involved in the procedure to the extent necessary to safeguard his or her legitimate interests. . . .

We shall now examine how the Court has applied these basic necessities.

First, regarding the institutional independence of investigators, the Court in *Gulec v Turkey,*[50] was unanimous in finding that the two gendarmerie officers appointed by the Provincial Governor to investigate the killing of the applicant's son, during the suppression of a demonstration by gendarmes opening fire with an armoured vehicle, did not satisfy this condition. This was because the investigating officers were also gendarmes and the hierarchical superiors of the gendarmes whose actions were under scrutiny. An even more dramatic example of the Court finding a lack of independence during investigations undertaken by Turkish security personnel occurred in *Orhan v Turkey.*[51] The applicant alleged, *inter alia*, that his two brothers and son had been apprehended and killed by soldiers. For some time the investigation into his complaints was headed by the officer who had been in charge of the gendarme stations where it was alleged that the victims had been detained. By a large majority, six votes to one, the Court found that the investigations were seriously deficient[52] and consequently there had been a breach of Article 2.

A lack of independence was also found by the unanimous Court in respect of the Royal Ulster Constabulary's (RUC) investigation into the shooting dead of nine persons by SAS soldiers during an ambush of terrorists attacking an RUC police station at Loughgall in Northern Ireland.[53] In the Court's judgment:

> 114. . . . While the investigating officers did not appear to be connected structurally or factually with the soldiers under investigation, the operation at Loughgall was nonetheless conducted jointly with local police officers, some of whom were injured, and with the co-operation and knowledge of the RUC in that area. Even though it also appears that, as required by law, this investigation was supervised by the ICPC [Independent Commission for Police Complaints], an independent police monitoring authority, this cannot provide a sufficient safeguard where the investigation itself has been for all practical purposes conducted by police officers connected, albeit indirectly, with the operation under investigation. The Court notes the recommendation of the CPT [European Committee for the Prevention of Torture] that a fully independent investigating agency would help to overcome the lack of confidence in the system which exists in England and Wales and is in some respects similar. . . .

This ruling indicates that the Court demands a strict institutional independence of investigators from those state agents implicated in the killing and it is to be

---

[50]   1998-IV.
[51]   Judgment of 18 June 2002.
[52]   *Ibid* para 348.
[53]   *Kelly v UK*, above n 45.

welcomed as such a structural separation will contribute to the objective independence of the investigation and the public's acceptance of its legitimacy.[54]

The Court's judgment in *Kelly* also requires investigators to exercise 'practical independence', *i.e.* self-reliance, in ascertaining and evaluating evidence during their inquiries. In *Ergi v Turkey*,[55] the Chamber was critical of the prosecutor's failure to demonstrate such an approach:

> 83. . . . . the Court is struck by the heavy reliance placed by Mustafa Yuce, the public prosecutor who had the obligation to carry out an investigation into Havva Ergi's death, on the conclusion of the gendarmerie incident report that it was the PKK [Kurdish Workers' Party] which had shot the applicant's sister. . . . The prosecutor had explained to the delegates [of the Commission] that only if there had been any elements contradicting this conclusion would he have considered that any other investigatory measures would have been necessary. . . . He also seemed to consider that the onus was on the deceased's relatives to alert him to any suspicion of wrongdoing on the part of the security forces and they had not approached him. . . . In the absence of any such elements of suspicion, he had issued a decision of lack of jurisdiction indicating that the PKK was suspected of the killing, without having taken statements from members of the victim's family, villagers or any military personnel present during the operation. . . .

The need for practical independence in the conduct of investigations supplements the institutional dimension by seeking to ensure that investigators do not automatically accept the veracity and accuracy of reports or statements by state agents without conducting further relevant inquiries. Consequently, investigators must exercise a critical professional/independent assessment of evidence obtained from all sources.

Furthermore, the Court expects public authorities having the power to make decisions, such as whether to bring a prosecution against the state agents involved in the killing, on the basis of the investigation report also to be independent of those subject to the report. For example, in *Gulec*,[56] the Court was critical of the role played by the Provincial Administrative Council in deciding not to refer the case against the gendarmes involved in the shooting to the criminal courts. 'Such a conclusion cannot be accepted, regard being had to . . . the nature of the administrative authority concerned, which was chaired by the Provincial Governor (who appointed the investigation officers and was in charge of the local gendarmerie). . .'[57] The Court has repeated its criticism of the lack of independence of Turkish Provincial Administrative Councils in a number of subsequent cases.[58] Clearly, an institutional, or personal, connection between the decision-makers and the relevant state agents will undermine public confidence in the legitimacy of the inquiry/enforcement processes.

---

[54] Note, the Court found a similar lack of independence when the RUC investigated a joint RUC/Army operation which resulted in the death of the applicant's husband in *McShane v UK* (28 May 2002).

[55] Above n 6.

[56] Above n 50.

[57] *Ibid* para 80.

[58] See *Tas v Turkey* (14 November 2000) para 71.

The second general category of effective investigation requirements outlined in *Kelly* was concerned with the means and processes of inquiries. States must ensure that they have taken 'the reasonable steps available to them to secure the evidence concerning the incident'.[59] The Court then referred to a number of methods of obtaining evidence which states ought to have regard to when conducting Article 2 investigations. The most basic means of ascertaining the circumstances of a killing is via eye witnesses' testimony. However, in several cases the Court has found governmental investigators have failed to interview key witnesses. For instance, in *Gulec*, the Court determined that the investigating officer's inquiries were 'not thorough,'[60] in part, because he had failed to interview a number of fundamental witnesses including the driver of the armoured vehicle and the person who was standing next to the applicant's son when he was shot. This defect was one element in the Court concluding that the investigation did not satisfy the minimum requirements of Article 2. In *Velikova*,[61] the Court criticised the regional investigator for not examining 'a number of important witnesses' including the police officer who arrested the deceased and a person who had been detained in the police station at the same time as the deceased. Again, these omissions were factors in the Court's judgment that the investigation had not been effective. Similarly in *Akkoc v Turkey*,[62] the Court was unanimous in finding that the investigation into the shooting of the applicant's husband, a Kurdish teacher/union activist whilst on his way to school at seven o'clock one morning, did not comply with Article 2.

> 98. The Court recalls that following the killing of Zubeyir Akkoc and Ramazan Bilge the police arrived at the scene and commenced an investigation. According to the information provided by the Government however, only one statement was taken from a witness near the scene. Though the Government disputed that this was in any way remarkable due to the time of the incident, the Court notes that the witness concerned referred to a crowd being present at the location.

It is clear, therefore, that the Court expects investigators to take reasonable steps to obtain full testimony from all primary witnesses. Failure to meet this elementary requirement is likely to result in the Court determining that there has not been an effective investigation.

The second method of obtaining evidence noted in *Kelly* was through the utilisation of forensic science. There are a number of cases where the Court has determined that state officials have failed to undertake effective investigations due to the omission of rudimentary forensic tests. For instance, in *Kaya v Turkey*,[63] the applicant alleged that his brother had been deliberately shot dead by members of the security forces. The Court found that the public prosecutor had not ordered key forensic tests including; examining the scene of the death for spent bullet

---

[59] Above n 45 para 96.
[60] Above n 50 para 82.
[61] Above n 27 para 79.
[62] Above n 17.
[63] 1998-I.

cartridges (in order to ascertain whether there was confirmation of the government's assertion that the deceased was a terrorist who had been killed during an intense gun battle with the security forces) and testing the deceased's hands or clothing for gunpowder traces (to discover if he had fired a weapon).[64] Similarly in *Gul v Turkey*,[65] where the applicant complained about the shooting of his son by police officers, the Court found significant defects in the examinations and tests conducted at the scene of the killing and on items found at the scene.

> 89. . . . the Court notes that an investigation into the incident was carried out by the public prosecutor. Notwithstanding the seriousness of the incident however and the necessity to gather and record the evidence which would establish what had happened, there were a number of significant omissions. There was no attempt to find the bullet allegedly fired by Mehmet Gül at the police officers, which was their primary justification for shooting him. There was no proper recording of the alleged finding of two guns and a spent cartridge inside the flat, which was also relied on by the police in justifying their actions. The references in the police statements on this point were vague and inconsistent, rendering it impossible to identify which officer had found each weapon. No photograph was taken of the weapons at the alleged location. While a test was carried out on the Browning weapon to show that it had been recently fired, there was no testing of Mehmet Gül's hands for traces that would link him with the gun. Nor was the gun tested for prints. . . .

Therefore, it is clear that the Court expects states to ensure that investigators use well recognised forensic science methodology, such as the precise recording/photographing of the scene of the killing combined with subsequent laboratory tests on items found at the scene (including fingerprint, gunpowder and ballistic/metallurgic[66] analyses), in order to discover the facts of the killing. Obviously, which precise forensic tests should be undertaken depends upon the circumstances of the killing and the types of evidence found at the scene. Investigators must, however, take reasonable steps to record and recover all relevant items at the scene so that later laboratory tests can be conducted. As forensic science technology evolves, *e.g.* the use of DNA profiling, so the Court ought, where appropriate, to require Article 2 investigations to use the expanding techniques available.

The final aspect of the means of investigation referred to in *Kelly* concerned the conducting of a full autopsy examination of the deceased. There are several cases where the Court has concluded that such examinations have not been performed. An early example of the Court criticising the thoroughness of an autopsy was in *Kaya v Turkey*:[67]

> 89. . . . The autopsy report provided the sole record of the nature, severity and location of the bullet wounds sustained by the deceased. The Court shares the concern of the Commission about the incompleteness of this report in certain crucial respects, in particular the absence of any observations on the actual number of bullets which

---

[64] *Ibid* para 89.
[65] Judgment of 14 December 2000.
[66] See *Gulec*, above n 50 on the use of these tests to identify the type of weapon used.
[67] Above n 63.

struck the deceased and of any estimation of the distance from which the bullets were fired. It cannot be maintained that the perfunctory autopsy performed or the findings recorded in the report could lay the basis for any effective follow-up investigation or indeed satisfy even the minimum requirements of an investigation into a clear-cut case of lawful killing since they left too many critical questions unanswered.

Furthermore, the government's contention that the location of the body, in an area subject to terrorist attacks, justified the performing of a limited autopsy was rejected by the Court. The latter held that it was 'surprising' that the public prosecutor had not arranged the removal of the body to a safer location for a thorough examination. This rigorous approach by the Court is to be welcomed, otherwise governments would be able to circumvent the need for an adequate autopsy by reference to the location of the deceased who are often found in dangerous places (*e.g.* areas of terrorist activity in south-east Turkey or Northern Ireland). Where bodies are removed from their places of discovery, for detailed autopsies, the further examinations must seek to provide clear explanations for injuries/marks found on them. In *Mahmut Kaya v Turkey*,[68] the Court considered a second autopsy to be defective as it '. . . omitted however to provide explanations or conclusions regarding the ecchymoses [an area of discoloration due to bleeding under the skin] on the nailbases and the knees and ankle or the scratches on the ankle.'[69]

The Court's understanding of the broad objectives of a thorough autopsy were outlined in *Gul*.[70]

> 89. . . . The failure of the autopsy examination to record fully the injuries on Mehmet Gül's body hampered an assessment of the extent to which he was caught in the gunfire, and his position and distance relative to the door, which could have cast further light on the circumstances in which he was killed. The Government submitted that further examination was not necessary since the cause of death was clear. The purpose of a *post mortem* examination however is also to elucidate the circumstances surrounding the death, including a complete and accurate record of possible signs of ill-treatment and injury and an objective analysis of clinical findings (see in that respect the Model Autopsy Protocol annexed to The Manual on the Effective Prevention and Investigation of Extra-legal, Arbitrary and Summary Executions adopted by the United Nations in 1991, which emphasises the necessity in potentially controversial cases for a systematic and comprehensive examination and report to prevent the omission or loss of important details. . . .

This part of the judgment reveals that an adequate autopsy is not confined to discovering the basic cause of death, such as death from bullet wounds, but also, where possible, the events leading up to the death; *e.g.* how many bullets hit the deceased and from what range were they fired. The Court also implicitly gave its support to the United Nations' attempts to achieve universal good practice in the conduct of such autopsies.

[68] Above n 13.
[69] *Ibid* para 104.
[70] Above n 65.

In a subsequent case, *Tanli v Turkey*,[71] the Court was united in emphasising the importance of properly qualified personnel conducting autopsies. The applicant complained about the death of his healthy twenty-two year old son whilst being held in police detention.

> 150. . . . It also appears that the doctors who signed the *post mortem* report were not qualified forensic pathologists, notwithstanding the provision in the Code of Criminal Procedure which required the presence of a forensic doctor. The Government have relied on the second paragraph of that provision concerning emergencies. However, the Court is not satisfied that the perceived need for the examination to take place before rigor mortis set in justified proceeding without the involvement of a forensic doctor. The importance that an effective investigation be carried out into a death, possibly resulting from ill-treatment, necessitated that a properly qualified forensic expert be involved. Even if such a doctor was not available in the immediate aftermath of the death, no explanation has been given for failing to continue the examination in the presence of such an expert within the following days.

Having regard to a thorough autopsy's potential to provide investigators, and in due course prosecutors/trial courts, with crucial evidence regarding the killing of the deceased it is essential that these specialised examinations are undertaken by experts who are versed in contemporary best practice, as discussed above, and who will not overlook essential evidence or inadvertently destroy irreplaceable samples.

The third general requirement of effective investigations identified in *Kelly* is that of 'promptness and reasonable expedition'. A graphic example of an investigation failing to meet the necessity of promptness is *Tas v Turkey*.[72] The applicant petitioned the local prosecutor to investigate whether his son had been killed whilst in the custody of gendarmes. However, the Court found that an investigation was not commenced for two years. Consequently, the Court was unanimous in ruling that Turkey had not complied with its procedural obligation under Article 2.

It is not enough for domestic authorities to simply begin an investigation expeditiously they must also pursue their inquiries with determination and avoid undue delays. Consequently, in *Yasa v Turkey*,[73] the Court found that there had not been an adequate and effective investigation into armed attacks on the applicant and his uncle, who had been killed, even though both incidents had been subject to immediate police inquiries. This was because after two days of investigating the attack on the applicant the local police concluded that it was not possible to identify those responsible and in respect of the applicant's uncle the investigation appeared to have ceased after seven days. Therefore, the Court determined that, '. . . up till now, more than five years after the events, no concrete and credible progress has been made, the investigations cannot be

---

[71] Judgment of 10 April 2001.
[72] Above n 58.
[73] 1998-VI.

considered to have been effective as required by Article 2.'[74] Similarly in *Mahmut Kaya*[75] although inquiries began once the bodies were discovered:

106. The investigation was also dilatory. There were significant delays in seeking statements from witnesses. . . . There was no apparent activity between 5 May 1993 and September 1993 and no significant step taken from April 1994 until 13 March 1995.

107. The Court does not underestimate the difficulties facing public prosecutors in the south-east region at this time. It recalls that Judge Major Bulut who gave evidence to the Commission's Delegates explained that he had 500 other investigations under his responsibility. Nonetheless, where there are serious allegations of misconduct and infliction of unlawful harm implicating state security officers, it is incumbent on the authorities to respond actively and with reasonable expedition . . .

108. The Court is not satisfied that the investigation carried out into the killing of Hasan Kaya and Metin Can was adequate or effective. It failed to establish significant elements of the incident or clarify what happened to the two men and has not been conducted with the diligence and determination necessary for there to be any realistic prospect of the identification and apprehension of the perpetrators. . . .

The Court's rejection of the prosecutor's plea of overwork as an excuse for tardiness in the conduct of the investigation echoes the Court's refusal to countenance the progressive growth in caseload as an excuse for domestic judges failing to determine criminal or civil cases within a reasonable time as required by Article 6(1).[76] If states become aware of a significant rise in killings, especially if this occurs in one part of their territory, they should be expected to increase, or re-direct, investigative resources to ensure that prompt and thorough inquires can be undertaken into those deaths.

The final set of requirements noted in *Kelly* concerned the involvement of the victim's family in the investigation process and general public scrutiny of the inquiry, or its results. These elements are designed to safeguard against the dangers of introspective investigations leading to secret reports. In *Gulec*[77] the Court criticised the investigation into the death of the applicant's son, in part, because the former had not been able to participate in the process. The Court singled out the Provincial Administrative Council's failure to notify him of its decision that there was no case to be referred to the criminal courts in respect of those persons responsible for his son's death and the subsequent failure to inform the applicant that the Supreme Administrative Court had decided that it could not examine the case.

The Court expressed analogous criticism of the Northern Ireland Director of Public Prosecutions' failure to explain why he had decided not to initiate criminal proceedings against any of the security personnel involved in the shootings at Loughgall that were challenged in *Kelly*.

---

[74] 1998-VI para 107.
[75] Above n 13.
[76] See eg *Zimmermann v Switzerland* A.66 (1983) and below ch 5 n 27.
[77] Above n 50.

116. The Court recalls that the DPP is an independent legal officer charged with the responsibility to decide whether to bring prosecutions in respect of any possible criminal offences carried out by a police officer. He is not required to give reasons for any decision not to prosecute and in this case he did not do so. No challenge by way of judicial review exists to require him to give reasons in Northern Ireland, though it may be noted that in England and Wales, where the inquest jury may still reach verdicts of unlawful death, the courts have required the DPP to reconsider a decision not to prosecute in the light of such a verdict, and will review whether those reasons are sufficient. This possibility does not exist in Northern Ireland where the inquest jury is no longer permitted to issue verdicts concerning the lawfulness or otherwise of a death.

117. The Court does not doubt the independence of the DPP. However, where the police investigation procedure is itself open to doubts of a lack of independence and is not amenable to public scrutiny, it is of increased importance that the officer who decides whether or not to prosecute also gives an appearance of independence in his decision-making. Where no reasons are given in a controversial incident involving the use of lethal force, this may in itself not be conducive to public confidence. It also denies the family of the victim access to information about a matter of crucial importance to them and prevents any legal challenge of the decision.

118. In this case, nine men were shot and killed, of whom one was unconnected with the IRA and two others at least were unarmed. It is a situation which, to borrow the words of the domestic courts, cries out for an explanation. The applicants however were not informed of why the shootings were regarded as not disclosing a criminal offence or as not meriting a prosecution of the soldiers concerned. There was no reasoned decision available to reassure a concerned public that the rule of law had been respected. This cannot be regarded as compatible with the requirements of Article 2, unless that information was forthcoming in some other way. This however is not the case.[78]

The above reasoning indicates that the Court requires sufficient public accountability and involvement of the victims' family at some stage(s) in the investigation/prosecution processes if they are to satisfy the requirements of Article 2. This was confirmed in the later case of *Edwards*,[79] when the Court, unanimously, determined that the applicants inability to attend more than three days of the non-statutory inquiry in to the death of their son (56 days of hearings were held by the inquiry) coupled with the denial of the opportunity for the applicants to question witnesses contributed to the finding that the inquiry did not satisfy the procedural obligations of Article 2.

It may, however, be possible for a subsequent criminal prosecution against the state agents involved in a particular killing to satisfy the necessary elements of public scrutiny/family participation, even where the preliminary investigation did not meet these requirements. For example, in *Gul*[80] the Court considered whether the prosecution of three police officers on charges of causing death

[78] Above n 45.
[79] Above n 20.
[80] Above n 65.

by lack of attention and due precaution in respect of the shooting of the applicant's son, by many bullets fired through his front door, cured the defects in the
original inquiry. The judges were unanimous in concluding that the circumstances of this prosecution did not have a curative effect because, *inter alia*:

> 93. . . . . [t]he criminal court heard evidence from the three officers charged, whose
> brief statements added nothing of substance to their written statements. It called no
> other witnesses. The applicant and members of his family were not informed that the
> proceedings were going on and were not afforded the opportunity of telling the court
> of their very different version of events.

Hence, subsequent criminal proceedings must be rigorous and transparent if
they are to compensate for inadequate preliminary investigations.

We can conclude that in a relatively short period of time since the mid 1990s
the Court has created a wide ranging and relatively well defined positive obligation requiring states to undertake effective investigations into killings. This
obligation encompasses institutional elements (*e.g.* investigators must be
independent of those state agents involved in the killing) and procedural duties
(*e.g.* investigators should utilise appropriate forensic tests, such as ballistic
examinations of bullets found at the scene of the killing, to determine the facts
of the killing). Furthermore, it applies, depending upon the context of the
killing, to a number of agencies within the law enforcement and criminal justice
matrix including, civilian police and military investigators, public prosecutors,
coroners and criminal courts. As the previous analysis of the Strasbourg case
law reveals most of the breaches of this duty have occurred in the context of
anti-terrorist campaigns in Turkey and Northern Ireland. One of the values of
this obligation is that the Court's judgments make clear that even in such
dangerous situations all killings must be subject to thorough inquiries. Thereby,
hopefully, restraining state agents from abusing their powers through the deterrent effect of knowing that any killings in which they are involved will be subject to rigorous investigations and prosecutions in the criminal courts.

GENERAL CONCLUSIONS

Although the original Court only began to recognise the existence of positive
obligations under Article 2 in its final years of existence, innovative judgments,
such as *McCann*[81] and *Osman*,[82] established the jurisprudential foundations
upon which the full-time Court is constructing an ever expanding range of
obligations. These encompass both substantive obligations, for example to provide protection to persons known to be at immediate risk of being killed by state
agents or private individuals/groups (*e.g. Akkoc*)[83] and procedural obligations,

---

[81] Above n 1.
[82] Above n 12.
[83] Above n 17.

notably to undertake effective investigations into killings (*e.g. Kelly*).[84] It is remarkable how the Court has elaborated extensive guidelines on the needs of effective investigations, encompassing diverse components from the scope of autopsies (*Gul*)[85] to the involvement of the victims' families (*Edwards*),[86] within such a relatively short period of time. This judicial creativity is a worthy reflection of the importance of the right to life and there is considerable potential for future developments in the emerging obligation on states to provide medical services (see *Cyprus*).[87]

[84] Above n 45.
[85] Above n 65.
[86] Above n 20.
[87] Above n 32.

3

Article 3: Prohibition of torture

The text of this pithy, but crucial, provision states that:

No one shall be subjected to torture or to inhuman or degrading treatment or punishment.

PROTECTIVE MEASURES

The original Court held that under this Article states are obliged to take action to protect individuals from serious maltreatment which infringes the substantive prohibitions of the Article. In *A. v United Kingdom*,[1] when the applicant was six years' old, his mother's partner (subsequently her husband) was given a police caution after he admitted hitting A. with a cane. Three years later a medical examination revealed that A. had a number of bruises on his legs and bottom consistent with blows from a garden cane. A.'s stepfather was charged with assault occasioning actual bodily harm. The trial judge directed the jury that it was for the prosecution to prove that the defendant's conduct was not a reasonable punishment of a child by his stepfather. By a majority verdict the jury found the stepfather not guilty. A. complained to the Commission alleging that, *inter alia*, the UK had violated Article 3 by failing to protect him from illtreatment at the hands of his stepfather. The Commission was unanimous in finding a breach of Article 3. Before the Court, the British government accepted that there had been a breach of that Article in this case. The Court, unanimously, determined that the beating of A. fell within the scope of Article 3, though the Court did not specify which particular element was infringed (*i.e.* did the beating constitute 'inhuman' or 'degrading' treatment/punishment). It was then necessary to consider if the state was liable under the Convention for the stepfather's conduct.

22. ... The Court considers that the obligation on the High Contracting Parties under Article 1 of the Convention to secure to everyone within their jurisdiction the rights and freedoms defined in the Convention, taken together with Article 3, requires States to take measures designed to ensure that individuals within their jurisdiction are not

---

[1] 1998-VI.

subjected to torture or inhuman or degrading treatment or punishment, including such ill-treatment administered by private individuals (see, mutatis mutandis, the *H.L.R. v France* judgment of 29 April 1997, *Reports* 1997-III, p. 758, § 40). Children and other vulnerable individuals, in particular, are entitled to State protection, in the form of effective deterrence, against such serious breaches of personal integrity (see, *mutatis mutandis*, the *X and Y v the Netherlands* judgment of 26 March 1985, Series A no. 91, pp. 11–13, §§ 21–27; the *Stubbings and Others v the United Kingdom* judgment of 22 October 1996, Reports 1996-IV, p. 1505, §§ 62–64; and also the United Nations Convention on the Rights of the Child, Articles 19 and 37).

23. The Court recalls that under English law it is a defence to a charge of assault on a child that the treatment in question amounted to 'reasonable chastisement' . . .

24. In the Court's view, the law did not provide adequate protection to the applicant against treatment or punishment contrary to Article 3. Indeed, the Government have accepted that this law currently fails to provide adequate protection to children and should be amended.

In the circumstances of the present case, the failure to provide adequate protection constitutes a violation of Article 3 of the Convention.

Once again we discover the Court utilising the combination of Article 1 and a substantive Article of the Convention to create the jurisprudential foundations of another discrete positive obligation upon states. Significantly, this obligation requires states to take action to protect persons from serious ill-treatment originating from both state agents and private individuals. As to the types of protective measures mandated by this positive obligation, the judgment referred to 'effective deterrence' against serious infringements of personal integrity and the lack of 'adequate protection' provided by 'the law' in England. Therefore, in this case it appears that the Court envisaged the need for more extensive criminal law prohibitions on the use of corporal punishment by parents in respect of their children. Hence the enactment and enforcement of adequate criminal law offences safeguarding the physical (and psychological) well-being of individuals may be one form of action required by this Convention duty.

The full-time Court has endorsed and developed the positive obligation articulated in *A*. In *Z. and Others v United Kingdom*,[2] the four applicants were teenagers (born in 1982, 1984, 1986 and 1988). From 1987 the local social services were concerned about the applicants' welfare by their parents. Reports from neighbours and school authorities indicated that the applicants were not being properly fed or cared for (*e.g.* the applicants were dirty and slept in filthy conditions). At the end of 1989 a social work assistant was assigned to the family. Later reviews of the applicants' situation by the authorities concluded that their parents were not wilfully neglecting them (the parents had experienced poor upbringings) and the social services should seek to support the parents, rather than take the applicants into public care. Eventually the applicants were

---

[2] Judgment of 10 May 2001. Note, a later unanimous Chamber followed this judgment in finding a similar breach in respect of the numerous failings of various Scottish governmental agencies in *E v UK* (26 November 2002).

taken into emergency care in 1992 when their mother informed the social services that she could not cope and would batter them. The applicant complained to the Commission alleging, *inter alia*, that the authorities had failed to protect them from being subject to inhuman and degrading treatment by their parents. The Commission, unanimously, considered that the UK was in breach of its positive obligation under Article 3 to take effective steps to protect children from ill-treatment prescribed by the Article. The Grand Chamber of the Court was also united in finding a violation.

> 73. . . . The obligation on High Contracting Parties under Article 1 of the Convention to secure to everyone within their jurisdiction the rights and freedoms defined in the Convention, taken together with Article 3, requires States to take measures designed to ensure that individuals within their jurisdiction are not subjected to torture or inhuman or degrading treatment, including such ill-treatment administered by private individuals (see *A. v the United Kingdom* judgment of 23 September 1998, *Reports of Judgments and Decisions* 1998-VI, § 22). These measures should provide effective protection, in particular, of children and other vulnerable persons and include reasonable steps to prevent ill-treatment of which the authorities had or ought to have had knowledge (*mutatis mutandis*, the *Osman v the United Kingdom* judgment of 28 October 1998, Reports 1998-VIII, § 116).
>
> 74. There is no dispute in the present case that the neglect and abuse suffered by the four child applicants reached the threshold of inhuman and degrading treatment. . . . This treatment was brought to the local authority's attention, at the earliest in October 1987. It was under a statutory duty to protect the children and had a range of powers available to them, including removal from their home. The children were however only taken into emergency care, at the insistence of the mother, in 30 April 1992. Over the intervening period of four and a half years, they had been subject in their home to what the child consultant psychiatrist who examined them referred to as horrific experiences. . . . The Criminal Injuries Compensation Board had also found that the children had been subject to appalling neglect over an extended period and suffered physical and psychological injury directly attributable to a crime of violence. . . . The Court acknowledges the difficult and sensitive decisions facing social services and the important countervailing principle of respecting and preserving family life. The present case however leaves no doubt as to the failure of the system to protect these child applicants from serious, long-term neglect and abuse.
>
> 75. Accordingly, there has been a violation of Article 3 of the Convention.

This reasoning indicates that the positive obligation of protection under Article 3 may require states to do more than enact and enforce criminal law offences designed to safeguard personal integrity. Citing *Osman*[3] the Court held that the Article 3 duty obliges states to take 'reasonable steps' to prevent vulnerable persons from being subject to ill-treatment where the domestic authorities 'had or ought to have had knowledge' of that maltreatment. Consequently physical intervention by state agents (e.g. social workers removing Z. and her siblings from the family home at a much earlier stage in their neglect and abuse)

---

[3] Examined above, ch 2 n 12.

may be another necessary form of compliance with this positive obligation. This need for specific protective action by officials, where persons are known to be at risk of Article 3 ill-treatment, mirrors the Article 2 duty upon states to take preventive operational measures where individuals are known to be at immediate risk to life from others elaborated in *Osman*. In *Z. and Others* the numerous indications of serious ill-treatment being experienced by the applicants known to the authorities combined with the length of time during which the neglect/abuse persisted were crucial factors in the Court's conclusion that 'the system' (i.e. the network of relevant domestic authorities, including social services, schools and the police) had failed to provide adequate protection for these young children.

The limits of the positive obligation of protection were revealed in the tragic case of *Pretty v United Kingdom*.[4] Mrs Pretty was a forty-three year old grandmother suffering from advanced motor neurone disease. This disease results in the progressive weakening of muscles leading to respiratory failure. Sadly, at present, no treatment is available to prevent the progression of the disease. Mrs Pretty was diagnosed with the disease in 1999 and her condition deteriorated rapidly. By the time of the Court's judgment she was paralysed from the neck down, had virtually no speech (she used a voice synthesiser to speak) and needed to be fed through a tube. Her intellect and ability to make decisions were not impaired. Mrs Pretty's doctors had predicted that she only had a short time to live (a matter of weeks or months). She was frightened and distressed at the suffering and indignity she would endure if the disease was allowed to progress to her death. Therefore, she wished to be able to control how and when she died. Because of her physical incapacity she could not commit suicide alone (such behaviour is not a criminal offence in England), but would require the assistance of another person. However, it is a crime (punishable with a sentence of up to fourteen years' imprisonment) for a person to assist another to commit suicide.[5] Mrs Pretty wished her husband to help her commit suicide and in the summer of 2001 her lawyer wrote to the Director of Public Prosecutions (DPP) requesting an undertaking that he would not prosecute her husband if the latter assisted in her suicide. The Director refused to provide such a guarantee, because of the established policy of not granting immunities that condone future criminal behaviour. Mrs Pretty then sought judicial review of the Director's refusal, but the High Court refused her application finding that the Suicide Act 1961 was not incompatible with the Convention. The House of Lords also turned down her appeal.[6]

Before the Court, she contended that the Director's decision and the Suicide Act 1961 infringed a number of her Convention rights. Recognising the wider issues raised by the applicant, the President of the Chamber permitted written

[4] Judgment of 29 April 2002.
[5] The Suicide Act 1961, s 2(1).
[6] *R (Pretty) v Director of Public Prosecutions (Secretary of State for the Home Department intervening)* [2001] 3 WLR 1598.

submissions from the (UK) Voluntary Euthanasia Society and the Catholic Bishops' Conference of England and Wales. The respondent government submitted that the application was manifestly ill-founded. However, the Court declared the application admissible because of the serious questions of law raised by Mrs Pretty. Her major argument was that the suffering she faced from motor neurone disease amounted to degrading treatment and the British authorities were under a positive obligation, derived from Article 3, to take steps to protect her from that suffering. The Court acknowledged that previous judgments had upheld the existence of positive obligations upon states under this Article. Furthermore,

> 55. The Court cannot but be sympathetic to the applicant's apprehension that without the possibility of ending her life she faces the prospect of a distressing death. It is true that she is unable to commit suicide herself due to physical incapacity and that the state of law is such that her husband faces the risk of prosecution if he renders her assistance. Nonetheless, the positive obligation on the part of the State which is invoked in the present case would not involve the removal or mitigation of harm by, for instance, preventing any ill-treatment by public bodies or private individuals or providing improved conditions or care. It would require that the State sanction actions intended to terminate life, an obligation that cannot be derived from Article 3 of the Convention.

> 56. The Court therefore concludes that no positive obligation arises under Article 3 of the Convention to require the respondent Government either to give an undertaking not to prosecute the applicant's husband if he assists her to commit suicide or to provide a lawful opportunity for any other form of assisted suicide. There has, accordingly, been no violation of this provision.

The unanimous judgment of the Chamber indicated that Mrs Pretty's claim went too far beyond the acceptable parameters of the positive obligations arising under Article 3.[7] Her contention that the authorities were obliged to provide for assisted suicides was contrary to both the domestic[8] and European[9] parliamentary consensus and the paramount duty upon states to protect life under Article 2.[10] Mrs Pretty decided not to petition the Grand Chamber for a rehearing, under Article 43, and she died in a hospice from her illness a few weeks after the delivery of the Court's judgment.

---

[7] Note, the Court (unanimously) also rejected all her complaints under other arts of the Convention.

[8] Including, the *Report of the House of Lords' Select Committee on Medical Ethics,* HL Paper 21–1 (31 January 1994).

[9] Recommendation 1418 (1999) of the Parliamentary Assembly of the Council of Europe.

[10] Above n 4, para 39.

PROVISION OF ACCEPTABLE CONDITIONS OF DETENTION

During recent years the Court has been willing to rule that the detention of persons in poor conditions can infringe Article 3. In *Dougoz v Greece*[11] the applicant was a Syrian national who had been imprisoned for drugs related offences. The domestic court authorised his early release on licence combined with an order expelling him from Greece. He was placed in police detention pending his expulsion. Between July 1997 and April 1998 he was held in Drapetsona detention centre. He alleged that the centre was severely over-crowded (100 detainees held in 20 cells),there were no beds, mattresses or blankets, no fresh air or daylight entered the centre and no activities were provided for detainees. From April 1998 until his expulsion to Syria in December 1998 he was detained in Alexandras Avenue Police Headquarters. Dougoz asserted that the conditions there were similar to Drapetsona, but he had natural light and air in his police cell. He complained that his conditions of detention in both institutions violated Article 3. The government did not contest Dougoz's allegations regarding overcrowding , a lack of beds and bedding. The Court, unanimously, held that:

> 46. . . . conditions of detention may sometimes amount to inhuman or degrading treatment. In the *Greek case* (Yearbook of the European Convention on Human Rights no. 12, 1969), the Commission reached this conclusion regarding overcrowding and inadequate facilities for heating, sanitation, sleeping arrangements, food, recreation and contacts with the outside world. When assessing conditions of detention, account has to be taken of the cumulative effects of these conditions, as well as of specific allegations made by the applicant. In the present case, although the Court has not conducted an on-site visit, it notes that the applicant's allegations are corroborated by the conclusions of the CPT [the European Committee for the Prevention of Torture and Inhuman or Degrading Treatment or Punishment] report of 29 November 1994 regarding the Police Headquarters in Alexandras Avenue. In its report the CPT stressed that the cellular accommodation and detention regime in that place were quite unsuitable for a period in excess of a few days, the occupancy levels being grossly excessive and the sanitary facilities appalling. Although the CPT had not visited the Drapetsona detention centre at that time, the Court notes that the Government had described the conditions in Alexandras as being the same as in Drapetsona, and the applicant himself conceded that the former were slightly better with natural light, air in the cells and adequate hot water.

> 47. Furthermore, the Court does not lose sight of the fact that in 1997 the CPT visited both the Alexandras Police Headquarters and the Drapetsona detention centre and felt it necessary to renew its visit to both places in 1999. The applicant was detained in the interim from July 1997 to December 1998.

> 48. In the light of the above, the Court considers that the conditions of detention of the applicant in the Alexandras Police Headquarters and the Drapetsona detention

---

[11] Judgment of 6 March 2001.

centre, in particular the serious overcrowding and absence of sleeping facilities, combined with the inordinate length of the period during which he was detained in such conditions, amounted to degrading treatment contrary to Article 3.

49. Accordingly, there has been a violation of Article 3 of the Convention.

In classifying Dougoz's conditions of detention as being sufficiently inadequate to constitute degrading treatment the Court was clearly influenced by the parallel findings and criticisms of its sibling (Council of Europe) body the CPT.[12] Furthermore, the fact that the CPT had made follow up visits to both places of detention and its reports had not been published (inspection reports can only be published if the relevant state gives its approval) suggested that the conditions in those institutions were continuing to be problematic. This was confirmed when the CPT reports were eventually published in September 2001.[13]

A few weeks later a different Chamber also found poor conditions in another Greek prison amounted to degrading treatment. The British applicant in *Peers v Greece*[14] was convicted of drugs offences in Greece. After his conviction he was detained in the segregation unit of the Delta wing of Koridallos prison for approximately two months, because he was suffering from drug withdrawal symptoms and later as he did not wish to be located in the ordinary wing where illegal drugs were circulating amongst the prisoners. During his imprisonment in the segregation unit Peers was required to share his cell, built for one person, with another prisoner. There was no natural light or ventilation in the cell. Also there was an 'asian-type' toilet in the cell with no screen to separate it from the sleeping area. He complained, *inter alia*, that his conditions of detention violated Article 3. The Commission, by twenty-six votes to one, considered that there had been a breach of this Article. The Court was unanimous in determining that:

> 74. . . . in the present case there is no evidence that there was a positive intention of humiliating or debasing the applicant. However, the Court notes that, although the question whether the purpose of the treatment was to humiliate or debase the victim is a factor to be taken into account, the absence of any such purpose cannot conclusively rule out a finding of violation of Article 3 (*V. v the United Kingdom* [GC], no. 24888/94, § 71, ECHR-IX).

> 75. Indeed, in the present case, the fact remains that the competent authorities have taken no steps to improve the objectively unacceptable conditions of the applicant's detention. In the Court's view, this omission denotes lack of respect for the applicant. The Court takes particularly into account that, for at least two months, the applicant had to spend a considerable part of each 24-hour period practically confined to his bed in a cell with no ventilation and no window which would at times become unbearably

---

[12] For an examination of the work of this organisation see MD Evans and R Morgan, *Preventing Torture* (Oxford, Clarendon Press, 1998).

[13] See, www.cpt.coe.int/en/reports/inf2001

[14] Judgment of 19 April 2001.

hot. He also had to use the toilet in the presence of another inmate and be present while the toilet was being used by his cellmate. The Court is not convinced by the Government's allegation that these conditions have not affected the applicant in a manner incompatible with Article 3. On the contrary, the Court is of the opinion that the prison conditions complained of diminished the applicant's human dignity and arose in him feelings of anguish and inferiority capable of humiliating and debasing him and possibly breaking his physical or moral resistance. In sum, the Court considers that the conditions of the applicant's detention in the segregation unit of the Delta wing of the Koridallos prison amounted to degrading treatment within the meaning of Article 3 of the Convention.

There has thus been a breach of this provision.

In terms of the implicit positive obligation upon states to provide acceptable conditions of detention it is important to note that in *Peers* the Court found that the authorities had 'taken no steps to improve the objectively unacceptable conditions of the applicant's detention'. Also the period of time that Peers was subject to these conditions (about two months) was considerably less than the time-frame at issue in *Dougoz* (nearly one and a half years).

Even a few days of detention in unacceptable conditions may be sufficient to constitute a violation of Article 3. The applicant in *Price v United Kingdom*[15] was a four-limb deficient victim of Thalidomide. On 20 January 1995 she refused to answer questions regarding her financial position during civil proceedings. The judge found her in contempt of court and ordered that she be committed to prison for seven days. She was held in the cells of Lincoln police station that night, as it was too late to send her to a prison. Price had to sleep in her wheelchair (she claimed that she could not sleep on the wooden bed as it would have been too painful for her hips) and was cold (extra blankets were provided and a doctor attended her). The next day she was moved to the health centre of New Hall Women's Prison, in Wakefield. Her cell had a wider wheelchair door access, hand pulls on the toilet and a hydraulic hospital bed. Constant nursing care was provided. Male officers were required to help the nurse lift Price on and off the toilet. She was released after four days (due to the rules on remission of sentences). Price alleged that her treatment during detention breached Article 3. The Court, unanimously, was critical of the domestic judge's conduct. '. . . [I]n accordance with English law and practice, the sentencing judge took no steps, before committing the applicant to immediate imprisonment, a particularly harsh sentence in this case, to ascertain where she would be detained or to ensure that it would be possible to provide facilities adequate to cope with her severe level of disability.'[16] After noting the factual circumstances of her detention the Court held that:

> 30. There is no evidence in this case of any positive intention to humiliate or debase the applicant. However, the Court considers that to detain a severely disabled person

[15] Judgment of 10 July 2001.
[16] *Ibid* para 25.

in conditions where she is dangerously cold, risks developing sores because her bed is too hard or unreachable, and is unable to go to the toilet or keep clean without the greatest of difficulty, constitutes degrading treatment contrary to Article 3. It therefore finds a violation of this provision in the present case.

In a separate opinion judges Bratza and Costa expressed the view that it was the domestic judge who was primarily responsible for the violation of the applicant's rights under Article 3.

> While there appear on the material before the Court to have been certain failings in the standard of care provided by the police and prison authorities, these stemmed in large part from the lack of preparedness on the part of both to receive and look after a severely handicapped person in conditions which were wholly unsuited to her needs. On the other hand, we can see no justification for the decision to commit the applicant to an immediate term of imprisonment without at the very least ensuring in advance that there existed both adequate facilities for detaining her and conditions of detention in which her special needs could be met.

The judgment in *Price* indicates that the Court will have regard to the needs of individual detainees when assessing if their conditions of detention infringed Article 3. Clearly the greater the physical/medical needs of disabled detainees the more states must do in terms of providing suitably adapted basic cell facilities, such as special beds, to satisfy their corresponding obligations under this Article. The section below examines the positive medical obligations of states in further detail.

The deplorable conditions in Russian prisons came under scrutiny by the Court in *Kalashnikov v Russia*.[17] The applicant had been held on remand in a detention facility, in the city of Magadan, for over four years. The Court found that there was only 0.9–1.9 sq.m. space per inmate in the cell where the applicant had been detained (the CPT has issued guidelines recommending 7 sq. m. per prisoner as desirable)[18] and he had to share a bed with two other inmates (they occupied it on an eight hour shift system). However, it was difficult to sleep due to constant lighting and the noise caused by the overcrowding. There was inadequate ventilation in the cell and it was infested with pests. At times the cell was occupied by persons suffering from serious contagious diseases (including tuberculosis and syphilis), but the applicant did not contract any of these. There was a toilet in one corner of the cell which had to be used by between 11–24 inmates. The Court, unanimously, concluded that, '. . . the applicant's conditions of detention, in particular the severely overcrowded and insanitary environment and its detrimental effect on the applicant's health and well-being, combined with the length of the period during which the applicant was detained in such conditions, amounted to degrading treatment.'[19]

---

[17] Judgment of 15 July 2002.
[18] 2nd General Report, CPT/Inf (92) 3, 43.
[19] Above n 17, para 102.

The wider implications of *Kalashnikov* were revealed by the government's submissions that the conditions of the applicant's detention were no worse than those of most detainees in Russia and it was acknowledged that, because of economic difficulties, the very unsatisfactory conditions in Russian penal institutions were below the requirements of the Council of Europe. Although the government has adopted a number of programmes to improve these facilities, it is likely that the Court's finding of a breach of Article 3 in *Kalashnikov* will encourage other detainees in Russian prisons to bring similar complaints to Strasbourg.

Although the Court determines what are acceptable conditions on a case by case by case basis relevant factors include the length of time the detainee was subject to the poor conditions and the effect of those conditions upon the detainee (particularly if they caused him/her identifiable medical problems). Adverse reports by the CPT on the place of detention, regarding the conditions at the time when the complainant was being held there, may also encourage the Court to uphold the complainant's allegations under Article 3.

PROVISION OF ADEQUATE MEDICAL TREATMENT FOR DETAINEES

The former Commission expressed the opinion that Article 3 included such a positive obligation in *Hurtado v Switzerland*.[20] The applicant was a Colombian national who the Swiss police suspected of being a member of an international drug-trafficking gang. He was arrested by members of the Vaud cantonal police task force, used for special operations, after the police had detonated a stun grenade in the flat where he was staying. Two days after his arrest Hurtado asked to see a doctor , but he had to wait six more days before he was examined by a doctor. X-rays subsequently disclosed that he had a fractured rib. Hurtado complained, *inter alia*, that the failure to provide him with prompt medical treatment violated Article 3. The Commission, unanimously, considered that:

79. . . . Under Article 3 of the Convention the State has a specific positive obligation to protect the physical well-being of persons deprived of their liberty. The lack of adequate medical treatment in such a situation must be classified as inhuman treatment.

Taking account of the violent (but lawful) arrest of the applicant, his request for medical treatment and the delay of six days in providing a doctor, the Commission found a breach of Article 3. Subsequently, the Court struck-out the case[21] after a friendly settlement had been agreed between the applicant and Switzerland. Without admitting a violation of the Convention, the Swiss government agreed to pay the applicant SF 14,000 as an *ex gratia* payment.

The limited medical treatment and associated conditions of detention of a mentally disturbed offender in a prison psychiatric wing were examined by the

---

[20] A.280A (1994).
[21] Judgment of 26 January 1994.

original Court in *Aerts v Belgium*.[22] The applicant was found to have assaulted his ex-wife at a time when he was suffering from 'a severe mental disturbance'. Therefore, the Liege court ordered his detention in an institution to be designated by the local mental health board. In the meantime the court required Aerts to be held in the psychiatric wing of Lantin Prison. Two months later a psychiatrist informed the board that it was 'urgent' for Aerts to be relocated to an institution 'better equipped to calm the constant anxiety he feels at the moment.' A few days later the board designated a particular social protection centre as the institution where he should be detained. However, it was not until seven months later (in October 1993) that Aerts was moved from the prison to the centre. Aerts complained that, *inter alia*, his detention in the prison psychiatric wing violated Article 3. The CPT visited Lantin in November 1993 and its report, published in 1994, found contacts between detainees and the psychiatrist to be basic and brief. The CPT concluded that, '. . . keeping mental patients detained for lengthy periods in the conditions described above carries an undeniable risk of causing their mental state to deteriorate.'[23] The Commission, by seventeen votes to fourteen, considered that there had been a breach of Article 3. Before the Court the applicant argued that he had not received any regular medical or psychiatric attention whilst in Lantin prison and the conditions of detention had caused a deterioration of his mental health in breach of Article 3. However, the majority, seven votes to two, rejected his claim.

65. It was not contested that the general conditions in the psychiatric wing of Lantin Prison were unsatisfactory and not conducive to the effective treatment of the inmates. The CPT considered that the standard of care given to the patients placed in the psychiatric wing at Lantin fell below the minimum acceptable from an ethical and humanitarian point of view and that prolonging their detention at Lantin for lengthy periods carried an undeniable risk of a deterioration of their mental health . . .

66. In the present case there is no proof of a deterioration of Mr Aerts's mental health. The living conditions on the psychiatric wing at Lantin do not seem to have had such serious effects on his mental health as would bring them within the scope of Article 3. Admittedly, it is unreasonable to expect a severely mentally disturbed person to give a detailed or coherent description of what he has suffered during his detention. However, even if it is accepted that the applicant's state of anxiety, described by the psychiatrist in a report of 10 March 1993 . . . was caused by the conditions of detention in Lantin, and even allowing for the difficulty Mr Aerts may have had in describing how these had affected him, it has not been conclusively established that the applicant suffered treatment that could be classified as inhuman or degrading.

67. In conclusion, the Court considers that there has been no breach of Article 3.

Judge Pekkanen, joined by Judge Jambrek, issued a partly dissenting opinion in which he expressed the view that as the applicant had been in urgent need of appropriate psychiatric care, which was not available in Lantin prison, to detain him in the prison for nine months amounted to inhuman treatment.

[22] 1998-V 1939.
[23] *Ibid* para 28.

The judgment of the Court in *Aerts* was unduly lenient to the state. Despite the evidence of minimal psychiatric treatment being given to a mentally disturbed detainee for a period of many months, the majority was not willing to find a breach of Article 3. This conclusion is hard to justify when the domestic mental health board had determined that Aerts should be placed in a special centre in the early months of his detention and the expert CPT had produced a damning assessment of the regime and lack of facilities in Lantin prison soon after his period of imprisonment there. We may speculate that the Court was being tolerant of a poor level of psychiatric care by prison authorities because of the endemic nature of this deficiency in many member states and the consequent large financial costs of raising mental health provision standards in such institutions.

A unanimous Grand Chamber of the full-time Court found the authorities' delay in providing adequate medical treatment to a seriously injured detainee to be a contributory factor in classifying his mal-treatment as torture in *Ilhan v Turkey*.[24] The applicant's brother, Abdullatif, was apprehended by gendarmes during an anti-terrorist operation in his village. Abdullatif was kicked and hit with rifles by a number of gendarmes. He sustained major injuries, including brain damage which resulted in permanent loss of function on his left side. However, the authorities did not take Abdullatif to hospital for treatment until thirty-six hours after his apprehension. The Court concluded that:

> 87. Having regard to the severity of the ill-treatment suffered by Abdullatif Ilhan and the surrounding circumstances, including the significant lapse in time before he received proper medical attention, the Court finds that he was a victim of very serious and cruel suffering that may be characterised as torture . . .

So the failure to provide reasonably prompt medical care to a visibly injured detainee was considered to be an aggravating element for the purpose of classifying the type of breach occurring under Article 3.

In the subsequent case of *Kudla v Poland*,[25] the Court sought to expound upon both the limits and requirements of the obligation to provide detainees with adequate medical care. The applicant was held in Cracow Remand Centre between August 1991 and July 1992 and then again between October 1993 and October 1996 whilst awaiting trial on a number of fraud charges. He attempted suicide twice whilst detained in the Centre. The authorities arranged for him to be examined by psychiatric experts on a number of occasions (from the beginning of 1995 he was seen by a psychiatrist at least once a month). He complained to the Court that, *inter alia*, the Centre did not have a psychiatric ward and that no serious effort had been made by the authorities to treat his chronic depression with the consequence that he had suffered inhuman and degrading treatment in violation of Article 3. The Grand Chamber was unanimous in holding that:

---

[24] Judgment of 27 June 2000.
[25] Judgment of 26 October 2000, and for the important art 13 aspect of this case see below ch 8.

93. . . . Nor can that Article be interpreted as laying down a general obligation to release a detainee on health grounds or to place him in a civil hospital to enable him to obtain a particular kind of medical treatment.

94. Nevertheless, under this provision the State must ensure that a person is detained in conditions which are compatible with respect for his human dignity, that the manner and method of the execution of the measure do not subject him to distress or hardship of an intensity exceeding the unavoidable level of suffering inherent in detention and that, given the practical demands of imprisonment, his health and well-being are adequately secured by, among other things, providing him with the requisite medical assistance (see, *mutatis mutandis*, the *Aerts v Belgium* judgment of 30 July 1998, *Reports* 1998-V, p. 1966, §§ 64 et seq.).

Taking account of the regular examinations of the applicant by expert doctors the Court determined that there had not been a breach of Article 3. This judgment makes it plain that states must provide detainees with 'requisite medical assistance' but when assessing whether that standard of provision has been delivered the Court will also have regard to the 'practical demands of imprisonment'. The latter factor potentially enables states to invoke matters such as security risks to justify restrictions on the types of medical treatment given to particular detainees.

The evidential significance of medical records in determining if an appropriate level of medical care has been provided for detainees was considered in *Tas v Turkey*.[26] The applicant's son, Muhsin, was shot in the knee and taken into custody by gendarmes during a security operation. Within one hour of Muhsin's arrest he was taken to the local hospital for treatment. Hospital records showed that due to the complexity of treating the wound the doctor recommended transfer to a specialist at another hospital. Records at the Dirnak Military Hospital indicated that Muhsin was seen at some time that day. However, the doctor who treated him had no recollection of the treatment. The doctor subsequently told the Commission that a splint would have been applied to Muhsin's leg and he would have been given antibiotics. Furthermore, the wound would have to be dressed every three days. There were no records of any further medical care being given to Muhsin. The government claimed that three weeks later he escaped from custody whilst assisting gendarmes to find PKK shelters in the Gabar mountains. Muhsin was not seen again. The applicant contended, *inter alia*, that the failure to provide Muhsin with necessary medical treatment violated Article 3. This claim was rejected:

76. The Court observes that the applicant's son did receive prompt and effective medical treatment for the injury to his knee as he was taken immediately to Cizre State Hospital and then received specialist care at Dirnak Military Hospital. It agrees with the Commission that in these circumstances the lack of records as to his subsequent care is an insufficient basis to conclude that he was the victim of treatment contrary to Article 3 of the Convention.

[26] Judgment of 14 November 2000.

Although it may seem that the Court was being very lenient in exonerating the respondent government, despite the fact that there were no records confirming that the necessary continuing medical treatment of Muhsin's injury had been provided, we can speculate that this approach was taken because the Court went on to find Turkey liable for the death of Muhsin in breach of Article 2. When compared with the gravity of the latter violation the failure to provide follow-up medical care of his wound is of much less significance. Nevertheless, it is to be regretted that the Court did not take the opportunity to emphasise the need for states to provide detainees with both prompt and, where necessary, continuing medical care.

The Court also examined the continuing medical care of a detainee in *Rehbock v Slovenia*.[27] The applicant, a German body-building champion, was arrested by thirteen Slovenian police officers on suspicion of drugs smuggling. The day after his arrest Rehbock complained of headaches. He was seen by a doctor who recommended that he be examined by a specialist. On the same day he was taken to the facial surgery department of the local hospital where x-rays revealed a double fracture of his jaw. The doctor advised surgery, under a general anaesthetic, but Rehbock refused to give his consent. He underwent regular examinations at the hospital and analgesics were prescribed. Several months later Rehbock was convicted of dealing in narcotics and sentenced to seventeen months' imprisonment. He complained several times to the governor of the prison where he was detained that the guards had refused to provide him with the analgesics prescribed and, consequently, he suffered from severe pain and depression. The Court, unanimously, dismissed his contention that the authorities' omissions breached Article 3.

> 80. In the Court's view, the treatment to which the applicant was subjected in prison, namely the prison staff's failure to provide him with pain-killing medication on several occasions, did not attain a degree of gravity warranting the conclusion that his rights under Article 3 was thereby infringed.

Again the Court was exhibiting tolerance of omissions in the continuing care of injured detainees. If Rehbock really did suffer severe pain through the repeated failure of the guards to supply him with his prescribed medication it was surely not a trivial matter?

The Court found a number of failures in the continuing medical care of a seriously mentally ill prisoner contributed to a breach of Article 3 in *Keenan v United Kingdom*.[28] The applicant's son, Mark, had a history of mental illness, including symptoms of paranoia, violence and deliberate self-harm. In April 1993 he was convicted of assaulting his former girlfriend and sentenced to four months' imprisonment. He was admitted to Exeter Prison and sent to the prison health centre. The prison's senior doctor consulted the psychiatrist who had

---

[27] Judgment of 28 November 2000.
[28] Judgment of 3 April 2001.

been treating Mark. Several attempts were made to transfer Mark to the ordinary cells but he resisted (by barricading himself in the ward on one occasion). At the end of April the prison's visiting psychiatrist recommended a change in Mark's medication. The next day Mark's condition deteriorated and a prison doctor, with no psychiatric training, ordered a return to his original medication. Later that day Mark assaulted two prison hospital officers (one was seriously injured). The next day another prison doctor, who had six months psychiatric training, certified Mark as being fit for disciplinary proceedings in respect of the assaults and for placement in the segregation unit within the prison's punishment block. A deputy governor ordered Mark's placement in the segregation unit, where he was locked up for 23 hours each day. He was visited each day by a doctor, the prison chaplain and the prison governor. Mark asked to see a prisoner trained by the Samaritans (to counsel inmates who may be suicidal) and threatened to harm himself. He was put on a 15 minute watch by prison staff. Prison doctors recorded that he was a hazard to staff. No further entries were made in Mark's medical record from 3 May 1993. However, the segregation unit's occurrence book had several entries regarding his behaviour, stating that he was being aggressive to staff and acting strangely. On 14 May he was subject to a disciplinary adjudication, after being certified as medically fit for the hearing by one of the prison doctors, and found guilty of assaulting the officers. The deputy governor sentenced him to 28 additional days in prison and seven days in the segregation unit. During the next day Mark was visited by a friend and he appeared to be in good spirits. However, that evening Mark was found hanged in his cell (the relevant prison officer had been absent in the toilet for a few minutes prior to the discovery of Mark's suicide). The applicant contended that, *inter alia*, there had been wholly insufficient psychiatric care given to her son whilst in prison and that violated his rights under Article 3. The Court, by five votes to two, held that:

110. It is relevant in the context of the present application to recall also that the authorities are under an obligation to protect the health of persons deprived of liberty (*Hurtado v Switzerland*, Comm. Report 8 July 1993, Series A no. 280, p. 16, § 79). The lack of appropriate medical treatment may amount to treatment contrary to Article 3 (see *Ilhan v Turkey* [GC] no. 22277/93, ECHR 2000-VII, § 87). In particular, the assessment of whether the treatment or punishment concerned is incompatible with the standards of Article 3 has, in the case of mentally ill persons, to take into consideration their vulnerability and their inability, in some cases, to complain coherently or at all about how they are being affected by any particular treatment (see e.g. the *Herczegfalvy v Austria* judgment of 24 September 1992, Series A no. 244, § 82; the *Aerts v Belgium* judgment of 30 July 1998, Reports 1998-V, p. 1966, § 66).

113. In this case, the Court is struck by the lack of medical notes concerning Mark Keenan, who was an identifiable suicide risk and undergoing the additional stresses that could be foreseen from segregation and, later, disciplinary punishment. From 5 May to 15 May 1993, when he died, there were no entries in his medical notes. Given that there were a number of prison doctors who were involved in caring for Mark

Keenan, this shows an inadequate concern to maintain full and detailed records of his mental state and undermines the effectiveness of any monitoring or supervision process. The Court does not find the explanation of Dr Keith—that an absence of notes indicates that there was nothing to record—a satisfactory answer in the light of the occurrence book entries for the same period.

114. Further, while the prison senior medical officer consulted Mark Keenan's doctor on admission and the visiting psychiatrist, who also knew Mark Keenan, had been called to see Mark Keenan on 29 April 1993, the Court notes that there was no subsequent reference to a psychiatrist. Even though Dr Rowe had warned on 29 April 1993 that Mark Keenan should be kept from association until his paranoid feelings had died down, the question of returning to normal location was raised with him the next day. When his condition proceeded to deteriorate, a prison doctor, unqualified in psychiatry, reverted to Mark Keenan's previous medication without reference to the psychiatrist who had originally recommended a change. The assault on the two prison officers followed. Though Mark Keenan asked the prison doctor to point out to the governor at the adjudication that the assault occurred after a change in medication, there was no reference to a psychiatrist for advice either as to his future treatment or his fitness for adjudication and punishment.

115. The lack of effective monitoring of Mark Keenan's condition and the lack of informed psychiatric input into his assessment and treatment disclose significant defects in the medical care provided to a mentally ill person known to be a suicide risk. The belated imposition on him in those circumstances of a serious disciplinary punishment—seven days' segregation in the punishment block and an additional 28 days to his sentence imposed two weeks after the event and only nine days before his expected date of release—which may well have threatened his physical and moral resistance, is not compatible with the standard of treatment required in respect of a mentally ill person. It must be regarded as constituting inhuman and degrading treatment and punishment within the meaning of Article 3 of the Convention.

Accordingly, the Court finds a violation of this provision.

The above judgment is important for disclosing the Court's endorsement of the duty upon states to safeguard the health of detainees, originally articulated by the Commission in *Hurtado*. Furthermore in *Keenan* the Court was according greater weight to the absence of medical records concerning the care given to a seriously ill prisoner than in *Tas*. Where there are a number of different medical personnel responsible for the treatment of such a detainee, as is likely to be the situation in most large institutions, the judgment suggests that good practice requires the maintenance of regular notes recording the condition of the detainee. The judgment also indicates that the Court may be becoming more sensitive to the needs of 'vulnerable' mentally ill detainees Indeed one of the general issues behind the applicant's complaint to Strasbourg was 'the acute concern caused by the high rate of suicide in the European prison population.'[29]

Overall we can conclude that the Court has been rather cautious in finding that states have failed to provide adequate medical care for detainees. Violations

---

[29] Judgment of 3 April 2001, para 105.

of this duty under Article 3 have tended to be found where there were defects in the medical treatment combined with other unacceptable actions, such as serious assaults by state agents (as in *Ilhan*) or the imposition of severe disciplinary punishment (as in *Keenan*). The Court has not always been strict in evaluating the significance of defects in the follow-up care of detainees (*e.g.* in *Tas* and *Rehbock*). Whilst, from the perspective of states, they can best seek to satisfy this positive obligation by ensuring that they provide medical care as soon as possible after it is requested by the detainee (*Rehbock*), or it becomes apparent that the detainee is unwell (*Ilhan*), and that where necessary specialist medical experts are involved in the treatment of detainees (*Kudla*).

THE DUTY TO INVESTIGATE ALLEGATIONS OF SERIOUS ILL-TREATMENT
BY STATE AGENTS

Counsel for the applicant in *Aydin v Turkey*,[30] argued that the authorities' failure to conduct an effective investigation into her complaint of torture (including an act of rape) by officials amounted to a distinct breach of this Article. Furthermore, in its written submissions to the Court, Amnesty International drew attention to the requirements of Articles 12 and 13 of the 1984 United Nations' Convention against Torture and Other Cruel, Inhuman or Degrading Treatment or Punishment. These provisions oblige states to ensure that individuals, who allege that they have been tortured in any territory under the jurisdiction of the relevant state, have the right to complain and to have their cases 'promptly and impartially examined' by competent authorities. However, the Grand Chamber decided that it 'would be appropriate'[31] to examine this aspect of her case under Article 13. Unfortunately, the Court did not elaborate upon the reasons why it considered Article 3 to be an unsuitable Convention basis for the applicant's procedural complaint.

Nevertheless, one year later a unanimous Chamber[32] endorsed the existence of a positive duty of investigation under Article 3. In *Assenov and Others v Bulgaria*,[33] the first applicant, who was aged fourteen at the time of the alleged incidents, was arrested by the police on suspicion of illegal gambling. He asserted that the police assaulted him whilst he was held in detention at the local police station. A few days after he was released his mother, the second applicant, filed a complaint with the District Directorate of Internal Affairs requesting the prosecution of the police officers who had allegedly beaten her son. A colonel in the Directorate ordered written statements from the police officers who had arrested Assenov and had been in charge of his detention. He reached

[30] 1997-VI 1889.
[31] *Ibid* para 88.
[32] Note, six members of the Chamber (President Bernhardt and Judges: Pettiti, Palm, Baka, Makarczyk and Gotchev) had also been members of the Grand Chamber in *Aydin*.
[33] 1998-VIII.

the view that Assenov had been beaten by his father and not by the police. The Director of the Directorate subsequently informed the second applicant that no criminal proceedings would be brought against the police officers. She renewed her request for the officers to be prosecuted by complaining to the Regional Military Prosecution Office. A military investigation officer received copies of the Directorate's earlier inquiries and recommended that no prosecution should be initiated. Later, both the Regional and General Military Prosecution Offices determined that no public prosecution of the police officers should take place.

Before the Court the applicants submitted that, *inter alia*, '. . . wherever there were reasonable grounds to believe that an act of torture or inhuman or degrading treatment or punishment had been committed, the failure of the competent domestic authorities to carry out a prompt and impartial investigation in itself constituted a violation of Article 3.'[34] Again, this expansive interpretation of Article 3 was supported by written comments from Amnesty International. In response, the Court held that:

> 102. . . . where an individual raises an arguable claim that he has been seriously ill-treated by the police or other such agents of the State unlawfully and in breach of Article 3, that provision, read in conjunction with the State's general duty under Article 1 of the Convention to 'secure to everyone within their jurisdiction the rights and freedoms in [the] Convention', requires by implication that there should be an effective official investigation. This obligation, as with that under Article 2, should be capable of leading to the identification and punishment of those responsible (see, in relation to Article 2 of the Convention, the *McCann and Others v the United Kingdom* judgment of 27 September 1995, Series A no. 324, p. 49, § 161, the *Kaya v Turkey* judgment of 19 February 1998, Reports 1998-I, p. 297, § 86 and the *Yasa v Turkey* judgment of 2 September 1998, Reports 1998-VI, p. 2411, § 98). If this were not the case, the general legal prohibition of torture and inhuman and degrading treatment and punishment, despite its fundamental importance . . . would be ineffective in practice and it would be possible in some cases for agents of the State to abuse the rights of those within their control with virtual impunity.

The Court considered that the applicants had raised such an arguable claim in respect of the alleged police beating of Assenov. But, in its judgment, the subsequent investigations by the Bulgarian authorities were not sufficiently thorough to meet the minimum requirements of Article 3. In particular the Court was critical of the Directorate's failure to question those persons (including about fifteen fellow Roma and twenty bus drivers) who had witnessed the arrest of Assenov at the bus station. Additionally, the Military Prosecution Offices' investigations 'were even more cursory.'[35] The Court was especially damning of the military prosecutors' failure to critically evaluate the police account of Assenov's arrest.

---

[34] 1998-VIII, para 90.
[35] *Ibid* para 104.

104. . . . The Court finds it particularly striking that the [General Military Prosecution Office] could conclude, without any evidence that Mr Assenov had not been compliant, and without any explanation as to the nature of the alleged disobedience, that 'even if the blows were administered on the body of the juvenile, they occurred as a result of disobedience to police orders'. . . . To make such an assumption runs contrary to the principle under Article 3 that, in respect of a person deprived of his liberty, recourse to physical force which has not been made strictly necessary by his own conduct is in principle an infringement of his rights . . .

Therefore, the Court concluded that there had been a violation of the effective official investigation obligation embodied in Article 3.

Significantly the judgment in *Assenov* had many similarities with the Court's earlier articulation of an analogous positive investigatory duty under Article 2 from *McCann* onwards.[36] Under both Articles the obligation to undertake effective investigations is an implied duty. Also the jurisprudential justifications for the Court to develop these obligations are derived from a combination of the substantive Convention right allied with the general duty of member states to 'secure' Convention rights and freedoms to all persons in their jurisdictions. Whilst the pragmatic reason for subjecting states to duties of investigation was to seek to ensure that the basic rights to life and freedom from torture, inhuman or degrading treatment/punishment by state agents are respected and enforced in practice.

A united Chamber of the full-time Court, which contained only Judge Baka from the Chamber that gave judgment in *Assenov*, endorsed and applied the *Assenov* positive obligation in *Sevtap Veznedaroglu v Turkey*.[37] The applicant, a public law student, was arrested in 1994 on suspicion of membership of the PKK (Kurdistan Workers Party). She alleged that whilst in detention she was interrogated by 15 policemen who, *inter alia*, undressed her, hung her up by her arms and subjected her to electric shocks. After eleven days she was brought before the State Security Court. She complained that she had been tortured during her detention. Neither the public prosecutor nor the judge pursued her complaints. The Strasbourg Court determined that:

35. . . . in the circumstances the applicant had laid the basis of an arguable claim that she had been tortured. It is to be noted also that the applicant persisted in her allegations right up to the stage of trial. . . . The inertia displayed by the authorities in response to her allegations was inconsistent with the procedural obligation which devolves on them under Article 3 of the Convention. In consequence, the Court finds that there has been a violation of that Article on account of the failure of the authorities of the respondent State to investigate the applicant's complaint of torture.

Two months later, however, a Grand Chamber[38] sought to discourage the invocation of a duty of investigation under Article 3 in *Ilhan v Turkey*.[39] The

---

[36] Above ch 2 n 37.

[37] Judgment of 11 April 2000.

[38] Note, Judges Bonello, Baka and Golcuklu had also been members of the Chamber in *Sevtap Veznedaroglu* and Judges Baka and Makarczyk had previously been members of the Chamber in *Assenov*.

applicant's brother sustained serious head injuries during his arrest by gendarmes. Before the Court, the applicant contended that, *inter alia*, in breach of Article 3 there had not been an effective investigation into his brother's ill-treatment. The Court held:

89. In the *Assenov* case . . . the Court made a finding of a procedural breach of Article 3 due to the inadequate investigation made by the authorities into the applicant's complaints that he had been severely ill-treated by the police. It had regard, in doing so, to the importance of ensuring that the fundamental prohibition against torture and inhuman and degrading treatment and punishment be effectively secured in the domestic system.

90. However, in that case, the Court had been unable to reach any conclusion as to whether the applicant's injuries had in fact been caused by the police as he alleged. The inability to make any conclusive findings of fact in that regard derived at least in part from the failure of the authorities to react effectively to those complaints at the relevant time. . . .

91. Procedural obligations have been implied in varying contexts under the Convention, where this has been perceived as necessary to ensure that the rights guaranteed under the Convention are not theoretical or illusory but practical and effective. The obligation to provide an effective investigation into the death caused, *inter alios*, by the security forces of the State was for this reason implied under Article 2 which guarantees the right to life (see *McCann and Others v the United Kingdom* . . .). This provision does however include the requirement that the right to life be 'protected by law'. It also may concern situations where the initiative must rest on the State for the practical reason that the victim is deceased and the circumstances of the death may be largely confined within the knowledge of state officials.

92. Article 3 however is phrased in substantive terms. Furthermore, though the victim of an alleged breach of this provision may be in a vulnerable position, the practical exigencies of the situation will often differ from cases of the use of lethal force or suspicious deaths. The Court considers that the requirement under Article 13 of the Convention for a person with an arguable claim of a violation of Article 3 to be provided with an effective remedy will generally provide both redress to the applicant and the necessary procedural safeguards against abuses by state officers. The Court's caselaw establishes that the notion of effective remedy in this context includes the duty to carry out a thorough and effective investigation capable of leading to the identification and punishment of those responsible for any ill-treatment and permitting effective access for the complainant to the investigatory procedure, (see *Aksoy v Turkey* . . .). Whether it is appropriate or necessary to find a procedural breach of Article 3 will therefore depend on the circumstances of the particular case.

93. In the present case, the Court has found that the applicant has suffered torture at the hands of the security forces. His complaints concerning the lack of any effective investigation by the authorities into the cause of his injuries fall to be dealt with in this case under Article 13 of the Convention.

---

[39] Above n 24.

This judgment indicates a potentially important retreat from *Assenov*, with applicants only being able to successfully assert a duty of effective investigation under Article 3 in exceptional cases. The Grand Chamber's ruling suggests that the Article 3 duty may well be restricted to cases where the Court, due to a lack of conclusive evidence, is unable to reach a finding in respect of the applicants' substantive complaints (*i.e.* whether they had been subject to torture or inhuman treatment *etc.* in violation of Article 3). Indeed, in the earlier cases of *Assenov* and *Sevtap Veznedaroglu* the Court was not able to determine if the applicants had been ill-treated by officials as they claimed, but went on to find breaches of the effective investigation obligation under Article 3.

Yet in *Satik and Others v Turkey*,[40] a unanimous Chamber[41] found breaches of Article 3 in both its substantive and investigatory duty forms. The applicant prisoners asserted that they had been attacked by about fifty gendarmes and thirty prison officials with truncheons and wooden planks, because they refused to allow their shoes to be searched. The Court rejected the Turkish government's claim that the applicants were injured by falling down some stairs as contemporaneous medical reports indicated that many of the applicants had been 'hit on the head and/or other parts of the body'. The Court determined that the applicants' maltreatment violated Article 3. Furthermore, the Court was critical of a number of facets of the subsequent domestic investigation into the attack upon the applicants. These included the loss of the case file after it was sent to gendarmes at the prison. In the Court's view, '[t]he authorities' failure to secure the integrity of important case documents must be considered a most serious defect in the investigative process.'[42] Additionally, the role of the Izmir Administrative Council in overseeing the investigation, despite the fact that it exercised control over the relevant security forces being investigated, undermined the independence of the investigation. Therefore, the Court concluded that:

> The inadequacy of that investigation is in itself inconsistent with the duty devolving on the authorities of a respondent State under Article 3 of the Convention to initiate an investigation into an arguable claim that an individual has been seriously ill-treated at the hands of its agents, which investigation should be capable of leading to the identification and punishment of those responsible (see the . . . *Assenov* judgment . . .).[43]

Hence the Court finding a substantive violation of Article 3 does not always exclude the possibility of it also determining that there has been a breach of the effective investigation obligation.

---

[40] Judgment of 10 October 2000.
[41] Including Judges Casadevall, Maruste and Golcuklu who had previously been members of the Grand Chamber in *Ilhan*.
[42] Above n 40, para 60.
[43] *Ibid* para 62.

The vagaries of the Court's response to applicants' complaints involving both substantive and investigative elements of Article 3 was further illustrated in *Denizci and Others v Cyprus*.[44] The applicants were nine Turkish Cypriots who alleged, *inter alia*, that they were unlawfully detained, beaten and expelled to the northern (Turkish occupied) part of Cyprus by agents of the Republic of Cyprus. The Chamber was unanimous in determining that the applicants had been subjected to inhuman treatment by the Cypriot authorities. It then dismissed the applicants' procedural claim under Article 3 in the following terms; '[i]t does not deem it necessary to make a separate finding under Article 3 in respect of the alleged lack of an effective investigation.'[45] It is to be regretted that the Court did not elaborate upon why it did not examine the complaint in respect of the absence of an effective investigation. Indeed, the Chamber's approach is even more inexplicable when we appreciate that it also failed to examine if there was an effective domestic inquiry as required by Article 13.

In *Anguelova v Bulgaria*,[46] the unanimous Chamber found a substantive violation of Article 3 in respect of the injuries to the applicant's son who died whilst in police custody. However, the Court's justification for declining to examine whether there had been an effective investigation under Article 3 was that it had already dealt with that issue under Article 2.

We may conclude that whilst the Court has recognised an implied positive obligation upon states to conduct effective investigations into arguable claims of serious ill-treatment by state agents violating Article 3's substantive prohibitions, the application of this duty by different Chambers has been problematic. In particular the circumstances when the Court will scrutinise domestic investigations under this Article, in contrast to utilising Article 13, remain obscure. Additionally, the willingness of the Court to reach decisions on complaints relating to allegations of breaches of both the substantive prohibitions and effective investigation duties enshrined in Article 3 does not follow a consistent pattern. Consequently, the effective investigation obligation under Article 3 is less well developed and more uncertain in its application at Strasbourg that the corresponding obligation created via Article 2.

GENERAL CONCLUSIONS

We can discern a considerable similarity in the development of positive obligations under this Article and those that we have already explored in the previous chapter under Article 2. Examples include the requirement upon public authorities to take protective measures to safeguard individuals (especially vulnerable persons such as children) from serious ill-treatment by others (*e.g.* as in *Z. and*

---

[44] Judgment of 23 May 2001.
[45] *Ibid* para 388.
[46] Judgment of 13 June 2002.

Others)[47] and the corresponding Article 2 obligation to protect individuals at immediate risk to their lives (*Osman v United Kingdom*).[48] Also, the duty to provide adequate medical care to detainees under both Article 3 (e.g. in *Keenan*)[49] and the parallel requirement under Article 2 (*e.g.* in *Anguelova*).[50] The obligation, under Article 3, to undertake effective investigations into arguable claims of serious ill-treatment by state agents (*e.g. Assenov*)[51] is, however, narrower than the corresponding obligation under Article 2 (as the latter requires effective investigations to be undertaken into all killings irrespective of the status of the perpetrator; *e.g. Ergi v Turkey*)[52] and we have discovered that the Court's application of the Article 3 obligation is more uncertain. Nevertheless, the Court's jurisprudential justification for the above positive obligations has often been identical, namely the combined requirements of Article 1 and the relevant substantive Article.

A significant enhancement in the full-time Court's application of positive obligations under Article 3 has been the willingness to find inadequate prison conditions to be in breach of this Article (*e.g.* in *Kalashnikov*).[53] When evaluating the acceptability of detention facilities under this provision the Court has found valuable guidance in the inspection reports and guidelines promulgated by its sibling body, the European Committee for the Prevention of Torture and Inhuman or Degrading Treatment or Punishment. With the relentless geo-political expansion of state parties to the European Convention on Human Rights we can reasonably expect a large increase in the number of complaints alleging breach of the obligation to provide acceptable conditions of detention.

---

[47] Above n 2.
[48] 1998-VIII.
[49] Above n 28.
[50] Above n 46.
[51] Above n 33.
[52] 1998-IV.
[53] Above n 17.

4

Article 5: Right to liberty and security

This lengthy article provides that:

(1) Everyone has the right to liberty and security of person. No one shall be deprived of his liberty save in the following cases and in accordance with a procedure prescribed by law:

(a) the lawful detention of a person after conviction by a competent court;

(b) the lawful arrest or detention of a person for non-compliance with the lawful order of a court or in order to secure the fulfilment of any obligation prescribed by law;

(c) the lawful arrest or detention of a person effected for the purpose of bringing him before the competent legal authority on reasonable suspicion of having committed an offence or when it is reasonably considered necessary to prevent his committing an offence or fleeing after having done so;

(d) the detention of a minor by lawful order for the purpose of educational super-vision or his lawful detention for the purpose of bringing him before the compe-tent legal authority;

(e) the lawful detention of persons for the prevention of the spreading of infectious diseases, of persons of unsound mind, alcoholics or drug addicts or vagrants;

(f) the lawful arrest or detention of a person to prevent his effecting an unauthorised entry into the country or of a person against whom action is being taken with a view to deportation or extradition.

(2) Everyone who is arrested shall be informed promptly, in a language which he understands, of the reasons for his arrest and of any charge against him.

(3) Everyone arrested or detained in accordance with the provisions of paragraph (1)(c) of this article shall be brought promptly before a judge or other officer author-ised by law to exercise judicial power and shall be entitled to trial within a reasonable time or to release pending trial. Release may be conditioned by guarantees to appear for trial.

(4) Everyone who is deprived of his liberty by arrest or detention shall be entitled to take proceedings by which the lawfulness of his detention shall be decided speedily by a court and his release ordered if the detention is not lawful.

(5) Everyone who has been the victim of arrest or detention in contravention of the provisions of this article shall have an enforceable right to compensation.

THE DUTIES TO ACCOUNT FOR DETAINEES AND TAKE EFFECTIVE MEASURES TO
SAFEGUARD AGAINST THE RISK OF THEIR DISAPPEARING WHILST IN CUSTODY

These related implied obligations were first identified within the express Convention guarantees accorded to detainees by the original Court in *Kurt v Turkey*.[1] By a majority, of six votes to three, the Chamber accepted the Commission's findings of fact that the applicant saw her son outside a fellow villager's house on the morning of 25 November 1993 and that he was surrounded by soldiers and village guards. At that time there was an anti-terrorist operation being conducted in the village by the authorities and three terrorists together with one member of the security forces were killed during the operation. The applicant's son was never seen again. She contended, *inter alia*, that the disappearance of her son involved multiple breaches of Article 5. The Court noted that Article provided a number of substantive rights, particularly regarding judicial supervision and scrutiny of the legality of an individual's detention under Article 5(3) and 5(4), intended to minimise the dangers of arbitrary detention. Furthermore:

> 124. The Court emphasises in this respect that the unacknowledged detention of an individual is a complete negation of these guarantees and a most grave violation of Article 5. Having assumed control over that individual it is incumbent on the authorities to account for his or her whereabouts. For this reason, Article 5 must be seen as requiring the authorities to take effective measures to safeguard against the risk of disappearance and to conduct a prompt effective investigation into an arguable claim that a person has been taken into custody and has not been seen since.

The Court then elaborated the practical measures that states must take in respect of safeguarding the custody of detainees, '. . . the absence of holding data recording such matters as the date, time and location of detention, the name of the detainee as well as the reasons for the detention and the name of the person effecting it must be seen as incompatible with the very purpose of Article 5 of the Convention.'[2] The majority went on to conclude that as the authorities had failed to provide any credible explanation for the whereabouts of the applicant's son after his detention they had breached their obligation to account for him and 'it must be accepted that he has been held in unacknowledged detention in the complete absence of the safeguards contained in Article 5.'[3]

The above element of the judgment in *Kurt* was a significant development of the Court's jurisprudence which sought to enhance the protection of detainees by defining the types of custody records that authorities must maintain in respect of every person detained by state agents. Of course, the purpose of this duty is not that of simple record keeping but of providing accurate accounts of

---

[1] 1998-III 1187.
[2] *Ibid* para 125.
[3] *Ibid* para 128.

the location (and related information) of detainees. These records should be available to both senior officials who have responsibility for supervising the detention of persons (*e.g.* prison governors) and relevant non-state persons (*e.g.* the detainee's lawyer). Such forms of access will help to ensure the whereabouts and treatment of detainees can be monitored to facilitate compliance with their Convention rights. Conversely, the failure to maintain efficient custody records can exacerbate the potential danger of detainees disappearing without trace (possibly being murdered) as the facts of *Kurt* graphically illustrated.

Subsequently, a Chamber of the full-time Court was united in finding a breach of this obligation in *Anguelova v Bulgaria*.[4] The applicant's seventeen year old son had died whilst in police custody, following his arrest in connection with suspected thefts from cars. The Court applied *Kurt* and stated that the custody record obligation was derived from the 'requirement of lawfulness'[5] found within Article 5(1). As the son's detention was not initially recorded in the police station register, and later an attempt was made to forge such an entry, the Court found a violation of the 'requirements implicit in Article 5 of the Convention for the proper recording of deprivations of liberty.'[6]

Another Chamber found systematic failings in the custody records of Turkish gendarme stations. The applicant in *Orhan v Turkey*[7] alleged, *inter alia*, that two of his brothers and his son were taken away by soldiers in 1994 and they have never been seen since. The Court was unanimous in concluding that serious deficiencies had been found in the practice of recording custody in those premises.

> 372. . . . The first established deficiency is not allowed by domestic law namely, the gendarme practice of detaining persons for various reasons in their stations without being entered in the custody records. The second and third failing further underline the unreliability of custody records as those records will not show whether one is apprehended by military forces and may not show the date of release from the gendarme station. These three deficiencies attest to the absence of effective measures to safeguard against the risk of disappearances of individuals in detention.

Hence the Court determined that the applicant's relatives had been held in unacknowledged detention in violation of Article 5. Clearly, this judgment indicates a widespread undermining of rigorous custody record keeping by Turkish state agents during the last decade. It also demonstrates how the obligation to maintain thorough custody records is at the heart of states' duties to account for detainees and safeguard them against disappearance.

---

[4] Judgment of 13 June 2002.
[5] *Ibid* para 154.
[6] *Ibid* para 157.
[7] Judgment of 18 June 2002.

THE DUTY TO INVESTIGATE ALLEGATIONS THAT PERSONS IN CUSTODY
HAVE DISAPPEARED

This positive obligation, which is closely related to those in the previous section, is concerned with the situation where it is alleged that a person has been taken into custody by state agents and the detained person has not been seen again. Obviously such circumstances involve the underlying apprehension that the detained person may have been unlawfully killed. The duty of investigation in regard to alleged disappeared persons was also first articulated by the Court in *Kurt*.[8] The majority concluded that there had been 'no meaningful investigation' into the applicant's petition to the local public prosecutor that her son had been detained by state agents and that she was concerned about his fate. This contributed to the majority's judgment that: '[t]he Court, accordingly, like the Commission, finds that there has been a particularly grave violation of the right to liberty and security of person guaranteed under Article 5 raising serious concerns about the welfare of Uzeyir Kurt.'[9]

Once again we learn that a positive obligation of investigation is impliedly contained within the express rights of a Convention Article. Although the Court did not make reference to the analogous implied obligations of investigation under Articles 2 and 3,[10] the *Kurt* duty has a similar practical objective of seeking to discourage state agents from violating detainees' basic rights by the deterrent consequences of the state's obligation to undertake an effective investigation into arguable claims that a detainee has disappeared.

A Chamber of the full-time Court applied *Kurt* in *Tas v Turkey*,[11] where the applicant complained that his son had been shot in the leg and detained by gendarmes, during another anti-terrorist operation in south-east Turkey, and he had never been seen again. The majority, six votes to one, found a number of deficiencies in the Turkish authorities' inquiries into the applicant's petition regarding the whereabouts of his son. These included the local public prosecutor failing to undertake any investigations for two years and a lack of independence, openness and vigour in the subsequent investigation by the provincial administrative council. Consequently the Court held that the domestic investigation was 'neither prompt nor effective' and contributed towards 'a particularly grave' violation of Article 5.

Later a Grand Chamber of the full-time Court also endorsed the *Kurt* positive investigation obligation in *Cyprus v Turkey*.[12] The applicant state argued, *inter alia*, that the respondent state authorities (in both the occupied territory of

---

[8] Above n 1.
[9] *Ibid* para 129.
[10] Above chs 2–3.
[11] Judgment of 14 November 2000.
[12] Judgment of 10 May 2001.

northern Cyprus and on the Turkish mainland) had failed to undertake effective investigations into the detention and subsequent disappearance of a large, but indefinite, number (many hundreds) of Greek-Cypriot persons who disappeared during the Turkish military invasion of 1974. The former Commission concluded that Turkey had failed to comply with this obligation. Also, '[t]he Commission stressed that there could be no limitation in time as regards the duty to investigate and inform, especially as it could not be ruled out that detained persons who had disappeared might have been the victims of the most serious crimes, including war crimes or crimes against humanity.'[13] An overwhelming majority of the Court, sixteen votes to one, supported this expansive view of the *Kurt* investigation duty.

> 150. The Court concludes that, during the period under consideration, there has been a continuing violation of Article 5 of the Convention by virtue of the failure of the authorities of the respondent State to conduct an effective investigation into the whereabouts and fate of the missing Greek-Cypriot persons in respect of whom there is an arguable claim that they were in custody at the time they disappeared.

The dissentient, Judge Fuad the *ad hoc* Turkish judge, advocated a shorter duration of the duty to conduct an investigation into alleged disappeared persons.

> 25. ... The events which the majority of the Court held to have given rise to an obligation to conduct effective investigations occurred in July and August 1974. This was some fifteen years before the operative date of Turkey's declaration. Neither the Commission nor the Court found sufficient evidence to hold that the missing persons were still in the custody of the Turkish authorities at the relevant time. In my opinion, it cannot be right to treat the Convention obligation which arises in certain circumstances to conduct a prompt and effective investigation as having persisted for fifteen years after the events which required investigation so that, when Turkey did become bound by the Convention, her alleged failure to date to conduct appropriate investigations can be regarded as a violation of the Convention. In my view, the concept of continuing violations cannot be prayed in aid to reach such a result. It seems to me that such an approach would be to apply an obligation imposed by the Convention retrospectively and to divest the time limitation in the declaration of its effect.

Although this case was atypical (due to a range of factors, including the numbers of persons alleged to have disappeared, the context of their detention/disappearance and the inter-state form of the case) it is submitted that in principle the approach of the Commission and Court was correct and the duty upon states to effectively investigate arguable complaints of disappearances should be an enduring one. For the families and friends of such persons their legitimate desire to know the whereabouts and fate of the disappeared has no cut-off date.

An example of a unanimous Chamber finding a violation of the effective investigation duty occurred in *Akdeniz and Others v Turkey*.[14] The applicants

---

[13] *Ibid* para 145.
[14] Judgment of 31 May 2001.

were the relatives of eleven villagers detained during a major security operation in south-east Turkey during October 1993. The detainees have not been seen since. The Court found that, *inter alia*, the public prosecutors were unwilling to pursue any lines of enquiry concerning the security forces' involvement in the disappearance of the applicants' relatives. Therefore, the Court held that there had not been an effective investigation and that contributed towards a 'particularly grave violation' of Article 5.

This implied positive obligation has many similarities in terms of the requirements of promptness and effectiveness with the parallel duties of investigation under Articles 2 and 3. As we have already observed, these duties also share the common aim, amongst a number, of seeking to discourage state agents from violating the fundamental rights of persons in their custody. Hence these obligations are a progressive judicial attempt to buttress the legal safeguards of potentially vulnerable persons.

THE DUTY TO INFORM PROMPTLY DETAINED PERSONS OF THE REASONS FOR THEIR DETENTION

Article 5(2) expressly requires that, 'everyone who is arrested shall be informed promptly, in a language which he understands, of the reasons for his arrest and of any charge against him.' The original Court significantly extended the ambit of this positive obligation in *Van der Leer v Netherlands*.[15] In September 1983 the applicant was committed to a psychiatric hospital on the orders of the local Burgomaster. A few days later the District Court refused to extend her confinement. However, Mrs Van der Leer continued to stay in the hospital as a voluntary patient. In November 1983, on the application of her husband, the Cantonal Court ordered her compulsory confinement in the hospital for six months. Mrs Van der Leer was not informed of the order and first became aware of it when, ten days later, she was placed in isolation within the hospital. She immediately contacted her lawyer and after several court hearings the order was revoked in May 1984. Mrs Van der Leer contended that her detention violated several aspects of Article 5. The Commission unanimously found, *inter alia*, that there had been a breach of Article 5(2). Before the Court, the Dutch government contended that the wording of that provision indicated that it only applied to detentions under the criminal law. The Chamber held that:

> 27. The Court is not unmindful of the criminal-law connotation of the words used in Article 5(2). However, it agrees with the Commission that they should be interpreted 'autonomously,' in particular in accordance with the aim and purpose of Article 5, which are to protect everyone from arbitrary deprivations of liberty. Thus the 'arrest' referred to in paragraph 2 of Article 5 extends beyond the realm of criminal-law measures. Similarly, in using the words 'any charge' ('tout accusation') in this provision,

---

[15] A.170 (1990).

the intention of the drafters was not to lay down a condition for its applicability, but to indicate an eventuality of which it takes account.

28. The close links between paragraphs 2 and 4 of Article 5 supports this interpretation. Any person who is entitled to take proceedings to have the lawfulness of his detention decided speedily cannot make effective use of that right unless he is promptly and adequately informed of the reasons why he has been deprived of his liberty. . . .

Paragraph 4 does not make any distinction as between persons deprived of their liberty on the basis of whether they have been arrested or detained. There are therefore no grounds for excluding the latter from the scope of paragraph 2.

The Court went on to hold that neither the manner nor the time involved in informing the applicant of her compulsory detention satisfied the requirements of this positive obligation. The judgment in *Van der Leer* greatly widened the scope of detainees who could now invoke this obligation as it was not limited to those being held under criminal law powers. This was, therefore, a desirable extension of a basic informational safeguard to potentially vulnerable persons being detained under civil law provisions.

A few months later another Chamber reduced the burdens of this obligation upon police officers in *Fox, Campbell and Hartley v United Kingdom*.[16] The first two applicants were arrested together in Belfast. They were informed that they had been arrested under section 11 of the Northern Ireland (Emergency Provisions) Act 1978, because they were suspected of being terrorists. About five hours later they were separately questioned about their suspected involvement in courier and intelligence gathering activities on behalf of the Provisional IRA. They were released, without being charged, two days later. The third applicant was arrested, at his home in Northern Ireland, under the same section. He too was informed by the arresting officer that he was suspected of being a terrorist. About four hours later he was interviewed, at a police station, about a kidnapping believed to be connected with the IRA. Hartley was not charged and he was released after thirty hours of detention. The applicants complained, *inter alia*, of a breach of Article 5(2) as they asserted that they had not been given adequate information regarding the grounds of their arrest at the time of their arrest and the authorities had not complied with the duty to inform detainees of the grounds where the latter had to deduce that information from subsequent police questioning. However, the Court defined the requirements of Article 5(2) in the following terms:

40. . . . any person arrested must be told, in simple, non-technical language that he can understand, the essential legal and factual grounds for his arrest, so as to be able, if he sees fit, to apply to a court to challenge its lawfulness in accordance with paragraph 4. . . . Whilst this information must be conveyed 'promptly' . . . it need not be related in its entirety by the arresting officer at the very moment of the arrest. Whether the content and promptness of the information conveyed were sufficient is to be assessed in each case according to its special features.

---

[16] A.182 (1990).

The judges, and the government, acknowledged that the information provided to the applicants by their arresting officers did not satisfy the demands of Article 5(2). But, taking account of the subsequent police questioning of the applicants in respect of specific criminal acts.

> 41. . . . There is no ground to suppose that these interrogations were not such as to enable the applicants to understand why they had been arrested. The reasons why they were suspected of being terrorists were thereby brought to their attention during their interrogation.

Furthermore, in the determination of the Court those interrogations had taken place within a few hours of the applicants arrest and therefore the information had been conveyed to them promptly. Hence no breach of Article 5(2) had occurred.

In the above judgment the Court rejected the applicants' contention that states could not satisfy the information provision element of Article 5(2) by police interrogations of detainees concerning particular suspected offences. To enable states to claim that they had 'informed' detainees of the grounds for their arrest by virtue of subsequent police questioning was a very generous interpretation in their favour. Undoubtedly, the legitimate response of states to terrorism was a significant factor in the Court's application of this positive obligation in *Fox*.

> 28. . . . The Court has already recognised the need, inherent in the Convention system, for a proper balance between the defence of the institutions of democracy in the common interest and the protection of individual rights (see the *Brogan and Others v United Kingdom judgment*, A.145-B (1988), para. 48). Accordingly, when examining these complaints the Court will, as it did in the *Brogan* judgment, take into account the special nature of terrorist crime and the exigencies of dealing with it, as far as is compatible with the applicable provisions of the Convention in the light of their particular wording and its overall object and purpose.

A Grand Chamber endorsed the *Fox* interpretation of Article 5(2) in *Murray v United Kingdom*.[17] Mrs Murray was arrested at her home by an army Corporal, who had been briefed that the applicant was suspected of being involved in the illegal collection of money for the purchase of arms by the IRA. The Corporal simply informed the applicant that she was being arrested under section 14 (of the Northern Ireland (Emergency Provisions) Act 1978, which empowered a member of the British armed forces on duty to arrest, and detain for up to four hours, any person he suspected to be committing, having committed or being about to commit any offence). After being taken to an army screening centre the applicant was questioned, by another soldier, about her brothers and her contacts with them (a few weeks earlier her brothers had been convicted in the USA of arms offences connected with the purchase of weapons for the IRA). She refused to answer any questions and was released, without

---

[17] A.300-A (1994).

charge, two hours after her arrest. Before the Court she claimed that, *inter alia*, at the time of her arrest and during her detention she had not been given sufficient information as to the grounds of her arrest in breach of the obligation under Article 5(2). A large majority of the Court, thirteen votes to five, rejected her claim.

> 77. . . . In the Court's view, it must have been apparent to Mrs Murray that she was being questioned about her possible involvement in the collection of funds for the purchase of arms for the Provisional IRA by her brothers in the USA. Admittedly, 'there was never any probing examination of her collecting money'—to use the words of the trial judge- but, as the national courts noted, this was because of Mrs Murray's declining to answer any questions at all beyond giving her name. The Court therefore finds that the reasons for her arrest were sufficiently brought to her attention during her interview.

In his partly dissenting opinion Judge Mifsud Bonnici was scathing in his condemnation of the majority's interpretation of Article 5(2).

> 5. In my opinion this decision reduces the meaning of Article 5(2) to such a low level that it is doubtful whether in fact it can, if it is adhered to in this form, have any possible concrete application in the future.
>
> In fact what is being held here is that through the contents of an interrogation an accused person can, by inference or deduction, arrive, on his own, to understand 'the reasons for his arrest and . . . any charge against him.' Since the Convention obliges the investigating officer 'to inform' the arrested person, I cannot agree that the duty imposed on the investigating officer can be satisfied by the obligation of the arrested person to carry out a logical exercise so that he will thereby know of the charge against him- surmising both, from the contents of the interrogation.

Despite this cogent criticism the full-time Court has continued to follow the *Fox* and *Murray* approach.[18]

Overall, the Court's jurisprudence regarding this obligation has been somewhat mixed. The scope of the obligation has been extended to encompass civil forms of detention, *e.g.* in respect of psychiatric patients, but the Court has also allowed states to satisfy the information provision element of this obligation via the questioning of detainees regarding particular criminal acts. However, the cases on the provision of the reasons for an arrest have involved persons suspected of involvement in terrorism and here the Court has been quite understanding of the difficulties faced by states in combating this scourge.

THE DUTY TO BRING DETAINEES SUSPECTED OF HAVING COMMITTED A CRIMINAL OFFENCE PROMPTLY BEFORE A JUDGE OR JUDICIAL OFFICER

Article 5(3) expressly imposes this obligation upon states. As we shall examine below, the underlying purpose of this obligation is to require the domestic

---

[18] For example in *Kerr v UK*, admissibility decision, (7 December 1999).

judiciary to review whether the deprivation of the suspects' liberty is justified. The leading authority on the assessment of the promptness element of the obligation is the plenary Court judgment in *Brogan and Others v United Kingdom*.[19] The four applicants had been arrested on suspicion of involvement in terrorist crimes in Northern Ireland. They were detained by the police for questioning for variable periods of time (from four days and six hours up to six days and sixteen hours) before being released without charge. Before, the Court they argued, *inter alia*, that they had not been brought promptly before a judge in breach of Article 5(3). The Court held that:

59. The obligation expressed in English by the word 'promptly' and in French by the word '*aussitôt*' is clearly distinguishable from the less strict requirement in the second part of paragraph 3 (art. 5-3) ('reasonable time'/'*délai raisonnable*') and even from that in paragraph 4 of Article 5 ('speedily'/'*à bref délai*'). The term 'promptly' also occurs in the English text of paragraph 2 (art. 5-2), where the French text uses the words '*dans le plus court délai*'. As indicated in the *Ireland v the United Kingdom* judgment (18 January 1978, Series A no. 25, p. 76, para. 199), 'promptly' in paragraph 3 (art. 5-3) may be understood as having a broader significance than '*aussitôt*', which literally means immediately. Thus confronted with versions of a law-making treaty which are equally authentic but not exactly the same, the Court must interpret them in a way that reconciles them as far as possible and is most appropriate in order to realise the aim and achieve the object of the treaty (see, *inter alia*, the *Sunday Times* judgment of 26 April 1979, Series A no. 30, p. 30, para. 48, and Article 33 para. 4 of the Vienna Convention of 23 May 1969 on the Law of Treaties).

The use in the French text of the word '*aussitôt*,' with its constraining connotation of immediacy, confirms that the degree of flexibility attaching to the notion of 'promptness' is limited, even if the attendant circumstances can never be ignored for the purposes of the assessment under paragraph 3 (art. 5-3). Whereas promptness is to be assessed in each case according to its special features (see the above-mentioned *de Jong, Baljet and van den Brink* judgment, Series A no. 77, p. 25, para. 52), the significance to be attached to those features can never be taken to the point of impairing the very essence of the right guaranteed by Article 5 para. 3 (art. 5-3), that is to the point of effectively negativing the State's obligation to ensure a prompt release or a prompt appearance before a judicial authority.

Whilst the Court accepted the government's contention that the investigation of terrorist crimes presented special problems for the authorities, a majority (twelve votes to seven) concluded that:

62. As indicated above (paragraph 59), the scope for flexibility in interpreting and applying the notion of 'promptness' is very limited. In the Court's view, even the shortest of the four periods of detention, namely the four days and six hours spent in police custody by Mr McFadden falls outside the strict constraints as to time permitted by the first part of Article 5 para. 3. To attach such importance to the special features of this case as to justify so lengthy a period of detention without appearance before a judge or other judicial officer would be an unacceptably wide interpretation

---

[19] A.145-B (1988).

of the plain meaning of the word 'promptly.' An interpretation to this effect would import into Article 5 para. 3 a serious weakening of a procedural guarantee to the detriment of the individual and would entail consequences impairing the very essence of the right protected by this provision. The Court thus has to conclude that none of the applicants was either brought 'promptly' before a judicial authority or released 'promptly' following his arrest. The undoubted fact that the arrest and detention of the applicants were inspired by the legitimate aim of protecting the community as a whole from terrorism is not on its own sufficient to ensure compliance with the specific requirements of Article 5 para. 3.

There has thus been a breach of Article 5 para. 3 (art. 5-3) in respect of all four applicants.

The dissentients, taking account of the exceptional circumstances of terrorist violence in Northern Ireland, considered that the periods of detention in the applicants' cases satisfied the test of promptness.

The Court's judgment in *Brogan* is highly significant because the majority rejected the Commission's established guidelines on the notion of promptness in respect of this obligation (up to four days of detention prior to bringing a detainee before a judge/releasing him in ordinary criminal cases or five days in exceptional cases was compatible with Article 5(3)). It also reflected a tougher stance towards state claims of leeway to counter terrorism than that exhibited in the Court's jurisprudence regarding the obligation under Article 5(2) discussed previously.

The Court has also elaborated upon the institutional features required of the 'officer authorised by law to exercise judicial power' who can review the detention of suspects under Article 5(3). In *Huber v Switzerland*,[20] the applicant challenged the impartiality of the District Attorney who questioned her about a prostitution network, then ordered her detention and subsequently instituted criminal proceedings against her. She contended that this multiplicity of roles undermined his impartiality when exercising powers of detention over her and therefore he did not satisfy the requirements of Article 5(3). The plenary Court overwhelmingly, twenty-one votes to one, upheld her complaint.

> 43. . . . . Clearly the Convention does not rule out the possibility of the judicial officer who orders the detention carrying out other duties, but his impartiality is capable of appearing open to doubt . . . if he is entitled to intervene in the subsequent criminal proceedings as a representative of the prosecuting authority.
>
> Since that was the situation in the present case, there has been a breach of Article 5(3).

This decision represented a higher standard of institutional impartiality of judicial officers than had been demanded in the earlier case law.[21] The full-time Court endorsed the *Huber* impartiality test in *Hood v United Kingdom*.[22] The applicant was a soldier in the British army who had a history of being absent

---

[20] A.188 (1990).

[21] In the previous case of *Schiesser v Switzerland* A.34 (1979), the Court had upheld the exercise of detention powers by another District Attorney.

[22] Judgment of 18 February 1999.

without leave. He was arrested by the police and taken to his barracks. After being brought before his commanding officer the latter ordered that Hood be held in military custody until the time of his court martial. Hood challenged the impartiality of his commanding officer to make decisions about his detention because of the other roles of the officer (including overseeing the subsequent prosecution of Hood and the officer's general responsibility for discipline in his command). The Court was united in concluding that those other responsibilities undermined the commanding officer's ability to comply with the institutional requirements of Article 5(3).

Judicial officers must also satisfy the requirement of independence. In *Assenov and Others v Bulgaria*,[23] the first applicant had been arrested and the next day, in the presence of his lawyer and a prosecutor, he was questioned by an investigator in regard to a series of robberies and burglaries. Assenov admitted committing most of the burglaries but denied involvement in the robberies. The investigator decided to remand Assenov in custody to await trial. Subsequently, Assenov contended that his detention had not been authorised by an independent judicial officer. The Court was unanimous in finding a breach of Article 5(3).

> 148. . . . . It notes that, under Bulgarian law, investigators do not have the power to make legally binding decisions as to the detention or release of a suspect. Instead, any decision made by an investigator is capable of being overturned by the prosecutor, who may also withdraw a case from an investigator if dissatisfied with the latter's approach. It follows that the investigator was not sufficiently independent properly to be described as an 'officer authorised by law to exercise judicial power' within the meaning of Article 5(3).

Hence, the officer making detention decisions must possess authority under domestic law to reach binding determinations, subject of course to possible appeals to a higher judicial body, if that officer is to satisfy the Court's institutional requirement of independence. Furthermore, the element of independence also necessitates that the judicial officer must not be part of the government. In *Niedbala v Poland*,[24] the applicant had been remanded in custody on suspicion of car theft by a District Prosecutor. Before the Court, Niedbala challenged the independence of this official. In the unanimous judgment of the Court:

> 49. Thus, the 'officer' must be independent of the executive and of the parties. . . .
>
> 52. . . . In this respect, the Court notes the Government's submission that prosecutors in Poland were at the material time, and, indeed, still are, subordinate to the Prosecutor General, who at the same time carries out the function of the Minister of Justice. It is therefore indisputable that the prosecutors, in the exercise of their functions, are subject to supervision of an authority belonging to the executive branch of the Government.

Consequently, there had been a violation of Article 5(3).

[23] 1998-VIII 3187.
[24] Judgment of 4 July 2000.

A Grand Chamber of the full-time Court articulated the purpose and contemporary features (both substantive and procedural) of this obligation in *T.W. v Malta*.[25] The applicant was arrested one evening, the next day (Friday 7 October 1994) he was brought before a magistrate. He was charged with sexual and physical abuse of his minor daughter. He pleaded not guilty. The magistrate had no power to order his release. Eventually, another magistrate granted him bail on 25 October 1994. The applicant alleged, *inter alia*, that he had suffered a violation of Article 5(3) because the magistrate whom he had originally been brought before had no power to authorise his release. The judges were united in holding that:

41. As the Court has pointed out on many occasions, Article 5 § 3 of the Convention provides persons arrested or detained on suspicion of having committed a criminal offence with a guarantee against any arbitrary or unjustified deprivation of liberty (see, *inter alia*, the *Assenov and Others v Bulgaria* judgment of 28 October 1998, *Reports of Judgments and Decisions* 1998-VIII, p. 3187, § 146). It is essentially the object of Article 5 § 3, which forms a whole with paragraph 1 (c), to require provisional release once detention ceases to be reasonable. The fact that an arrested person had access to a judicial authority is not sufficient to constitute compliance with the opening part of Article 5 § 3. This provision enjoins the judicial officer before whom the arrested person appears to review the circumstances militating for or against detention, to decide by reference to legal criteria whether there are reasons to justify detention, and to order release if there are no such reasons. . . . In other words, Article 5 § 3 requires the judicial officer to consider the merits of the detention.

42. To be in accordance with Article 5 § 3, judicial control must be prompt. Promptness has to be assessed in each case according to its special features. . . . However, the scope of flexibility in interpreting and applying the notion of promptness is very limited (see the *Brogan and Others v the United Kingdom* judgment of 29 November 1988, Series A no. 145-B, pp. 33-34, § 62).

43. In addition to being prompt, the judicial control of the detention must be automatic. . . . It cannot be made to depend on a previous application by the detained person. Such a requirement would not only change the nature of the safeguard provided for under Article 5 § 3, a safeguard distinct from that in Article 5 § 4, which guarantees the right to institute proceedings to have the lawfulness of detention reviewed by a court. . . . It might even defeat the purpose of the safeguard under Article 5 § 3 which is to protect the individual from arbitrary detention by ensuring that the act of deprivation of liberty is subject to independent judicial scrutiny (see, *mutatis mutandis*, the *Kurt v Turkey* judgment of 25 May 1998, *Reports* 1998-III, p. 1185, § 123). Prompt judicial review of detention is also an important safeguard against ill-treatment of the individual taken into custody (see the *Aksoy v Turkey* judgment of 18 December 1996, *Reports* 1996-VI, p. 2282, § 76). Furthermore, arrested persons who have been subjected to such treatment might be incapable of lodging an application asking the judge to review their detention. The same could hold true for other vulnerable categories of arrested persons, such as the mentally weak or those who do not speak the language of the judicial officer.

[25] Judgment of 29 April 1999.

44. Finally, by virtue of Article 5 § 3 the judicial officer must himself or herself hear the detained person before taking the appropriate decision . . .

Although the applicant's appearance before the magistrate on the day following his arrest satisfied the requirement of promptness, the magistrate's inability to review the merits of his continued detention and order his release if appropriate meant that there had been a breach of Article 5(3). The judgment vividly demonstrates that this positive obligation is not satisfied by a mere symbolic prompt appearance before a judge or judicial officer, to meet the requirements of the Court the hearing must examine the lawfulness of the detainee's detention.

Because of the crucial role performed by domestic judicial supervision of the detention of criminal suspects in protecting such persons' liberty and well-being, the Court has developed an extensive set of criteria under Article 5(3) which those authorities must comply with. As we have seen, they include strict time constraints (*Brogan*), the institutional requirements of impartiality (*Huber*) and independence (*Assenov*) for judicial officers, procedural elements (*e.g.* an automatic hearing before the judge/judicial officer, *T.W.*) and substantive necessities (*e.g.* consideration of the merits of the suspect's detention, *T.W.*). The creation of the above jurisprudence has ensured that this positive obligation provides effective protection for such detainees.

TO GRANT DETAINEES BAIL UNLESS THERE ARE PUBLIC INTEREST GROUNDS JUSTIFYING THEIR CONTINUED DETENTION PENDING TRIAL

The Grand Chamber in *T.W.* held, 'that the question of bail is a distinct and separate issue, which only comes into play when the arrest and detention are lawful.'[26] In the very early case of *Wemhoff v Germany*,[27] the original Court interpreted Article 5(3) as requiring states to justify the reasonableness of the decision(s) to refuse bail and the length of the remand period. The applicant had been arrested in November 1961, on suspicion of breach of trust, his applications for bail were refused on numerous occasions by the German courts and he was committed for trial in July 1964. In April 1965 he was convicted of serious breach of trust and sentenced to six-and-a-half-years' imprisonment (his period of detention on remand was deducted from this term). The Court considered that:

5. In other words it is the provisional detention of accused persons which must not, according to Article 5(3), be prolonged beyond a reasonable time . . .

10. The reasonableness of an accused person's continued detention must be assessed in each case according to its special features.

---

[26] Judgment of 29 April 1999, para 49.
[27] A.7 (1968).

An overwhelming majority of the Court, six votes to one, concluded that the German authorities had not breached these requirements. The majority accepted the reasonableness of the domestic courts' refusals of bail due to the perceived dangers that Wemhoff might flee or destroy evidence. Also, the nearly four year period of pre-trial detention was deemed reasonable given the complexity of investigating Wemhoff's criminal behaviour.

In contemporary times the Court has become more strict in its evaluation of decisions refusing detainees bail. For example, in *Kalashnikov v Russia*,[28] the applicant was charged with misappropriating a large number of shares, he was the president of a bank, in February 1995. In June 1995 he was remanded in custody on the ground that he had obstructed the investigation into his alleged criminal conduct. Despite numerous requests the courts refused to grant him bail. In August 1999 he was convicted and sentenced to five-and-a-half years' imprisonment (he was released from prison in June 2000 under an amnesty). In respect of his complaint of a breach of Article 5(3), the Court held that:

> 114. . . . the question of whether or not a period of detention is reasonable cannot be assessed in the abstract. Whether it is reasonable for an accused to remain in detention must be examined in each case according to its special features. Continued detention can be justified in a given case only if there are specific indications of a genuine requirement of public interest which, notwithstanding the presumption of innocence, outweighs the rule in respect for individual liberty laid down in Article 5 of the Convention . . .
>
> It falls in the first place to the national judicial authorities to ensure that, in a given case, the pre-trial detention of an accused person does not exceed a reasonable time. To this end they must, paying due regard to the principle of the presumption of innocence, examine all the facts arguing for or against the existence of the above-mentioned requirement of public interest justifying a departure from the rule in Article 5, and must set them out in their decisions on the applications for release. It is essentially on the basis of the reasons given in these decisions, and any well-documented facts stated by the applicant in his appeals, that the Court is called upon to decide whether or not there has been a violation of Article 5(3) . . .
>
> The persistence of a reasonable suspicion that the person arrested has committed an offence is a condition *sine qua non* for the lawfulness of the continued detention, but after a certain lapse of time it no longer suffices. The Court must then establish whether the other grounds given by the judicial authorities continued to justify the deprivation of liberty. Where such grounds were 'relevant' and 'sufficient', the Court must also be satisfied that the national authorities displayed 'special diligence' in the conduct of proceedings. The complexity and special characteristics of the investigation are factors to be considered in this respect . . .

The judges were united in determining that the ground relied upon by the Russian courts to deny Kalashnikov bail lost its relevant and sufficient character during the course of his lengthy detention. The Court considered that as the investigation progressed his ability to obstruct the collection of evidence was

---

[28] Judgment of 15 July 2002.

correspondingly reduced. Furthermore, the Court found that the applicant's period of pre-trial detention exceeded a reasonable time due to a poor quality investigation which had delayed proceedings. Therefore, a breach of Article 5(3) had occurred.

It is clear that now national authorities must grant detainees bail unless there are cogent public interest grounds for refusing to release particular detainees. In such cases the domestic courts are obliged to monitor the ongoing justification of these detainees' detention and they cannot be held on remand for more than a reasonable period of time.

ACCESS TO A COURT FOR THE SPEEDY DETERMINATION OF THE
LAWFULNESS OF A PERSON'S DETENTION

Article 5(4) guarantees that, 'everyone who is deprived of his liberty by arrest or detention shall be entitled to take proceedings by which the lawfulness of his detention shall be decided speedily by a court and his release ordered if the detention is not lawful.' An early judgment of the original Court, sitting in plenary session, established the basic requirements of this positive obligation in *De Wilde, Ooms and Versyp v Belgium (the 'Vagrancy' cases).*[29] The applicants voluntarily surrendered themselves to different police stations in Belgium as vagrants (they had no homes, means of subsistence nor regular trades or professions). Within twenty-four hours they were brought before police courts. The courts held public hearings during which the identity, age, physical and mental state and manner of life of each applicant were determined. The applicants had the opportunity to reply to these questions. At the end of the hearings the courts ordered that as vagrants the applicants be detained 'at the disposal of the government' for up to two years. Subsequently, the applicant complained to the Commission alleging, *inter alia*, a breach of Article 5(4). By nine votes to two the Commission found that the proceedings before the police courts failed to satisfy the requirements of Article 5(4). The Court first addressed the issue whether this obligation necessitated a second set of judicial proceedings where a court had ordered a person's detention at first-instance (*e.g.* after convicting him/her of committing a criminal offence).

> 76. . . . it is clear that the purpose of Article 5 (4) is to assure to persons who are arrested and detained the right to a judicial supervision of the lawfulness of the measure to which the[y] are thereby subjected; the word 'court' ('*tribunal*') is there found in the singular and not in the plural. Where the decision depriving a person of his liberty is one taken by an administrative body, there is no doubt that Article 5 (4) obliges the Contracting States to make available to the person detained a right of recourse to a court; but there is nothing to indicate that the same applies when the decision is made by a court at the close of judicial proceedings. In the latter case the supervision

[29] A.12 (1971).

required by Article 5(4) is incorporated in the decision; this is so, for example, where a sentence of imprisonment is pronounced after 'conviction by a competent court' (Article 5 (1) (a) of the Convention). It may therefore be concluded that Article 5 (4) is observed if the arrest or detention of a vagrant, provided for in paragraph (1)(e), is ordered by a 'court' within the meaning of paragraph (4).

It results, however, from the purpose and object of Article 5, as well as from the very terms of paragraph (4) ('proceedings', *'recours'*), that in order to constitute such a 'court' an authority must provide the fundamental guarantees of procedure applied in matters of deprivation of liberty. If the procedure of the competent authority does not provide them, the State could not be dispensed from making available to the person concerned a second authority which does provide all the guarantees of judicial procedure.

In sum, the Court considers that the intervention of one organ satisfies Article 5 (4), but on condition that the procedure followed has a judicial character and gives to the individual concerned guarantees appropriate to the kind of deprivation of liberty in question.

The Court acknowledged that the magistrates who presided over the Belgian police courts satisfied the organisational requirement of independence from the executive and the parties to the vagrancy proceedings. However, a majority of the Court, nine votes to seven, did not consider that the summary procedure followed in vagrancy cases provided adequate procedural safeguards for the applicants.

79. . . . This procedure undoubtedly presents certain judicial features, such as the hearing taking place and the decision being given in public, but they are not sufficient to give the magistrate the character of a 'court' within the meaning of Article 5(4) when due account is taken of the seriousness of what is at stake, namely a long deprivation of liberty attended by various shameful consequences.

As the applicants did not have access to a higher court with the ability to fully examine the lawfulness of their detention there had been a breach of Article 5(4).

The above judgment interpreted Article 5(4) to require at least one opportunity for detainees to seek judicial scrutiny of the legality of their detention. The Court demanded institutional independence of the judicial body conducting the domestic review together with the observance of procedures commensurate to the nature of the specific individual's detention. In respect of the vagrancy applicants, the Belgian police courts did not offer sufficient procedural safeguards, such as adjournments to allow detainees to seek legal advice or representation, given the potentially lengthy periods of loss of liberty involved in placing vagrants at the disposal of the government. This was a robust judgment by the Court that revealed the importance of Article 5(4) in protecting detainees from the arbitrary deprivation of their liberty.

The Court further enhanced the requirements of this obligation in *Winterwerp v Netherlands*.[30] The applicant suffered from serious mental

[30] A.33 (1979).

problems following an accident which had caused him severe brain damage. In June 1968 he was committed to a psychiatric hospital on the emergency orders of the local burgomaster. The next month his wife applied to the District Court for the continued detention of her husband at the hospital because of his mental health (her application was supported by a doctor who had examined Mr Winterwerp). The Court approved his continued detention. In November 1968 Mrs Winterwerp applied to the Regional Court for a one year detention order in respect of her husband. After receiving his medical records the Regional Court granted the order. Subsequently, the Regional Court renewed, at the request of the public prosecutor, the annual detention orders in respect of the Mr Winterwerp. Eventually, the applicant complained to the Commission alleging, *inter alia*, a breach of Article 5(4) as he had not been heard by the Regional Court or notified of its detention orders. The Commission was unanimous in finding a breach of this provision. Very significantly, the Court accepted the Commission's view that the prolonged detention of persons of 'unsound mind' needed to be accompanied by periodic court reviews to comply with Article 5(4).

> 55. . . . As is indicated earlier in the present judgment, the reasons initially warranting confinement of this kind may cease to exist [where the mental disorder is cured or no longer sufficiently serious to justify detention]. Consequently, it would be contrary to the object and purpose of Article 5 to interpret paragraph 4 thereof, read in its context, as making this category of confinement immune from subsequent review of lawfulness merely provided that the initial decision issued from a court. The very nature of the deprivation of liberty under consideration would appear to require a review of lawfulness to be available at reasonable intervals.

Regarding the nature of the review procedure:

> 60. . . . The judicial proceedings referred to in Article 5 para. 4 need not, it is true, always be attended by the same guarantees as those required under Article 6 para. 1 for civil or criminal litigation (see the above-mentioned *De Wilde, Ooms and Versyp* judgment, p. 42, para. 78 in fine). Nonetheless, it is essential that the person concerned should have access to a court and the opportunity to be heard either in person or, where necessary, through some form of representation, failing which he will not have been afforded 'the fundamental guarantees of procedure applied in matters of deprivation of liberty' (see the last-mentioned judgment, p. 41, para. 76). Mental illness may entail restricting or modifying the manner of exercise of such a right . . . but it cannot justify impairing the very essence of the right. Indeed, special procedural safeguards may prove called for in order to protect the interests of persons who, on account of their mental disabilities, are not fully capable of acting for themselves.

As neither the applicant nor his representative had been heard by the Regional Court during its annual renewals of his psychiatric detention the Court was unanimous in determining that Article 5(4) had been violated.

Winterwerp introduced the requirement under this obligation of periodic reviews of the necessity of the continued detention of mentally ill patients. Because of the potential for such patients' mental health to improve during their treatment in detention the Court, sensibly, held that a single judicial proceeding at the time of their initial confinement would not be enough to satisfy Article 5(4). As we shall see below, this approach has later been extended to other categories of detainees whose personalities are liable to change during their periods of detention. Furthermore, *Winterwerp* emphasised that the procedures followed by the court must be tailored to the nature of the detainee so as to ensure, as far as possible, that he/she is accorded effective access to the court. Clearly, in the context of persons suffering from serious mental illness/disabilities this may necessitate the appointment of professional representation if the detainees cannot adequately present their own cases.

The nature of the review(s) to be undertaken in respect of mentally ill detainees was further elaborated in *X. v United Kingdom*.[31] The applicant had been convicted of a serious crime of violence and ordered, by the trial court, to be detained in a special mental hospital because of his mental condition. Several years later he was discharged from the hospital, but after three years he was recalled to the hospital, by the Home Secretary, based on evidence that his mental health had deteriorated. After failing to obtain his release through habeas corpus proceedings the applicant complained to Strasbourg. The Court stated that:

> 58. . . . Article 5(4), the Government are quite correct to affirm, does not embody a right to judicial control of such scope as to empower the court, on all aspects of the case, to substitute its own discretion for that of the decision-making authority. The review should, however, be wide enough to bear on those conditions which, according to the Convention, are essential for the 'lawful' detention of a person on the ground of unsoundness of mind, especially as the reasons capable of initially justifying such a detention may cease to exist. . . . This means that in the instant case, Article 5(4) required an appropriate procedure allowing a court to examine whether the patient's disorder still persisted and whether the Home Secretary was entitled to think that a continuation of the compulsory confinement was necessary in the interests of public safety.

Taking account of the limited range of legal factors considered in the applicant's habeas corpus proceedings the Court was united in concluding that Article 5(4) had been breached. Hence states are obliged to ensure that their relevant judicial bodies have sufficiently extensive jurisdictions to examine the substantive grounds of the need for the continued detention of specific patients in psychiatric institutions.

The *Winterwerp* requirement to provide for regular court reviews of the continuing need for the detention of persons whose personalities were susceptible to change was applied to recidivists 'placed at the government's disposal' under the Belgian Social Protection Act 1964 in *Van Droogenbroeck v Belgium*.[32] The applicant had a history of convictions for property offences and when he was

[31] A.46 (1981).
[32] A.44 (1982).

convicted of theft by the Bruges criminal court in 1970 he was sentenced to two years' imprisonment and placed at the government's disposal for a further period of ten years. During the latter period the government released him on numerous occasions from prison to participate in schemes of work and other rehabilitation programmes but he continued to commit crimes and was consequently repeatedly recalled to prison. He alleged a violation of Article 5(4) as he was unable to challenge the legality of his detention under the 1964 Act. The plenary Court, like the Commission, was unanimous in finding a violation of this provision. Taking account of the long time period involved in the applicant's social protection order and the possibility that the conditions justifying the making of the order might have changed during the period of detention the Court held that he must have access to a court to review the lawfulness of his detention, '. . . once a certain period has elapsed since the detention began and thereafter at reasonable intervals- and also at the moment of any return to detention after being at liberty.'[33] Consequently, this was another form of detention which necessitated more than one instance of court review.

In *Sanchez-Reisse v Switzerland*,[34] the Court was unwilling to require that a detainee should always be provided with a hearing before the court at which he/she or his/her representative could argue against the lawfulness of the detention. The applicant had been detained, on the orders of the Federal Police Office, in pursuance of an extradition request by the Argentine government. Through his lawyer he sought provisional release from detention. The Federal Police Office rejected the request and passed it on, together with its own comments, to the Federal Court. The latter body rejected the application, after thirty-one days, without holding a hearing. Before the Strasbourg institutions Sanchez-Reisse complained that he had been a victim of a breach of Article 5(4) due to the lack of a properly adversarial procedure followed by the Federal Court and its delay in determining his application. In regard to the applicant's complaint that he had not been accorded a hearing before the domestic court, the Strasbourg Court held that:

> 51. . . . The possibility for a detainee 'to be heard either in person or, where necessary, through some form of representation' (see the above-mentioned *Winterwerp* judgment, Series A no. 33, p. 24, para. 60) features in certain instances among the 'fundamental guaranteees of procedure applied in matters of deprivation of liberty' (see the *De Wilde, Ooms and Versyp* judgment of 18 June 1971, Series A no. 12, p. 41, para. 76). Despite the difference in wording between paragraph 3 (right to be brought before a judge or other officer) and paragraph 4 (right to take proceedings) of Article 5, the Court's previous decisions relating to these two paragraphs have hitherto tended to acknowledge the need for a hearing before the judicial authority (*see, inter alia*, in addition to the above-mentioned *Winterwerp* judgment, the *Schiesser* [v Switzerland] judgment of 4 December 1979, Series A no. 34, p. 13, paras. 30–31). These decisions concerned, however, only matters falling within the ambit of sub-paragraphs (c) and

---

[33] A.44 (1982), para 48.
[34] A.107 (1986).

(e) in fine of paragraph 1 (art. 5-1-c, art. 5-1-e). And, in fact, 'the forms of the procedure required by the Convention need not . . . necessarily be identical in each of the cases where the intervention of a court is required' (see the above-mentioned judgment, Series A no. 12, pp. 41–42, para. 78).

But taking account of the applicant's inability to respond to the Federal Police Office's comments upon his request for release the Court, by five votes to two, concluded that the Swiss procedure had violated Article 5(4). In a concurring opinion Judges Ganshof van der Meersch and Walsh expressed their disagreement with the majority's reasoning concerning the need for hearings.

> . . . In our view, a procedure exclusively in writing is not sufficient to satisfy the requirements of Article 5 para. 4 of the Convention, even if the person concerned is assisted by a lawyer and has the right to challenge the lawfulness of his detention in the appropriate courts.
>
> Although Article 5 para. 4 is silent on the point, it seems to us that this provision is fully satisfied only if the detainee has an opportunity to be heard in person. The Article in question (art. 5-4) is based on the institution of habeas corpus, which is based on the principle that the person concerned appears in flesh and blood before the court.
>
> Such a view is moreover consistent with previous decisions of the Court, which has hitherto tended—as the judgment points out—to recognise the need for a court hearing. Admittedly, the case-law so far concerns only the eventualities contemplated in sub-paragraphs (c) and (e) in fine of paragraph 1 (art. 5-1-c, art. 5-1-e), but we see no reason why it should not also apply to a person 'against whom action is being taken with a view to . . . extradition' (sub-paragraph (f)) (art. 5-1-f).
>
> In short, the applicant's appearance in person before the Federal Court was necessary in the instant case.

It is submitted that this interpretation is the one which more fully realises the underlying purpose of Article 5(4). It is to be deprecated that the Court was not willing to articulate the general principle that detainees, or where appropriate their representatives- for example in respect of detainees whose medical conditions prevent them from participating in the proceedings, should be given a hearing before the court determining the legality of their detention.

The judgment in *Sanchez-Reisse* also dealt with the Court's methodology regarding the Article 5(4) requirement that domestic courts determine these proceedings 'speedily'. 'In the Court's view, this concept cannot be defined in the abstract; the matter must- as with the 'reasonable time' stipulation in Article 5(3) and Article 6(1)—be determined in the light of the circumstances of each case.'[35] By a large majority, six votes to one, the Court concluded that the thirty-one days taken by the Federal Court to decide the applicant's relatively straightforward application for release was in breach of this requirement. This strict approach to the application of the concept of 'speedily' is to be welcomed.

Where the legal system of a member state provided appellate proceedings in respect of challenges to detention decisions reached by first-instance courts the

[35] *Ibid* para 55.

original Strasbourg Court required the appellate proceedings to comply with the obligations of Article 5(4). In *Toth v Austria*,[36] the applicant had been remanded in custody, on suspicion of having committed aggravated fraud, by the Salzburg Regional Court. Prior to reaching that decision the Regional Court had held a hearing attended by the applicant and his lawyer. Toth challenged the detention decision before the Linz Court of Appeal. That court, after hearing the views of the public prosecutor, dismissed Toth's appeal without hearing him or his lawyer. Toth complained to Strasbourg alleging, *inter alia,* a breach of Article 5(4) due to the absence of adversarial proceedings before the Linz Court of Appeal. The Strasbourg Court held that:

> 84. . . . Article 5(4) does not compel the Contracting States to set up a second level of jurisdiction for the examination of applications for release from detention. Nevertheless, a State which institutes such a system must in principle accord to the detainees the same guarantees on appeal as at first instance.

An overwhelming majority of the Court, eight votes to one, concluded that the proceedings before the Linz Court of Appeal had infringed the requirement of equal treatment (as the applicant had not been able to rebut the submissions of the public prosecutor) embodied in the concept of adversarial proceedings mandated by Article 5(4). This principle, has subsequently been expressly endorsed and applied by the full-time Court.[37]

A Grand Chamber of the original Court re-stated the variable nature of the requirements of Article 5(4) in *Chahal v United Kingdom*.[38] The first applicant complained about his detention pending deportation. In part he contended that because the British government had sought to justify his detention/deportation on national security grounds the domestic courts had been unable to adequately examine the lawfulness of his detention. The Court re-affirmed that, 'The scope of the obligations under Article 5(4) is not identical for every kind of deprivation of liberty . . . this applies notably to the extent of the judicial review afforded.'[39] However, the Court was not willing to allow governments general immunity from judicial scrutiny in respect of detention decisions made on national security grounds.

> 131. The Court recognises that the use of confidential material may be unavoidable where national security is at stake. This does not mean, however, that the national authorities can be free from effective control by the domestic courts whenever they choose to assert that national security and terrorism are involved . . .

After acknowledging how Canada had adopted special procedures, involving security-cleared counsel and closed hearings, to enable its courts to handle such cases the Court unanimously concluded that the applicant's proceedings before

---

[36] A.224 (1991).
[37] For example, in *Migon v Poland* (25 June 2002).
[38] 1996-V 1855. For the art 13 aspect of this case see below ch 8 n 7.
[39] *Ibid* para 127.

British judicial and non-judicial bodies had not satisfied Article 5(4). This judgment is notable for the Court's firm support for effective domestic judicial scrutiny, albeit possibly utilising special procedures, of detention decisions involving the most sensitive issues of national security. Given the amorphous nature of the notion of national security and the danger that some states might abuse its invocation the above ruling is an important safeguard for detainees.

The full-time Court has ruled that detainees being held on suspicion of having committed a criminal offence must be provided with a hearing before the court that is reviewing the lawfulness of their continued detention. In *Nikolova v Bulgaria*,[40] the applicant had worked as an accountant in a state-owned enterprise. She was arrested and charged with misappropriation of a large amount of funds. An investigator ordered her detention on remand. Several weeks later she appealed to the Regional Court against that decision. One month later, without the participation of the applicant or the prosecution authorities, the Regional Court dismissed her appeal. Before the Strasbourg Court, Nikolova complained that the Regional Court's conduct violated Article 5(4). The Grand Chamber was united in upholding her complaint. 'In the case of a person whose detention falls within the ambit of Article 5(1)(c) a hearing is required.'[41] Hence, this category of detainees have a basic procedural right which may not be accorded to all detainees (see, *Sanchez-Reisse* above).

Both the original and full-time Courts have had to deal with a number of cases involving the different types of life sentences imposed by British courts.[42] The first type of life sentence to come before the original Court under Article 5(4) was that of the discretionary life sentence, which can be imposed by judges in respect of defendants who have been convicted of specified offences. In *Weeks v United Kingdom*,[43] this sentence had been imposed on a seventeen-year-old youth who had stolen thirty five pence during a robbery using a starting pistol. The judge imposed this sentence because of the emotional immaturity of the defendant. After ten years' of imprisonment Weeks was released on licence by the Home Secretary, acting on the advice of the Parole Board. However, Weeks was recalled to prison, and subsequently released, several times due to his commission of other minor offence. Each time he was recalled, by the Home Secretary, Weeks was entitled to have his re-detention considered by the Parole Board. Also during his imprisonment Weeks was able to apply to the Parole Board for regular reviews of the need for his continuing detention. He complained to Strasbourg alleging, *inter alia*, that the recall and review procedures did not comply with Article 5(4). A large majority, thirteen votes to four, of the

---

[40] Judgment of 25 March 1999.

[41] *Ibid* para 58.

[42] One explanation for the prevalence of these cases is that the UK has more prisoners serving life sentences than the rest of Europe together: submission of *Justice* to the Court in *Stafford v UK* (28 May 2002) para 54. On 31 December 2001, in the UK there were 3,171 male and 114 female mandatory life prisoners, 228 men and 11 women serving a sentence of detention at Her Majesty's pleasure and 1,424 male and 25 female discretionary life prisoners: *Ibid* para 29.

[43] A.114 (1987).

Court found breaches of that provision. Very significantly the Court held that because of the reasons for the imposition of the discretionary life sentence on Weeks, namely social protection and rehabilitation, he was entitled to judicial examinations of his recalls and regular reviews of his imprisonment.

> 58. ... unlike the case of a person sentenced to life imprisonment because of the gravity of the offence committed, the grounds relied on by the sentencing judges for deciding that the length of the deprivation of Mr Week's liberty should be subject to the discretion of the executive for the rest of his life are by their nature susceptible of change with the passage of time. ... It follows that by virtue of paragraph 4 of Article 5, Mr Weeks was entitled to apply to a 'court' having jurisdiction to decide 'speedily' whether or not his deprivation of liberty had become 'unlawful' in this sense; this entitlement should have been exercisable by him at the moment of any return to custody after being at liberty and also at reasonable intervals during the course of his imprisonment.

The Court concluded that the examination of Weeks' recalls undertaken by the Parole Board did not satisfy Article 5(4) because of procedural weaknesses, such as the Board's failure to disclose to Weeks all the adverse material it had concerning his circumstances. Furthermore, the Board's reviews of his continuing imprisonment failed to comply with this provision as the Board only had advisory powers (the Home Secretary possessed the power of release). Consequently, the judgment in effect determined that the domestic 'judicial' scrutiny of the implementation of discretionary life sentences fell well below the institutional and procedural requirements of Article 5(4).

Subsequently, in *Thynne, Wilson and Gunnell v United Kingdom*,[44] a plenary Court applied *Weeks* to discretionary life prisoners who had been convicted of serious sexual offences. Each of the applicants had been subjected to this form of sentence because their trial judges concluded that they were unstable and likely to commit similar offences in the future if released. Under domestic law and practice discretionary life sentences were divided into a 'tariff'[45] period, *i.e.* the length of time of imprisonment necessary for punishment of the offender, and a post-tariff period during which the offender remained in detention if he/she continued to pose a threat to the public. All the applicants were in the post-tariff period of their sentences and contended that they did not have access to a 'court' to review the lawfulness of their continued imprisonment. The Court held that:

> 76. ... the detention of the applicants after the expiry of the punitive periods of their life sentences is comparable to that at issue in the *Van Droogenbroeck* and *Weeks* cases: the factors of mental instability and dangerousness are susceptible to changes over the passage of time and new issues of lawfulness may thus arise in the course of

---

[44] A.190 (1990).

[45] Note, in 2002 the Lord Chief Justice, Lord Woolf, announced that this term had been misunderstood and therefore it would be replaced by the phrase 'minimum term': *Practice Statement (Crime: Life Sentences)* [2002] 1 WLR 1789.

detention. It follows that at this phase in the execution of their sentences, the applicants are entitled under Article 5(4) to take proceedings to have the lawfulness of their continued detention decided by a court at reasonable intervals and to have the lawfulness of any re-detention determined by a court.

An overwhelming majority, eighteen votes to one, concluded that requirement had been violated as no such judicial remedy was available to the applicants.

The full-time Court, unanimously, found a two-year delay between reviews of the continuing imprisonment of a post-tariff discretionary life prisoner did not satisfy the need for these reviews to be undertaken at 'reasonable intervals' in *Oldham v United Kingdom*.[46] The applicant had been convicted of manslaughter, whilst suffering from a mental abnormality induced by alcohol, in 1970. He was released and recalled to prison several times from the late 1980s. In July 1996 he was recalled by the Home Secretary on the ground that he had injured his partner after a drinking binge. The Parole Board Discretionary Lifer Panel that examined his recall expressed the view that he should remain in custody, as he posed a risk to the public and that he should undertake work in respect of alcohol abuse and the management of anger . The Home Secretary informed Oldham that the Parole Board would review his detention in two years' time. Within eight months of his recall Oldham completed courses on the specified topics. In 1998 the applicant had another hearing before the Discretionary Lifer Panel and it recommended his release (the Homes Secretary duly released him on licence). Oldham claimed that the delay in reviewing his detention was unreasonable and thereby violated Article 5(4). The Court stated that:

> 31. It is true that the question of whether periods comply with the requirement must—as with the reasonable time stipulation in Article 5 § 3 and Article 6 § 1—be determined in the light of the circumstances of each case (see the *Sanchez-Reisse v Switzerland* judgment of 21 October 1986, Series A no. 107, p. 55, § 55). It is therefore not for this Court to attempt to rule as to the maximum period of time between reviews which should automatically apply to this category of life prisoner as a whole. It notes that the system as applied in this case has a flexibility which must reflect the realities of the situation, namely, that there are significant differences in the personal circumstances of the prisoners under review.

After observing that Oldham had completed his courses within eight months of the previous review the Court concluded that his having to wait a further sixteen months before having his case reconsidered by the Discretionary Lifer Panel was not reasonable, hence the lawfulness of his continuing detention had not been decided 'speedily' as mandated by Article 5(4). This judgment indicates that national review procedures should not be primarily governed by automatic timetables but by the personal conditions of individual prisoners.

The ultimate power of the Home Secretary to authorise the release on licence of discretionary life prisoners transferred to a mental hospital under sections 47

---

[46] Judgment of 26 September 2000.

and 49 of the Mental Health Act 1983 was found to be incompatible with Article 5(4) in *Benjamin and Wilson v United Kingdom*.[47] Whilst discretionary life prisoners, like the applicants, could apply to a Mental Health Review Tribunal to examine the need for their continued detention in a mental hospital the Tribunal only had advisory powers in respect of such persons. The government argued, before the Court, that the Home Secretary had a policy of following the recommendations of Tribunals in respect of the discharge of these persons (and that this policy was enforceable in administrative law proceedings). But the Court did not accept that this practice satisfied the Convention obligations.

> 36. . . . In this case, the power to order release lay with the Secretary of State, even though he may have been under some constraints of administrative law as regarded the situations in which he could or could not depart from a policy that had created legitimate expectations. The ability of an applicant to challenge a refusal by the Secretary of State to follow his previous policy in the courts would not remedy the lack of power of decision in the Tribunal. Article 5 § 4 presupposes the existence of a procedure in conformity with its provisions without the necessity to institute separate legal proceedings in order to bring it about. . . .

Therefore, the Court was unanimous in finding a violation of Article 5(4). So in yet another discretionary lifer context we see the historically ubiquitous powers of the Home Secretary to be in breach of this provision's fundamental requirement of a judicial body determining the lawfulness of such prisoners' continued detention.

The second type of life sentence examined by the Court was the sentence of detention 'during Her Majesty's pleasure' automatically imposed on juveniles convicted of murder. Again, this sentence contained a tariff period (set by the Home Secretary after consultation with the judiciary). In *Hussain v United Kingdom*,[48] the applicant, when aged sixteen, had been convicted of the murder of his young brother. The Home Secretary had set a tariff of fifteen years. After the expiry of that term Hussain was kept in prison and his case was periodically examined by the Parole Board. He challenged that process on the grounds, *inter alia*, that the Board had only advisory powers and did not follow a fully adversarial procedure (*e.g.* he was not able to appear before the Board). The Court determined that this form of life sentence should be equated to that of the discretionary life sentence imposed upon adult offenders.

> 53. . . . In the case of young persons convicted of serious crimes, the corresponding sentence undoubtedly contains a punitive element and accordingly a tariff is set to reflect the requirements of retribution and deterrence. However an indeterminate term of detention for a convicted young person, which may be as long as that person's life, can only be justified by considerations based on the need to protect the public. . . .
>
> 54. Against this background the Court concludes that the applicant's sentence, after the expiration of his tariff, is more comparable to a discretionary life sentence. . . . The

---

[47] Judgment of 26 September 2002.
[48] 1996-I 252. Note, a similar judgment was also given in *Singh v UK* 1996-I 280.

decisive ground for the applicant's continued detention was and continues to be his dangerousness to society, a characteristic susceptible to change with the passage of time. Accordingly, new issues of lawfulness may arise in the course of detention and the applicant is entitled under Article 5(4) to take proceedings to have these issues decided by a court at reasonable intervals. . . .

All the judges were united in concluding, following *Weeks* and *Thynne, Wilson & Gunnell*, that the Parole Board's advisory powers and existing procedures failed to meet the criteria of a 'court' thereby breaching Article 5(4).

A Grand Chamber of the full-time Court developed *Hussain* to find a breach of Article 5(4) in respect of the situation of a pre-tariff juvenile murder. In *V. v United Kingdom,*[49] the applicant, when aged ten, had (together with a friend of the same age) abducted and killed a two-year-old boy. V. had been convicted and sentenced to detention at Her Majesty's pleasure. The Home Secretary had controversially imposed a tariff of fifteen years (the Lord Chief Justice had recommended a period of ten years). V. contended, *inter alia*, that he was the victim of a breach of Article 5(4) as since his conviction he had not been able to have the lawfulness of his continued detention reviewed by a judicial body. The Court, unanimously, upheld his complaint.

120. . . . [G]iven that the sentence of detention during Her Majesty's pleasure is inde-terminate and that the tariff was initially set by the Home Secretary rather than the sentencing judge, it cannot be said that the supervision required by Article 5(4) was incorporated in the trial court's sentence. . . .

Consequently no 'court' had determined or reviewed the period of time that V. was actually required to serve in detention. Therefore, as with the discretionary life sentence for adult offenders, the Home Secretary's dominant role in deter-mining how long persons sentenced to detention during Her Majesty's pleasure should serve in custody violated the judicial element of Article 5(4).

The third type of British life sentence brought before the Court has been the mandatory sentence that is required, by legislation,[50] to be imposed on adults convicted of murder. In *Wynne v United Kingdom,*[51] the applicant had been convicted of murder during the mid 1960s and released from prison, on licence, in 1980. He then killed an elderly person in 1981 and was convicted of manslaughter, on the ground of diminished responsibility, with a discretionary life sentence being imposed on him. The trial court also revoked his licence in respect of the previous mandatory life sentence. By 1992 his tariffs in respect of both the mandatory life sentence and the discretionary life sentence had expired. However, the Home Secretary (who had sole authority to order the release on licence of mandatory life prisoners) refused to authorise his release in accord-ance with a recommendation from the Parole Board. Wynne claimed that his

---

[49] 1999-IX. Note, the parallel judgment in *T v UK* 1999-IX brought by V's co-defendant.
[50] Originally under the Murder (Abolition of Death Penalty) Act 1965.
[51] A.294-A (1994).

inability to have a 'court' review the lawfulness of his continued detention violated Article 5(4). The Court accepted the government's submission that mandatory life sentences were distinguishable from discretionary life sentences and not subject to the latter's need for periodic reviews of prisoners' continuing detention by a judicial body.

35. ... However, the fact remains that the mandatory sentence belongs to a different category from the discretionary sentence in the sense that it is imposed automatically as the punishment for the offence of murder irrespective of considerations pertaining to the dangerousness of the offender. ...

36. Against the above background, the Court sees no cogent reasons to depart from the finding in the *Thynne, Wilson & Gunnell* case that, as regards mandatory life sentences, the guarantee of Article 5(4) was satisfied by the original trial and appeal proceedings and confers no additional right to challenge the lawfulness of continuing detention or re-detention following revocation of the life licence. ...

Therefore, the Chamber unanimously found no breach of this provision. The judgment can be criticised for denying mandatory life prisoners access to a 'court' for the regular determination of the continuing need for their detention. Instead, that power was allowed to remain with a senior politician.

In 2002 a Grand Chamber of the full-time Court declined to follow the approach in *Wynne*. *Stafford v United Kingdom*,[52] concerned a person convicted of murder in 1967. He was released on licence in 1979 but broke his parole conditions by leaving the country. During 1989 he returned to the UK and was arrested in possession of a false passport. He was fined and remained in custody because his licence had been revoked. After eighteen months imprisonment the Parole Board recommended his release on licence. The Home Secretary authorised Stafford's release. In 1994 he was convicted of conspiracy to forge travellers' cheques and passports and sentence to six years' imprisonment. His licence was again revoked. In 1996 the Parole Board recommended his release on licence as it considered the risk of him re-offending was low. However, the Home Secretary refused to release him. In July 1997 the applicant would have been released from prison in respect of his fraud sentence but he remained in custody due to the revocation of his life sentence licence. The Home Secretary approved his release on licence in December 1998. Stafford contended that the Court should reconsider the judgment in *Wynne* and hold that Article 5(4) required a judicial body to determine the continuing need for a mandatory lifer to be held in custody. The Court observed that:

78. ... The abolition of the death penalty in 1965 and the conferring on the Secretary of State of the power to release convicted murderers represented, at that time, a major and progressive reform. However, with the wider recognition of the need to develop and apply, in relation to mandatory life prisoners, judicial procedures reflecting standards of independence, fairness and openness, the continuing role of the Secretary of State in fixing the tariff and in deciding on a prisoner's release following its expiry, has

---

[52] Judgment of 28 May 2002.

become increasingly difficult to reconcile with the notion of separation of powers between the executive and the judiciary, a notion which has assumed growing importance in the case-law of the Court (*mutatis mutandis*, the *Incal v Turkey* judgment of 9 June 1998, *Reports* 1998–IV).

79. The Court considers that it may now be regarded as established in domestic law that there is no distinction between mandatory life prisoners, discretionary life prisoners and juvenile murderers as regards the nature of tariff-fixing. It is a sentencing exercise. The mandatory life sentence does not impose imprisonment for life as a punishment. The tariff, which reflects the individual circumstances of the offence and the offender, represents the element of punishment. The Court concludes that the finding in Wynne that the mandatory life sentence constituted punishment for life can no longer be regarded as reflecting the real position in the domestic criminal justice system of the mandatory life prisoner.

Furthermore, the Court determined that after the expiry of the tariff the continued detention of mandatory lifers depended upon:

87. . . . elements of dangerousness and risk associated with the objectives of the original sentence of murder. These elements may change with the course of time, and thus new issues of lawfulness arise requiring determination by a body satisfying the requirements of Article 5 § 4. It can no longer be maintained that the original trial and appeal proceedings satisfied, once and for all, issues of compatibility of subsequent detention of mandatory life prisoners with the provisions of Article 5 § 1 of the Convention.

Consequently the Grand Chamber unanimously found a breach of this requirement as Stafford had not had access to such a judicial body.

The judgment in *Stafford* is a forceful enhancement of the institutional rights of mandatory lifers and reflects a welcome willingness by the contemporary Court to reconsider lacunae in its predecessor's jurisprudence. From a Strasbourg perspective the central role of the Homes Secretary in determining the actual length of imprisonment served by mandatory lifers is becoming increasingly untenable. This approach is to be commended because on grounds of both constitutional principle and public policy such decisions should be left with independent judicial authorities and not in the hands of a minister subject to political pressures.[53]

Overall, the case law of the original and full-time Courts reveals that the positive obligation embodied in Article 5(4) has been invoked by an ever widening range of detainees, including vagrants, mentally ill patients, aliens facing deportation or extradition and criminals sentenced to life imprisonment. A major extension of this obligation was the original Court's development of the requirement for regular reviews by a 'court' of the need for the continuing detention of those detainees whose personal circumstances are liable to change over time,

---

[53] Note, in 1996 the Home Affairs Select Committee of the House of Commons made similar recommendations: *Ibid* para 52.

such as mentally ill patients, recidivists and British discretionary life prisoners. The current Court is continuing to reinforce this obligation (*e.g.* in *Stafford*).

GENERAL CONCLUSIONS

We have seen that Article 5 contains a number of express positive obligations encompassing, *inter alia*, informing detainees of the reasons for their arrest (Article 5(2)), bringing detainees arrested on suspicion of having committed an offence promptly before a judge (Article 5(3)) and providing access to a court for the speedy determination of the lawfulness of a person's detention (Article 5(4)). The jurisprudence of the Court has generally interpreted these obligations in ways which favour detainees, for example broadening the scope of the obligation under Article 5(2) to cover persons detained under civil law powers (such as a mentally ill patient in *Van der Leer*)[54] or recognising a right to periodic reviews of the need for the continuing detention of individuals whose personalities are liable to change over time (*e.g.* convicted juvenile murders as in *Hussain*).[55] In addition the Court has articulated several related implied positive obligations which are designed to give further protection to detainees. They include the obligations upon states to account for detainees (*Kurt*),[56] to take measures to safeguard detainees against disappearance whilst in the custody of public officials (*Orhan*)[57] and to undertake effective investigations into arguable claims that persons have disappeared whilst in state custody (*Cyprus v Turkey*).[58] The totality of these express and implied positive obligations applicable to the myriad of public authorities involved in the detention of persons (*e.g.* the police in *Fox, Campbell & Hartley*,[59] the District Attorney in *Huber*[60] and the Home Secretary in *Benjamin & Wilson*)[61] justifiably reflect the importance of the underlying right to liberty guaranteed by Article 5.

---

[54] Above n 15.
[55] Above n 48.
[56] Above n 1.
[57] Above n 7.
[58] Above n 12.
[59] Above n 16.
[60] Above n 20.
[61] Above n 47.

5

Article 6: Right to a fair trial

This elaborate provision specifies that:

(1) In the determination of his civil rights and obligations or of any criminal charge against him, everyone is entitled to a fair and public hearing within a reasonable time by an independent and impartial tribunal established by law. Judgment shall be pronounced publicly but the press and public may be excluded from all or part of the trial in the interests of morals, public order or national security in a democratic society, where the interests of juveniles or the protection of the private life of the parties so require, or to the extent strictly necessary in the opinion of the court in special circumstances where publicity would prejudice the interests of justice.

(2) Everyone charged with a criminal offence shall be presumed innocent until proved guilty according to law.

(3) Everyone charged with a criminal offence has the following minimum rights:

   (a) to be informed promptly, in a language which he understands and in detail, of the nature and causes of the accusation against him;

   (b) to have adequate time and facilities for the preparation of his defence;

   (c) to defend himself in person or through legal assistance of his own choosing or, if he has not sufficient means to pay for legal assistance, to be given it free when the interests of justice so require;

   (d) to examine or have examined witnesses against him and to obtain the attendance and examination of witnesses on his behalf under the same conditions as witnesses against him;

   (e) to have the free assistance of an interpreter if he cannot understand or speak the language used in court.

Article 6 is the source of the largest number of complaints made to the Court.[1] This can be explained, in part, by the scope of the provision which seeks to guarantee fair trials for both civil and criminal cases. As we examine the positive obligations derived from Article 6 we shall have to bear in mind the extent to which criminal proceedings are subject to more positive obligations due to the greater number of express rights conferred in respect of this type of proceedings. Our analysis of the major positive obligations under this Article will follow the order of the rights defined in the text of the Article.

---

[1] Jacobs and White *The European Convention on Human Rights,* 3rd edn C Ovey and RCA White (Oxford, OUP, 2002) 139.

ARTICLE 6(1)

A fair and public hearing for the determination of a person's civil rights and obligations or of any criminal charge against him/her

This is the first guarantee contained within Article 6(1) and there are considerable bodies of case law on the meanings of 'civil rights and obligations'[2] and 'criminal charge.'[3] Our focus, however, is on the nature of the positive obligations required of states to comply with this provision. In regard to civil proceedings the Court has held that a person's right of access to a court for the determination of his/her civil rights and obligations is inherent in the right to a fair trial under Article 6(1). Several applicants have contended that this element of the right to a fair hearing obliges states to provide legal aid for the bringing of civil proceedings. In *Airey v Ireland*,[4] the applicant was a married woman from a humble background with a modest income (£40 per week). Her husband had been convicted of assaulting her and for seven years she had been seeking to obtain a decree of judicial separation from him. However, such decrees were only available from the High Court and the costs of legal representation for her would have been between £500-1,200. She could not afford those fees and no civil legal aid was available in Ireland. Before the Court she contended that the above circumstances resulted in her being denied access to a court in breach of Article 6(1). The Irish government argued that she could have applied in person to the High Court for a decree. The Court emphasised that the Convention guarantees rights that are 'practical and effective.'[5] Taking account of the complexity of proceeding before the High Court, Mrs Airey's emotional involvement in her marital status and her background, the Court concluded that the possibility for her to apply in person did not provide her with an effective right of access to a court.

> 25. . . . Furthermore, fulfilment of a duty under the Convention on occasion necessitates some positive action on the part of the State; in such circumstances, the State cannot simply remain passive and 'there is . . . no room to distinguish between acts and omissions' (see, *mutatis mutandis*, the above-mentioned *Marckx* judgment, p. 15, para. 31, and the *De Wilde, Ooms and Versyp* judgment of 10 March 1972, Series A no. 14, p. 10, para. 22). The obligation to secure an effective right of access to the courts falls into this category of duty.
>
> 26. . . . The Court is aware that the further realisation of social and economic rights is largely dependent on the situation—notably financial—reigning in the State in question. On the other hand, the Convention must be interpreted in the light of pre-

---

[2] See, A Mowbray, *Cases & Materials on the European Convention on Human Rights* (London, Butterworths, 2001) 235–58.

[3] *Ibid* 259–78.

[4] A.32 (1979).

[5] *Ibid* para 24.

sent-day conditions (above-mentioned *Marckx* judgment, p. 19, para. 41) and it is designed to safeguard the individual in a real and practical way as regards those areas with which it deals. . . . Whilst the Convention sets forth what are essentially civil and political rights, many of them have implications of a social or economic nature. The Court therefore considers, like the Commission, that the mere fact that an interpretation of the Convention may extend into the sphere of social and economic rights should not be a decisive factor against such an interpretation; there is no water-tight division separating that sphere from the field covered by the Convention. . . .

The conclusion appearing . . . above does not therefore imply that the State must provide free legal aid for every dispute relating to a 'civil right'.

To hold that so far-reaching an obligation exists would, the Court agrees, sit ill with the fact that the Convention contains no provision on legal aid for those disputes, Article 6 para. 3 (c) dealing only with criminal proceedings. However, despite the absence of a similar clause for civil litigation, Article 6 para. 1 may sometimes compel the State to provide for the assistance of a lawyer when such assistance proves indispensable for an effective access to court either because legal representation is rendered compulsory, as is done by the domestic law of certain Contracting States for various types of litigation, or by reason of the complexity of the procedure or of the case.

In the light of Mrs Airey's predicament a majority, five votes to two, of the Court found that her right of access to a court had been violated.

The judgment in *Airey* clearly demonstrated, relatively early in the Court's case law, that Article 6(1) contained implied positive obligations. Whilst the Court was understandably cautious in explaining that it was not recognising a general right to legal aid for all civil proceedings falling within the Article, the decision opened up the possibility for other applicants to claim that their need for legal aid was analogous to that of Mrs Airey.

In the later case of *Andronicou and Constantinou v Cyprus*,[6] the Court rejected the applicants' claim that Article 6(1) required states to establish a system of civil legal aid. The applicants' son and daughter had been killed by police officers during an attempt to end an armed domestic hostage-taking crisis. Subsequently, the applicant families wished to sue the relevant public authorities for alleged negligence. There was no system of civil legal aid in Cyprus, but the government made an *ex gratia* offer, lasting just a few weeks, to fund the applicants legal action. The families did not consider that this offer satisfied the government's positive obligation under Article 6(1). However, the Court was united in holding that:

199. . . . whilst Article 6 § 1 of the Convention guarantees to litigants an effective right of access to the courts for the determination of their 'civil rights and obligations', it leaves to the State a free choice of the means to be used towards this end. The institution of a legal-aid scheme constitutes one of those means but there are others. It is not the Court's function to indicate, let alone stipulate, which measures should be taken. All that the Convention requires is that an individual should enjoy his effective right of access to the courts in conditions not at variance with Article 6 § 1 (see the *Airey v Ireland* judgment of 9 October 1979, Series A no. 32, pp. 14–15, § 26).

[6] 1997-VI for the art 2 aspect of this case see above ch 2 n 4.

In the determination of the Court, the government's offer to the applicants satisfied the former's Convention obligations. Hence, the Court was maintaining its earlier view that this implied positive obligation did not extend so far as to mandate the creation of general civil legal aid systems in member states. This would, presumably, be too onerous a burden to impose on states via an implied positive obligation.

Even where states establish civil legal aid systems the decisions of those authorities may be successfully challenged at Strasbourg if the determinations of the legal aid bodies prevent applicants gaining access to a court. For example, in *Aerts v Belgium*,[7] the applicant had been ordered to be temporarily detained in the psychiatric wing of a prison following his arrest in respect of a serious assault. The local Mental Health Board designated a specific social protection centre where he should be detained. However, due to a lack of places at the centre, he continued to be held in the prison. Subsequently, Aerts brought civil proceedings against the authorities for failing to place him in the designated social protection centre. Eventually, he applied to the Legal Aid Board of the Court of Cassation for funding to bring an appeal before that court (representation by counsel before the Court of Cassation was required by Belgian law). The Legal Aid Board accepted that he had insufficient means to pay for counsel but rejected his application as his appeal did not appear to be well-founded. The Strasbourg Court was united in holding that:

> 60. ... It was not for the Legal Aid Board to assess the proposed appeal's prospect of success; it was for the Court of Cassation to determine the issue. By refusing the application on the ground that the appeal did not at that time appear to be well-founded, the Legal Aid Board impaired the very essence of Mr Aert's right to a tribunal. There has accordingly been a breach of Article 6(1).

The combination of a detainee seeking to challenge governmental decisions concerning his right to liberty and the compulsion to have legal representation before the Court of Cassation were powerful factors underpinning the success of Aert's action before the European Court.

The full-time Court has endorsed the interpretation of its predecessor that there is no general right to civil legal aid under Article 6(1). In *Glaser v United Kingdom*,[8] the divorced applicant had been involved in protracted court proceedings to try and gain access to his children, who were in the custody of their mother. During the proceedings before English and Scottish courts the applicant had on occasions been represented by lawyers, paid for by the applicant, and in several proceeding he had represented himself. Before the Court he alleged, *inter alia*, that his ineligibility for legal aid, due to his financial situation, violated Article 6(1). A united Chamber dismissed this complaint.

---

[7] 1998-V 1939 for the art 3 aspect of this case see above ch 3 n 22.
[8] Judgment of 19 September 2000.

99. . . . . There is no right as such to receive legal aid in civil proceedings guaranteed under the Convention. However, a lack of legal aid may, in certain circumstances, deprive an applicant of effective access to court (see *Airey v Ireland*, A.32 (1979)). In this case, however, it appears that the applicant was represented during a substantial part of the proceedings. While he complains of the cost to him of obtaining representation, this by itself is not a relevant factor under Article 6(1) of the Convention. Furthermore, it does not appear that, where the applicant did appear on his own behalf, that he was unable to put forward his claims effectively.

Hence, states have considerable latitude under the Convention to choose whether to create general civil legal aid systems and where these are established to fix the criteria of financial eligibility.

The contemporary Court has extended *Airey* to apply to a defendant in civil proceedings. In *McVicar v United Kingdom*,[9] the applicant was a journalist who had written an article suggesting that a well known athlete had taken banned performance-enhancing drugs. The athlete sued the applicant, and his publisher, for defamation. English legal aid is not available to parties in defamation actions and consequently, for financial reasons, the applicant had to represent himself during most of the defamation proceedings. The jury, by a majority of ten to two, found in favour of the athlete. McVicar complained to the Court alleging, in part, that the unavailability of legal aid violated his right to a fair trial under Article 6(1). The Court ruled that:

48. . . . The question whether or not that Article requires the provision of legal representation to an individual litigant will depend upon the specific circumstances of the case and, in particular, upon whether the individual would be able to present his case properly and satisfactorily without the assistance of a lawyer.

50. Turning to the present case, the Court considers that the relevant question is not whether the applicant had access to court as such, since he was the defendant in the proceedings. Rather, the applicant's complaints relate to the fairness of the libel proceedings generally and his rights under Article 6(1) of the Convention to present an effective defence. However, the principles which apply to his complaint are identical to those which applied in the *Airey* case.

The Court determined that the applicant was a well-educated journalist, that legal representation was not compulsory in proceedings before the English High Court, the law of defamation was not sufficiently complex to require a person like the applicant to require legal assistance and the extent of the applicant's emotional involvement in the case was not incompatible with the degree of objectivity required of advocacy in court proceedings. Therefore, the unavailability of legal aid to the applicant had not denied him a fair trial as guaranteed by Article 6(1).

Whilst we should welcome the Court's express inclusion of civil defendants within the scope of *Airey*, the Court's assessment of the facts in *McVicar* is some what surprising. This is particularly so in regard to the Court's view that the law

---

[9] Judgment of 7 May 2002.

of defamation was not that complex.[10] Furthermore, the Court noted that the proceedings against McVicar had been brought by 'a comparatively wealthy and famous individual'[11] employing legal representation and 'the libel trial must have taken a significantly greater physical and emotional toll on the applicant than would have been the case in relation to an experienced legal advocate.'[12] Yet the Court found no breach of McVicar's right to a fair trial. The Court's evaluation of the personal competence of McVicar suggests that educated persons (he was a sociology graduate) will generally find it very difficult to convince the Court that they have been denied a fair hearing through the absence of civil legal aid.

A rare example of the full-time Court finding a breach of Article 6(1) through the lack of publicly funded legal representation in a civil case occurred in *P.,C. and S. v United Kingdom*.[13] The first two applicants were a married couple and S. was their daughter. P. had been convicted in California of endangering her son's health (the authorities believed that P. had inappropriately given her son laxatives and that she suffered from Munchausen Syndrome by Proxy).[14] A few years later, when she gave birth to S. in England, the local authority obtained an emergency protection order to remove S. to a place of safety away from her parents. Subsequently, the local authority applied to the High Court (because of the complexity of the case) for a care order to be made in respect of S. and then for an order freeing her for adoption. C. withdrew from the proceedings on health grounds. P. was represented by leading counsel and solicitors under the domestic legal aid scheme. Three days into the hearings P.'s legal representatives withdrew from the proceedings (because they considered that P. was requiring them to conduct her case in an unreasonable manner). The judge allowed P. an adjournment of four days but then required her to continue with the hearings conducting her own case (she was assisted by a lay advisor). After three weeks of proceedings the judge made a care order in favour of the local authority. A few days later the same judge made another order freeing S. for adoption. Before the European Court P. asserted that being obliged to represent herself in the above proceedings had violated her right to a fair hearing. The judges were united in finding a breach of Article 6(1).

> 95. Nonetheless, P. was required as a parent to represent herself in proceedings which as, the Court of Appeal observed, were of exceptional complexity, extending over the course of 20 days in which the documentation was voluminous and which required a review of highly complex expert evidence relating to the applicants, P. and C.'s, fitness

[10] See, E Barendt, *et al*, *Libel and the Media: The Chilling Effect* (Oxford, Clarendon Press, 1997).

[11] Above n 9 para 51.

[12] *Ibid.*

[13] Judgment of 16 July 2002.

[14] Defined by the Court as being 'a label sometimes used to describe a form of psychiatric illness, mainly found in women, who seek attention by inducing illness in their children or inventing accounts of illness in their children, and by repeatedly presenting their children to the medical authorities for investigation and treatment.' *Ibid* para 13.

to parent their daughter. Her alleged disposition to harm her own children, along with her personality traits, were at the heart of the case, as well as her relationship with her husband. The complexity of the case, along with the importance of what was at stake and the highly emotive nature of the subject matter, lead this Court to conclude that the principles of effective access to court and fairness required that P. receive the assistance of a lawyer. . . .

From the above judgments we can conclude that the Court has consistently held that states are not under a positive obligation to establish general schemes of legal aid for civil proceedings. However, in exceptional cases legal aid may be required under Article 6(1) for parties (claimants or defendants) to such actions. Relevant factors identifiable from the jurisprudence include: the person having a low level of education and/or a deep emotional involvement in the subject matter of the dispute, the case involves complex matters of law (*McVicar* applies a high threshold to this criterion) or elaborate court proceedings, or domestic law requires legal representation.

In criminal cases an important aspect of the right to a fair hearing is the positive obligation upon the prosecution to disclose relevant evidence to the defence, so that the latter may respond to potentially adverse material. This basic requirement was endorsed by a unanimous Grand Chamber of the full-time Court in *Rowe and Davis v United Kingdom*.[15] The applicants had been charged with murder, robbery and grievous bodily harm. The prosecution did not tell either the trial judge or the applicants that the police had investigated the applicants because of information supplied by an informant. The applicants were convicted. Several years later, when it was discovered that the prosecution had failed to disclose key evidence, the applicants complained to Strasbourg alleging a breach of the right to a fair trial under Article 6(1). The Court stated that:

60. It is a fundamental aspect of the right to a fair trial that criminal proceedings, including the elements of such proceedings which relate to procedure, should be adversarial and that there should be equality of arms between the prosecution and defence. The right to an adversarial trial means, in a criminal case, that both prosecution and defence must be given the opportunity to have knowledge of and comment on the observations filed and the evidence adduced by the other party. . . . In addition Article 6 § 1 requires, as indeed does English law . . . that the prosecution authorities disclose to the defence all material evidence in their possession for or against the accused . . .

61. However, as the applicants recognised . . . the entitlement to disclosure of relevant evidence is not an absolute right. In any criminal proceedings there may be competing interests, such as national security or the need to protect witnesses at risk of reprisals or keep secret police methods of investigation of crime, which must be weighed against the rights of the accused (see, for example, the *Doorson v the Netherlands* judgment of 26 March 1996, *Reports of Judgments and Decisions* 1996-II, p. 470, § 70). In some cases it may be necessary to withhold certain evidence from the defence so as

[15] Judgment of 16 February 2000.

to preserve the fundamental rights of another individual or to safeguard an important public interest. However, only such measures restricting the rights of the defence which are strictly necessary are permissible under Article 6 § 1 (see the *Van Mechelen and Others v the Netherlands* judgment of 23 April 1997, *Reports* 1997-III, p. 712, § 58). Moreover, in order to ensure that the accused receives a fair trial, any difficulties caused to the defence by a limitation on its rights must be sufficiently counterbalanced by the procedures followed by the judicial authorities (see the Doorson judgment cited above, p. 471, § 72, and the *Van Mechelen and Others* judgment cited above, p. 712, § 54).

As the prosecution had failed to inform the trial judge of the informant's role in the police investigation of the applicants, thereby depriving the judge of the opportunity to rule on whether that evidence should have been disclosed to the applicants, the Court concluded that the prosecution's omission had denied the applicants a fair trial in breach of Article 6(1). This judgment was, therefore, a forceful reminder of the obligation of disclosure resting upon prosecution authorities.

The obligation on state authorities to conduct civil and criminal trials in public is subject to a number of exceptions listed in Article 6(1); '. . . the press and public may be excluded from all or part of the trial in the interests of morals, public order or national security in a democratic society, where the interests of juveniles or the protection of the private life of the parties so require, or to the extent strictly necessary in the opinion of the court in special circumstances where publicity would prejudice the interests of justice.' This obligation was considered by a plenary Court in the context of 'civil' disciplinary proceedings taken against medical doctors in *Le Compte, Van Leuven and De Meyere v Belgium.*[16] Under a Royal Decree all disciplinary hearings before the Appeals Council of the Belgian Medical Association (*Ordre des medecins*) were to be conducted in private. The Council upheld disciplinary charges against the applicants concerning, *inter alia*, their contacts with the media. Before the Court, it was contended that the private proceedings in the applicants' cases violated the general obligation of holding public hearings. An overwhelming majority of the Court, sixteen votes to four, agreed that there had been a breach of Article 6(1). The Court did not consider that the nature of the charges against the applicants fell within the exceptions specified in that Article. Clearly, if the charges had concerned the applicants' treatment of individual patients then it would have been permissible for the Appeals Council to order private hearings under the exception applying to the protection of private life.

A contemporary examination of the obligation to hold public hearings for civil proceedings occurred in *B. and P. v United Kingdom.*[17] The applicants were fathers whose children resided with their mothers. Both applicants applied to the courts for residency orders in respect of their sons. The applicants requested that the proceedings be conducted in open court, however their requests were

---

[16]   A.43 (1981).
[17]   Judgment of 24 July 2001.

rejected by the judges as the Children Act 1989 established a presumption that such proceedings should be conducted in private. The applicants complained that the presumption violated the right to a public hearing in Article 6(1). The Court explained the justification for this obligation as being:

36. . . . The public character of proceedings protects litigants against the administration of justice in secret with no public scrutiny; it is also one of the means whereby confidence in the courts can be maintained. By rendering the administration of justice visible, publicity contributes to the achievement of the aim of Article 6 § 1, a fair hearing, the guarantee of which is one of the foundations of a democratic society. . . .

As to whether states could establish predetermined exceptions to the public hearing obligation the Court was divided. A majority, five votes to two, held that:

39. . . . while the Court agrees that Article 6 § 1 states a general rule that civil proceedings, *inter alia*, should take place in public, it does not find it inconsistent with this provision for a State to designate an entire class of case as an exception to the general rule where considered necessary in the interests of morals, public order or national security or where required by the interests of juveniles or the protection of the private life of the parties . . . although the need for such a measure must always be subject to the Court's control. . . . The English procedural law can therefore be seen as a specific reflection of the general exceptions provided for by Article 6 § 1.

From this perspective there had been no violation of the applicants' right to a public hearing. However, the dissentients, Judges Loucaides and Tulkens, believed that; . . . the general legal rule against public hearings applied in these cases is incompatible not only with the wording but also with the basic objective and philosophy of the requirement for public hearings under Article 6 . . .'[18] The approach of the majority allows states considerable freedom to establish broad class exemptions from the obligation to hold public hearings, but individuals should be able to apply to the national courts for their particular cases to be heard in public (as the applicants were able to do in this case). If the individuals consider that the domestic procedural rulings are not compatible with Article 6(1), *e.g.* their cases do not fall within the exceptions specified in the Article, then they have the possibility of making a complaint to Strasbourg.

The original Court considered the obligation of public hearings in respect of 'criminal' disciplinary proceedings against prisoners in *Campbell and Fell v United Kingdom*.[19] The first applicant was charged with mutiny and committing gross violence against an officer. The charges were determined by the Board of Visitors[20] of his prison (a group of magistrates and lay persons) and the hearing, in accordance with Home Office policy, took place in private inside the

---

[18] *Ibid* Dissenting Opinion, para 1.
[19] A.80 (1984).
[20] Note, the Criminal Justice Act 1991 removed the disciplinary function of Boards of Visitors and transferred it to prison governors. Disciplinary proceedings by governors were held to fall within art 6(1) as "criminal charges" in *Ezeh v UK* (15 July 2002).

prison. The Board of Visitors found him guilty and 'awarded' him 570 days' loss of remission (*i.e.* his early release on parole was delayed by that period of time). He alleged, *inter alia*, that the private hearing violated Article 6(1). The government sought to justify the nature of the proceedings as falling within the Article 6(1) exceptions applying to cases involving 'public order or national security'. A bare majority of the Court, four votes to three, accepted the government's submission.

> 87. . . . the Court cannot disregard the factors cited by the Government, notably the considerations of public order and the security problems that would be involved if prison disciplinary proceedings were conducted in public. Such a course would undoubtedly occasion difficulties of greater magnitude than those that arise in ordinary criminal proceedings. A Board's adjudications are, as befits the character of disciplinary proceedings of this kind, habitually held within the prison precincts and the difficulties over admitting the public to those precincts are obvious. If they were held outside, similar problems would arise as regards the prisoner's transportation to and attendance at the hearing. To require that disciplinary proceedings concerning convicted prisoners should be held in public would impose a disproportionate burden on the authorities of the State.

The dissentients, Judges Cremona, Macdonald and Russo, considered that the government had failed to produce evidence that security considerations in Campbell's particular cases necessitated a private hearing. The judgment of the majority subordinated prisoners' right to a public hearing to the asserted security needs of the prison administration.

The full-time Court revealed a far more protective attitude towards the right to public hearings of prisoners facing criminal charges in *Riepan v Austria*.[21] The applicant had been convicted of murder and during his subsequent imprisonment he was alleged to have made a number of threats against prison officers. The authorities responded by charging him with the crime of dangerous menace. The local Regional Court decided to hold the applicant's trial in the closed area of the prison where he was serving his existing sentence. As usual, in the week before the trial, the Public Prosecutor's Office at the Regional Court distributed a list of forthcoming cases (and their locations) including the applicant's to the media and made the list available to the public. The hearing took place in a small room within the prison. The applicant, represented by counsel, pleaded not guilty. After hearing from the relevant prison officers the judge found the applicant guilty and sentenced him to ten months' imprisonment. The trial lasted about half an hour and no members of the media/public were present. Before the Court the applicant complained that his trial breached the public hearing obligation under Article 6(1). A united Court held that:

> 27. . . . The public character of the proceedings assumes particular importance in a case such as the present where the defendant in the criminal proceedings is a prisoner,

---

[21] Judgment of 14 February 2001.

where the charges relate to the making of threats against prison officers and where the witnesses are officers of the prison in which the defendant is detained.

28. It was undisputed in the present case, that the publicity of the hearing was not formally excluded. However, hindrance in fact can contravene the Convention just like a legal impediment (see the *Airey v Ireland* judgment of 9 October 1979, Series A no. 32, p. 14, § 25). The Court considers that the mere fact that the trial took place in the precincts of Garsten Prison does not lead necessarily to the conclusion that it lacked publicity. Nor did the fact that any potential spectators would have had to undergo certain identity and possibly security checks in itself deprive the hearing of its public nature . . .

29. Nevertheless, it must be borne in mind that the Convention is intended to guarantee not rights that are theoretical or illusory but rights that are practical and effective (see the *Artico v Italy* judgment of 13 May 1980, Series A no. 37, p. 16, § 33). The Court considers a trial will only comply with the requirement of publicity if the public is able to obtain information about its date and place and if this place is easily accessible to the public. In many cases these conditions will be fulfilled by the simple fact that a hearing is held in a regular court room large enough to accommodate spectators. However, the Court observes that the holding of a trial outside a regular court room, in particular in a place like a prison to which the general public on principle has no access, presents a serious obstacle to its public character. In such a case, the State is under an obligation to take compensatory measures in order to ensure that the public and the media are duly informed about the place of the hearing and are granted effective access.

The Court did not find that such measures, for example directions in a special public/media notice issued by the Public Prosecutor as to how the media/public could reach the prison and what access conditions would apply, had been taken. Consequently, the Court determined that there had been a violation of the public hearing requirement of Article 6(1).

Whilst *Riepan* dealt with a criminal trial being held in a prison and *Campbell and Fell* applied to 'criminal' disciplinary charges against a prisoner being conducted in a prison, the judgment in *Riepan*[22] should be welcomed for its robust application of the right to a public hearing. Very significantly, the judgment increases the positive obligations upon states when trials are scheduled to be held in unusual locations. Hence the more difficult it is for the public/media to gain access to the particular trial location the greater the obligation on the authorities to provide advanced information about how access can be secured. Furthermore, this obligation may require more than the provision of official information/advice by demanding that domestic authorities ensure that extra-ordinary trial venues are physically equipped to accommodate the media/members of the public.[23]

---

[22] Note, *Jacobs and White* above n 1 p 164 consider that *Riepan* implicitly overrules *Campbell & Fell*.

[23] Above n 21 para 30.

To determine civil and criminal cases within a reasonable time

This obligation is the source of the majority of Court judgments in recent years.[24] As we shall discover below, this is mainly due to the persistent failure of Italy to establish effective civil and criminal justice systems. The original Court explained the factors to be taken into account when evaluating whether a particular case had been determined within a reasonable time in *Konig v Germany*.[25] The applicant was a medical doctor whose authorisations to operate a plastic surgery clinic and practise medicine were withdrawn by the provincial government. Konig challenged those decisions in civil proceedings before the Administrative courts. The first set of proceedings were still ongoing after nearly eleven years and the second set had been determined by the Hessen Administrative Court of Appeal after seven years. The plenary Court held that:

> 99. The reasonableness of the duration of proceedings covered by Article 6 para. 1 of the Convention must be assessed in each case according to its circumstances. When enquiring into the reasonableness of the duration of criminal proceedings, the Court has had regard, *inter alia*, to the complexity of the case, to the applicant's conduct and to the manner in which the matter was dealt with by the administrative and judicial authorities (above-mentioned *Neumeister [v Austria*, A.8 (1968)] judgment, pp. 42–43, paras. 20–21; above-mentioned *Ringeisen [v Austria*, A.13 (1971)] judgment, p. 45, para. 110). The Court, like those appearing before it, considers that the same criteria must serve in the present case as the basis for its examination of the question whether the duration of the proceedings before the administrative courts exceeded the reasonable time stipulated by Article 6 para. 1.

An overwhelming majority of the Court, fifteen votes to one, concluded that both sets of proceedings had not been determined within a reasonable time due to the dilatory conduct of the Administrative courts, therefore Konig had suffered a violation of his rights under Article 6(1).

The *Konig* judgment is significant for establishing that the factors to be analysed when establishing if proceedings have been determined within a reasonable time are similar for both civil and criminal cases. Additionally, the case confirmed that where national legal systems, civil and criminal, provide appellate courts the time taken by those higher tiers to determine individual cases must also be taken into account when the reasonable time obligation is applied.

Later the Court elaborated the obligation upon states to create and maintain effective civil and criminal justice systems in *Buchholz v Germany*.[26] The applicant complained that it had taken nearly five years for the German Labour courts to determine his claim of unjust dismissal. The government sought to justify the duration of the proceedings due to an unexpected growth in labour

---

[24] *Jacobs and White* above n 1 p 167 state that approximately two-thirds of the Court's judgments in 2000 related to complaints about the unreasonable length of domestic proceedings.

[25] A.27 (1978).

[26] A.42 (1981).

cases, of 60%, caused by a sudden economic recession. The authorities had responded by making an increase of 30% in the number of judges appointed to the Labour courts. The Court held that:

> 51. . . . the Convention places a duty on the contracting States to organise their legal systems so as to allow the courts to comply with the requirements of Article 6(1), including that of trial within 'a reasonable time'. Nonetheless, a temporary backlog of business does not involve liability on the part of the Contracting States provided they have taken reasonably prompt remedial action to deal with an exceptional situation of this kind.

All the judges were in agreement that the government had taken adequate remedial measures and therefore no breach of the reasonable time guarantee had occurred. In subsequent cases involving Switzerland[27] and Portugal[28] the Court found breaches of this provision as the authorities' responses to asserted exceptional situations were not deemed adequate by the Strasbourg judges.

A Grand Chamber of the full-time Court found the continuing failure of Italian courts to determine cases within a reasonable time amounted to a 'practice' in breach of the Convention in *Bottazzi v Italy*.[29] The applicant complained that it had taken the Court of Audit nearly seven years to determine his claim for a pension.

> 22. The Court notes at the outset that Article 6 § 1 of the Convention imposes on the Contracting States the duty to organise their judicial systems in such a way that their courts can meet the requirements of this provision (see the *Salesi v Italy* judgment of 26 February 1993, Series A no. 257-E, p. 60, § 24). It wishes to reaffirm the importance of administering justice without delays which might jeopardise its effectiveness and credibility (see the *Katte Klitsche de la Grange v Italy* judgment of 27 October 1994, Series A no. 293-B, p. 39, § 61). It points out, moreover, that the Committee of Ministers of the Council of Europe, in its Resolution DH (97) 336 of 11 July 1997 (Length of civil proceedings in Italy: supplementary measures of a general character), considered that 'excessive delays in the administration of justice constitute an important danger, in particular for the respect of the rule of law'.
>
> The Court next draws attention to the fact that since 25 June 1987, the date of the *Capuano v Italy* judgment (Series A no. 119), it has already delivered 65 judgments in which it has found violations of Article 6 § 1 in proceedings exceeding a 'reasonable time' in the civil courts of the various regions of Italy. Similarly, under former Articles 31 and 32 of the Convention, more than 1,400 reports of the Commission resulted in resolutions by the Committee of Ministers finding Italy in breach of Article 6 for the same reason.
>
> The frequency with which violations are found shows that there is an accumulation of identical breaches which are sufficiently numerous to amount not merely to isolated incidents. Such breaches reflect a continuing situation that has not yet been remedied and in respect of which litigants have no domestic remedy.

---

[27] *Zimmermann v Switzerland* A.66 (1983).
[28] *Guincho v Portugal* A.81 (1984).
[29] Judgment of 28 July 1999.

This accumulation of breaches accordingly constitutes a practice that is incompatible with the Convention.

The Court was united in concluding that the applicant had suffered a breach of Article 6(1).

Unfortunately, the number of complaints against Italy alleging breaches of the reasonable time obligation has risen dramatically in the years following *Bottazzi*. The Evaluation Group, established by the Committee of Ministers to examine the workload crisis facing the full-time Court,[30] found that in July 2001 there were approximately 10,000 provisional applications pending against Italy alleging violations of this provision.[31] This mountain of complaints vividly demonstrates both the systemic failures of the Italian civil and criminal courts and the scope of the institutional impact of this positive obligation.

An independent and impartial tribunal

Article 6(1) requires that the judicial bodies determining civil and criminal proceedings must possess these characteristics. In *Campbell and Fell*,[32] the Court defined its methodology for assessing if the criterion of independence was satisfied.

> 78. In determining whether a body can be considered to be 'independent'—notably of the executive and of the parties to the case (see, *inter alia*, the *Le Compte, Van Leuven and De Meyere* judgment of 23 June 1981, Series A no. 43, p. 24, para. 55)—, the Court has had regard to the manner of appointment of its members and the duration of their term of office (ibid., pp. 24–25, para. 57), the existence of guarantees against outside pressures (see the *Piersack* [*v Belgium*] judgment of 1 October 1982, Series A no. 53, p. 13, para. 27) and the question whether the body presents an appearance of independence (see the *Delcourt* [*v Belgium*] judgment of 17 January 1970, Series A no. 11, p. 17, para. 31).

Applying those factors the Court found that the appointment of members of the Boards of Visitors by the Home Secretary did not undermine their independence, because relevant ministers also had roles in the appointment of judges. That whilst the three year period of office of members of Boards was quite short, it was explicable as members were unpaid and might be reluctant to accept the position if it was for a longer duration. Whilst there was no formal guarantee regarding the irremovability of members in practice the Home Secretary would only require the resignation of a member in exceptional circumstances. The

---

[30] For details see A Mowbray, 'Proposals for Reform of the European Court of Human Rights' [2002] *Public Law* 252.

[31] Report of the Evaluation Group to the Committee of Ministers on the European Court of Human Rights, September 2001, para 22. In February 2002, the Committee of Ministers began a special programme of annual examinations of the general measures adopted or envisaged by Italy to remedy the problem of delays in domestic judicial proceedings

[32] Above n 19.

combination of adjudicatory and supervisory roles performed by Boards of Visitors did not, in the Court's view, justify legitimate doubts on the part of prisoners regarding the independence of members of those bodies. Therefore, the Court was unanimous in rejecting Campbell's claim that his case had not been determined by an independent body. Whilst the factors considered by the Court in *Campbell and Fell* were wide-ranging, the Court was quite accommodating to the state in its acceptance of governmental arguments regarding the status of members of Boards of Visitors. In particular, the Court's acceptance of the absence of formal guarantees concerning the security of tenure of members of Boards.

The requirement of impartiality was elaborated by the Court in *Piersack v Belgium*.[33] Piersack had been convicted of murder and sentenced to eighteen years' hard labour. The judge who presided over his trial had previously been the head of the section of the Brussels public prosecution office that had dealt with Piersack's case. The Court held that:

> 30. Whilst impartiality normally denotes absence of prejudice or bias, its existence or otherwise can, notably under Article 6 § 1 of the Convention, be tested in various ways. A distinction can be drawn in this context between a subjective approach, that is endeavouring to ascertain the personal conviction of a given judge in a given case, and an objective approach, that is determining whether he offered guarantees sufficient to exclude any legitimate doubt in this respect.

The subjective impartiality of a judge was to be presumed until evidence of personal bias was proven.[34] In this case no such evidence was provided. As to the objective impartiality of the judge in Piersack's trial, the Court found that his previous involvement in the prosecution meant that the impartiality of the trial court 'was capable of appearing open to doubt'[35] and, therefore, a breach of Article 6(1) had occurred. More generally, this judgment provided a salutary warning to those states where there were frequent career interchanges between prosecution and judicial offices that particular judges must not preside over cases where they have had a previous involvement as a prosecutor.

Later examples of the original Court finding violations of the independence and impartiality requirements occurred in respect of senior military 'convening officers' who performed a number of central roles in the British system of courts martial[36] and military judges who sat in National Security Courts trying civilians for alleged offences against the state.[37]

The full-time Court upheld a claim of breach of objective impartiality in regard to an exercise of the multifarious functions of the Guernsey Bailiff. This

---

[33] A.53 (1982).

[34] For the difficulty of substantiating a claim of subjective impartiality see Mowbray above n 2 p 311.

[35] Above n 33 para 31.

[36] *Findlay v UK* 1997-I.

[37] *Incal v Turkey* 1998-IV 1569.

senior position involved, *inter alia*, presiding over the island's highest court and parliament together with performing important governmental tasks. In *McGonnell v United Kingdom*,[38] the applicant landowner had sought to have his agricultural property reclassified as available for development. The local parliament, presided over by the Deputy Bailiff, Mr Dorey, decided to continue to zone the land as agricultural. Subsequently the applicant brought legal proceedings to challenge the authorities' refusal to allow him to develop his land. His case was heard by a court presided over by the Bailiff (a position now occupied by the former Deputy Bailiff). The Strasbourg Court was united in holding that:

> 55. . . . the Bailiff's non-judicial constitutional functions cannot be accepted as being merely ceremonial. With particular respect to his presiding, as Deputy Bailiff, over the [parliament] in 1990, the Court considers that any direct involvement in the passage of legislation, or of executive rules, is likely to be sufficient to cast doubt on the judicial impartiality of a person subsequently called on to determine a dispute over whether reasons exist to permit a variation from the wording of the legislation or rules at issue. . .

Consequently, the applicant had legitimate grounds for questioning the objective impartiality of the Bailiff when he sat as a judge hearing the applicant's planning case. This judgment should be welcomed as a firm indication of the Court's contemporary determination to ensure the visible independence and impartiality of domestic judges falling within Article 6.

To provide public judgments

Article 6(1) specifies that in civil and criminal proceedings subject to its ambit 'judgment shall be pronounced publicly'. A plenary Court interpreted this obligation in *Pretto v Italy*.[39] The applicant farmer had brought civil proceedings against his landlord to purchase the land he farmed. Eventually, Pretto appealed to the Court of Cassation. His appeal was dismissed and the full text of the Court of Cassation's judgment was made public by being deposited in the Court's registry (any person could consult or obtain copies of the Court's judgments so deposited on application to the registry). Pretto alleged that the above procedure violated the obligation expressed in Article 6(1). The Strasbourg Court was unanimous in holding that:

> 26. . . . many member States of the Council of Europe have a long-standing tradition of recourse to other means, besides reading out aloud, for making public the decisions of all or some of their courts, and especially of their courts of cassation, for example deposit in a registry accessible to the public. The authors of the Convention cannot have overlooked that fact, even if concern to take it into account is not so easily

---

[38] Judgment of 8 February 2000.
[39] A.71 (1983).

identifiable in their working documents as in the *travaux préparatoires* of the 1966 Covenant (see, for instance, document A/4299 of 3 December 1959, pp. 12, 15 and 19, §§ 38 (b), 53 and 63 (c) *in fine*).

The Court therefore does not feel bound to adopt a literal interpretation. It considers that in each case the form of publicity to be given to the 'judgment' under the domestic law of the respondent State must be assessed in the light of the special features of the proceedings in question and by reference to the object and purpose of Article 6 § 1.

Taking account of the availability to everyone, via the registry, of the full text of the Court of Cassation's judgment in Pretto's case was sufficient to satisfy Article 6(1) in the opinion of the European Court. This generous interpretation of the Convention ensured that well-established domestic judicial practices were compatible with the public judgment obligation.

A few months later a nearly identical plenary Court[40] developed the above approach in *Sutter v Switzerland*.[41] The applicant student had refused to have a haircut when called up for a refresher military conscription course. He was convicted of insubordination, after a public hearing, by a Divisional Court which sentenced him to ten days' imprisonment in a public judgment. He appealed to the Military Court of Cassation which later dismissed his appeal in a twenty page written judgment. He was sent a copy of the judgment. Any person who could establish an interest was able to consult or obtain a copy of the judgments of the Military Court of Cassation on application to the Chief Military Prosecutor or the registry of the Military Court. Sutter complained, *inter alia*, that the above procedure did not comply with the public judgment obligation. A large majority of the European Court, eleven votes to four, concluded that; '. . . the Convention did not require the reading out loud of the judgment delivered at the final stage of the proceedings.'[42] Therefore, there had been no breach of Article 6(1). Whereas the dissentients[43] felt it was:

. . . necessary to emphasise the particular importance of the accessibility of the judgment to the general public. If the basic underlying concept of public scrutability is to be a reality, a restricted access to judgments such as existed in the present case, i.e. restricted only to persons who could establish an interest to the satisfaction of a court official, falls short of what is required by that provision of the Convention. Public knowledge of court decisions cannot be secured by confining that knowledge to a limited class of persons.

The dissentients made a good point as the judgment of the majority in *Sutter* accepted a publication regime that was distinctly more limited than that upheld in *Pretto*.

---

[40] Judge Ryssdal had assumed Presidency of the Court and Judge Macdonald replaced former President Wiarda.
[41] A.74 (1984).
[42] *Ibid* para 34.
[43] Judges: Cremona, Ganshof van der Meersch, Walsh and Macdonald.

An example of the Court finding a breach of this obligation was *Campbell and Fell v United Kingdom*.[44] Campbell argued that the failure of the Board of Visitors to give a public judgment in his disciplinary case violated Article 6(1). The Court, by five votes to two, determined that as no steps had been taken to make public the Board's decision a violation had occurred.

A majority of the full-time Court found the English system of restricted access to civil judgments concerning children to be compatible with the public judgments obligation in *B. and P. v United Kingdom*.[45] Generally court orders and judgments concerning children are not made public, but any person with a legitimate interest can apply to the relevant court for permission to see and copy the text of orders and judgments. Also judgments of legal importance are published, in an anonymous form, in the law reports. In the light of these practices the Court, by five votes to two, held that:

> 48. . . . a literal interpretation of the terms of Article 6 § 1 concerning the pronouncement of judgments would not only be unnecessary for the purposes of public scrutiny but might even frustrate the primary aim of Article 6 § 1, which is to secure a fair hearing (see, *mutatis mutandis*, the above-mentioned *Sutter* judgment, § 34).

> 49. The Court thus concludes that the Convention did not require making available to the general public the residence judgments in the present cases, and that there has been no violation of Article 6 § 1 in this respect.

Judges Loucaides and Tulkens dissented as they considered that the obligation to pronounce judgments was expressed in unqualified terms by Article 6(1).

The above judgments reveal both the original and contemporary Court refusing to give a literal meaning to an express positive obligation. Rather than focus solely on whether a particular judgment was actually pronounced in public the Court has examined the form and degree to which the judgment has been made available to the public. Whilst this may be a realistic approach, given the practice of superior courts delivering written judgments in many member states, the Court can be criticised for tolerating considerable limitations on public access to judgments (*e.g.* in *Sutter* and *B. and P.*). In an ideal world all judgments should be made generally available to the public (technically more feasible in the modern digital era) with appropriate deletions of sensitive information (such as defence information- though not of military haircuts- or the identities of persons in family disputes).

ARTICLE 6(3)

This paragraph elaborates a number of minimum rights in respect of persons charged with criminal offences. The Court views these provisions as specific aspects of the general right to a fair trial enshrined in Article 6(1), that we have

---

[44] Above n 19.
[45] Above n 17.

examined above, and frequently considers complaints under Article 6(3) and 6(1) together.[46] Certain of the rights defined in Article 6(3) have also been held applicable to civil disciplinary proceedings, such as those concerning medical doctors, falling within the scope of Article 6(1).[47]

To inform promptly charged persons, in a language that they understand, of the detailed nature and cause of the accusations against them (Article 6(3)(a))

This is an expansion of the separate obligation, under Article 5(2),[48] on states to provide information to arrested persons regarding the reasons for their arrest and of any charges against them. The Court found a breach of Article 6(3)(a) in *Brozicek v Italy*.[49] The applicant was a German national who had been arrested in Italy for allegedly tearing down flags displayed by a political party and injuring one of the police officers who arrested him. Subsequently, the public prosecutor sent a letter, written in Italian, to Brozicek's home in Germany informing him that criminal proceedings had been brought against him for, *inter alia*, wounding the police officer. Brozicek replied to the prosecutor, in German, asking that the Italian authorities communicate with him in his mother tongue or one of the official languages of the United Nations. The prosecutor continued to write to Brozicek in Italian. Eventually, he was convicted *in absentia*. The Court held that as the Italian authorities had produced no evidence that Brozicek understood Italian they should have complied with his request for the documentation to be translated into a language that he comprehended. But, the content of the documentation sent was sufficient to comply with the level of detail required by the provision as it listed the offences he had been charged with, stated the date and place of the alleged offences, referred to the appropriate Articles of the Italian Criminal Code and disclosed the name of the alleged victim. This judgment determines that if a foreign national claims not to understand the national language the domestic authorities must provide the required information in a suitable language, unless they can prove that the person does in fact understand the national language.

In *Kamasinski v Austria*,[50] the Court ruled that this duty did not impose a general obligation on states to provide written translations of indictments for foreigners who could not understand the national language. The applicant was an American citizen who had been detained on suspicion of not paying various bills. He had been questioned, via an interpreter, about the alleged offences and an interpreter was present when the indictment was served on him during judicial proceedings. The European Court held that, 'whilst this provision does not

---

[46] See, for example, *Hadjianastassiou v Greece* A.252-A (1992).
[47] See, *Albert v Belgium* A.58 (1983).
[48] Examined above in ch 4.
[49] A.167 (1989).
[50] A.168 (1989).

specify that the relevant information should be given in writing or translated in written form for a foreign defendant, it does point to the need for special attention to be paid to the notification of the "accusation" to the defendant.'[51] As the charges against Kamasinski were simple and he had been questioned at length about the alleged offences by the police and the investigating judges, the Court held that the authorities had complied with their obligation under Article 6(3)(a). The significance of the authorities earlier questioning of Kamasinski about the alleged offences as a factor contributing to their satisfaction of the obligation under Article 6(3)(a) was echoed in the later case of *Fox, Campbell and Hartley v United Kingdom*[52] when the Court interpreted the analogous duty under Article 5(2).[53]

To enable defendants to have adequate time and facilities for the preparation of their defences (Article 6(3)(b))

A failure by a domestic court to provide adequate reasons for its decision with the consequence that a defendant was not able to effectively exercise a right of appeal was determined to be a breach of this provision in *Hadjianastassiou v Greece*.[54] The applicant, an officer, had been convicted by an Air Force Court of disclosing military secrets. He appealed to the Courts Martial Appeal Court which delivered a brief judgment which upheld his conviction but substituted a lighter sentence. The applicant requested a full record of the judgment and hearing. He was told that he would have to wait for it to be produced. Under Greek law he only had five days from the date of the Appeal Court's judgment to lodge an appeal with the Court of Cassation. He submitted a general appeal against the Court of Appeal's decision. The full record of the Court of Appeal's judgment and hearing was supplied to him several weeks later. Subsequently, the Court of Cassation dismissed his appeal because it was too vague. The European Court held that Article 6(3)(b) and 6(1) together required that national courts, '. . . indicate with sufficient clarity the grounds on which they base their decision.'[55] Here the combination of the abbreviated judgment given by the Appeal Court and the short duration of the period for making an appeal to the Court of Cassation resulted in such restrictions on the rights of the defence that these two provisions of Article 6 had been violated. Undoubtedly, the extremely limited timeframe for appeals exacerbated the significance of the Court of Appeal's failure to adequately explain the basis of its judgment on the day it was given.

---

[51] A.168 (1989), para 79.
[52] A.182 (1990).
[53] Above ch 4 n 16.
[54] Above n 46.
[55] *Ibid* para 33.

To provide free legal assistance to defendants when the interests of justice so require and they cannot afford to pay for it (Article 6(3)(c))

As we have already seen, in *McVicar*,[56] the Court has acknowledged that a defendant in civil proceedings might be able to invoke Article 6(1) to require a state to provide legal aid for such a person. However, in respect of impecunious defendants in complex and/or serious criminal proceedings this provision establishes an express positive obligation to do so. The original Court examined the nature of this obligation in *Artico v Italy*.[57] The applicant had been imprisoned for offences of dishonesty and he appealed against his convictions with a request that the Court of Cassation provide him with free legal representation. The Court of Cassation ordered that a named lawyer provide Artico with legal aid. That lawyer failed to provide any assistance to Artico, he claimed that he had other commitments and problems with his health prevented him taking on such an onerous case. Despite Artico's numerous requests for the Court of Cassation to designate another legal aid lawyer no one was appointed. Before the Court, the government claimed that it had fulfilled its obligations under Article 6(3)(c) by designating a legal aid lawyer for the applicant. The Court rejected that view of the obligation.

> 33. . . . The Court recalls that the Convention is intended to guarantee not rights that are theoretical or illusory but rights that are practical and effective; this is particularly so of the rights of the defence in view of the prominent place held in a democratic society by the right to a fair trial, from which they derive (see the *Airey* judgment of 9 October 1979, Series A no. 32, pp. 12–13, par. 24, and paragraph 32 above). As the Commission's Delegates correctly emphasised, Article 6 par. 3 (c) speaks of 'assistance' and not of 'nomination'. Again, mere nomination does not ensure effective assistance since the lawyer appointed for legal aid purposes may die, fall seriously ill, be prevented for a protracted period from acting or shirk his duties. If they are notified of the situation, the authorities must either replace him or cause him to fulfil his obligations. Adoption of the Government's restrictive interpretation would lead to results that are unreasonable and incompatible with both the wording of sub-paragraph (c) and the structure of Article 6 taken as a whole; in many instances free legal assistance might prove to be worthless.

> 36. . . . Admittedly, a State cannot be held responsible for every shortcoming on the part of a lawyer appointed for legal aid purposes but, in the particular circumstances, it was for the competent Italian authorities to take steps to ensure that the applicant enjoyed effectively the right to which they had recognised he was entitled. Two courses were open to the authorities: either to replace Mr. Della Rocca [the designated legal aid lawyer] or, if appropriate, to cause him to fulfil his obligations (see paragraph 33 above). They chose a third course—remaining passive -, whereas compliance with the Convention called for positive action on their part (see the above-mentioned *Airey* judgment, p. 14, par. 25 *in fine*).

[56] Above n 9.
[57] A.37 (1980).

Therefore, the Court found a breach of this obligation. The judgment in *Artico* is important for the Court's emphasis on the need for states to comply with the substance of their Convention duties and not merely undertake symbolic gestures of compliance. Hence, simply appointing a legal aid lawyer is not sufficient if he/she fails to provide any assistance and that omission is drawn to the attention of the authorities.

The 'interests of justice' element of this obligation was examined by the Court in *Pakelli v Germany*.[58] The applicant was a Turkish national who had been convicted of drugs offences whilst living in Germany. Pakelli appealed against his conviction and a lawyer requested the Federal Court to appoint him as Pakelli's representative in proceedings before that Court. However, the Federal Court determined that Pakelli's appeal did not justify the appointment of a legal representative. Subsequently, the European Court, unanimously, concluded that the interests of justice required that Pakelli should have been provided with legal representation as the Federal Court held a rare oral hearing in his appeal due to the complex issues raised by the case. It seems patently clear that in such circumstances a lay person, let alone a foreign national with a different mother tongue, would have been unable to effectively represent himself before the domestic court.

Similarly in *Granger v United Kingdom*,[59] the Court held that the interests of justice required that a convicted perjurer should have been provided with free legal assistance to aid him in presenting his complex appeal before Scotland's High Court of Justiciary. In the later Scottish cases of *Boner v United Kingdom*[60] and *Maxwell v United Kingdom*,[61] the Court also found that the interests of justice required legal assistance for appellants, even though they were making relatively simple appeals, because of the severity of the sentences that were at stake (eight years' imprisonment for robbery and five years' imprisonment for assault).

A unanimous Grand Chamber articulated a very important norm governing the application of this obligation in *Benham v United Kingdom*.[62] The applicant had been sentenced to thirty days' imprisonment by a magistrates' court for failing to pay his community charge ('poll tax'). He had not been provided with any legal representation before the magistrates. The European Court held that, '. . . where deprivation of liberty is at stake, the interests of justice in principle call for legal representation.'[63] Consequently, Benham should have received free legal representation and, therefore, Article 6(3)(c) had been breached.

The element of the defendant not having sufficient means to pay for legal representation was considered by the Court in *Croissant v Germany*.[64] Following

---

[58] A.64 (1983).
[59] A.174 (1990).
[60] A.300-B (1994).
[61] A.300-C (1994).
[62] 1996-III 753.
[63] *Ibid* para 61.
[64] A.273-B (1992).

the applicant's conviction for supporting a criminal organisation he was ordered to pay the costs of his defence lawyers, two selected by him and one appointed by the court. Under domestic law convicted persons were required to pay their defence costs, but those sums could be wholly or partly remitted by decision of a Minister. Croissant contended, *inter alia*, that requiring him to pay defence costs violated Article 6(3)(c). The Court ruled that, '. . . the burden of proving a lack of sufficient means should be borne by the person who pleads it.'[65] As domestic law would enable the remission of all or some of the defence costs, if Croissant could establish that he did not have sufficient funds, the Court did not find a breach of this obligation.

The full-time Court applied *Croissant* in *Morris v United Kingdom.*[66] The applicant was a soldier who had been absent without leave for over three years. After capture he was charged and sent for trial before a district court martial. He applied to the Army Criminal Legal Aid Authority for legal aid to pay for representation by a solicitor. The Authority granted him legal aid subject to him making a down-payment of £240 (Morris had informed the Authority that his weekly net income was £158). He declined the offer of legal aid. Before the Court he contended that the requirement to make a down-payment prior to being given legal aid violated Article 6(3)(c). The Court, unanimously, stated that *Croissant* had determined that it was not a breach of that obligation for states to make defendants pay a contribution towards the costs of legal representation provided they had sufficient means. The judges considered that the offer made to Morris was not 'arbitrary or unreasonable,'[67] consequently no breach of that provision had occurred. This judgment, therefore, confirms that states' obligation to provide free criminal legal assistance is not unconditional and reasonable contributions can be demanded of defendants who possess adequate financial resources.

A significant extension of the temporal scope of the obligation to provide free legal assistance occurred in *Berlinski v Poland.*[68] The two applicant body-builders refused to leave an athletics club with the consequence that the police were called. A violent struggle ensued with the applicants sustaining various injuries during their arrest by the police. Two days later the applicants requested that the prosecuting authorities appoint a free defence lawyer to help them. The prosecution did not respond. Some months later the applicants were charged with assaulting police officers. One year after the applicants had requested legal aid a court appointed a free lawyer to represent them. Two years later they were convicted and given suspended prison sentences. The applicants claimed, *inter alia*, to have suffered from a breach of Article 6(3)(c). A united Chamber held that:

---

[65] *Ibid* para 37.
[66] Judgment of 26 February 2002. For a commentary on other aspects of this case see, A Mowbray, 'The ECHR: The Abolition of Capital Punishment and Recent Cases' (2002) 2 *Human Rights Law Review* 319.
[67] *Ibid* para 89.
[68] Judgment of 20 June 2002.

75. The Court recalls that, even if the primary purpose of Article 6, as far as criminal matters are concerned, is to ensure a fair trial by a 'tribunal' competent to determine 'any criminal charge', it does not follow that this provision of the Convention has no application to pre-trial proceedings. Thus, Article 6—especially paragraph 3—may be relevant before a case is sent for trial if and so far as the fairness of the trial is likely to be seriously prejudiced by an initial failure to comply with its provisions. The manner in which Article 6 §§ 1 and 3 (c) is to be applied during the preliminary investigation depends on the special features of the proceedings involved and on the circumstances of the case . . .

77. The Court observes that it is undisputed that the applicants lacked means to employ a private representative in the context of criminal proceedings against them. It is also uncontested that the applicants' request for an official lawyer to be appointed was ignored by the authorities, with the result that they had no defence counsel for more than a year. Given that a number of procedural acts, including questioning of the applicants and their medical examinations, were carried out during that period . . . the Court finds no justification for this restriction which deprived the applicants of the right to adequately defend themselves during the investigation and trial.

Hence, there had been a breach of Article 6(1) and 6(3)(c). Consequently, where criminal justice authorities, such as prosecutors and judges, undertake important pre-trial tasks in regard to persons facing the likelihood of a subsequent criminal trial Article 6 requires the authorities to consider requests for legal aid made by those persons. It would appear that the greater the possible detriment to the suspect's defence posed by the task-in-hand the stronger will be the case for granting free legal assistance.

Overall we can conclude that the Court has applied this positive obligation to a broad range of criminal proceedings, encompassing major pre-trial events, trials and appellate processes. Provided that charged persons[69]/defendants can demonstrate that they do not have the financial resources to pay for legal assistance, the Court interprets Article 6(3)(c) as requiring states to provide legal representation where cases involve the potential imprisonment of the defendants and/or complex issues.

To provide defendants with an adequate opportunity to challenge adverse witnesses (Article 6(3)(d))

A number of applicants have alleged breaches of this provision following their convictions based upon the testimony of anonymous witnesses. In *Doorson v Netherlands*,[70] the Amsterdam Regional Court had found the applicant guilty of drug trafficking based upon the evidence of an identified witness, who had been subject to questioning by the prosecution and defence at the trial, and two

---

[69] For the Court's elaboration of the autonomous concept of a criminal charge under art 6 see, *Deweer v Belgium* A.35 (1980) and Mowbray above n 2 pp 277–78.

[70] 1996-II.

anonymous witnesses who had been heard by the investigating judge. During Doorson's appeal his lawyer was allowed to question the two anonymous witnesses in the presence of the investigating judge, however the identities of the witnesses were not disclosed. The Court of Appeal subsequently dismissed Doorson's appeal. The Strasbourg Court held that when national judges allowed prosecuting authorities to use the evidence of anonymous witnesses the domestic courts must adopt 'counterbalancing'[71] procedures designed to compensate the defence for the handicaps of challenging the evidence given by such persons. In this case the opportunity for Doorson's lawyer to question the anonymous witnesses satisfied the positive obligation under Article 6(3)(d) in the opinion of a large majority, seven votes to two, of the Court. The judgment also applied the important principle that:

> 76. Finally, it should be recalled that even when 'counterbalancing' procedures are found to compensate sufficiently the handicaps under which the defence labours, a conviction should not be based either solely or to a decisive extent on anonymous statements.

The Court determined that this principle had not been violated as the Dutch courts had taken account of the evidence of the identified witness as well as the testimony of the anonymous witnesses.

The judgment in *Doorson* revealed the Court seeking to find a fair balance between the conflicting interests of protecting vulnerable witnesses and ensuring that defendants have adequate opportunities to challenge the veracity of those witnesses. The counterbalancing procedures obligation is a key element of that equation. An example of a case where the modified procedure adopted by the national courts was found not to satisfy this requirement was *Van Mechelen and Others v Netherlands*.[72] The applicants had been convicted of attempted manslaughter and robbery. The prosecution had relied on written statements by anonymous police officers identifying the applicants as perpetrators of the relevant violent crimes. Before the Court of Appeal the police officers affirmed that they wished to remain anonymous, as they feared for the safety of their families and themselves. Therefore, the Court of Appeal arranged for the officers to be questioned via a sound link (each officer gave evidence in a room accompanied by an investigating judge whilst the defence and prosecution lawyers were located in another room). After these sessions the investigating judge reported that the officers' appeared to be truthful when answering the questions put to them. The Court of Appeal found the applicants guilty of attempted murder and robbery, and increased the length of their sentences. A majority of the European Court, six votes to three, determined that the sound link procedure was unsatisfactory because it deprived the defence of the possibility of observing the demeanour of the police officers as they were being questioned. Furthermore,

---

[71] *Ibid* para 75.
[72] 1997-III.

the applicants' convictions had impermissibly been based to a decisive extent on the evidence of anonymous witnesses.

The full-time Court has followed a similar approach. It found breaches of Article 6(3)(d) in *Birutis and Others v Lithuania*.[73] The three applicants were charged with organising and participating in a prison riot. The evidence against the first applicant consisted of written statements obtained by the investigating authorities from 17 anonymous witnesses, mostly other prisoners, statements made by three co-accused and evidence given at his trial by five members of the prison staff. The evidence against the second applicant was broadly the same, however the only evidence against the third applicant comprised of written statements by six anonymous witnesses. The trial court convicted all the applicants and imposed long prison sentences on them. The European Court held that:

> 28. ... as a general rule, paragraphs 1 and 3(d) of Article 6 require that the defendant be given an adequate and proper opportunity to challenge and question a witness against him, either when he makes his statements or at a later stage ...

The judges were united in concluding that the conviction of the third applicant solely on the basis of anonymous evidence violated the *Doorson* principle. Furthermore, the trial court had failed to implement counterbalancing procedures, such as questioning the anonymous witnesses or scrutinising how their evidence had been obtained, to safeguard the defence rights of the first and second applicants. Therefore, the Court found a breach of Article 6(3)(d) had occurred in respect of each applicant.

The above judgments show that normally the defence must be allowed to challenge prosecution witnesses. If there are strong reasons to justify the prosecution using anonymous witnesses (because of their vulnerable positions, such as prison inmates testifying against fellow prisoners) then an obligation is placed upon the trial court to adopt special procedures to safeguard defence rights. The decisions in *Van Mechelen* and *Birutis* demonstrate that the Court will rigorously examine whether adequate counterbalancing procedures have been utilised.

To provide the free assistance of an interpreter if a person charged with a criminal offence cannot understand or speak the language used in court (Article 6(3)(e))

This positive obligation is expressly stated in Article 6(3)(e). However, in *Luedicke, Belkacem and Koc v Germany*,[74] the government sought to advocate a restrictive interpretation of this provision. The applicants were foreign nation-

---

[73] Judgment of 28 June 2002.
[74] A.29 (1978).

als who had been convicted of various offences. As they did not understand German they had been provided with interpreters during their trials. After their convictions they were, in accordance with domestic law, required to pay the costs of the interpreters. The applicants contended that this requirement violated the right to free interpretation services. But, the government submitted that whilst Article 6(3)(e) exempted defendants from having to pay for interpretation expenses in advance it did not prevent those costs being recouped from defendants after they had been convicted. The Court, unanimously, rejected the government's interpretation as being contrary to both the ordinary meaning of the word 'free' and the overall object of Article 6 to safeguard the right to a fair trial. The judges also declined to accept the government's view that Article 6(3)(e) only applied to the provision of interpretation assistance at the oral hearing of a trial. The Court ruled that:

> 48. . . . Construed in the context of the right to a fair trial guaranteed by Article 6, paragraph (3)(e) signifies that an accused who cannot understand or speak the language used in court has the right to the free assistance of an interpreter for the translation or interpretation of all those documents or statements in the proceedings instituted against him which it is necessary for him to understand in order to have the benefit of a fair trial.

The judgment in *Luedicke* was a robust application of the wording of Article 6(3)(e). Unlike Article 6(3)(c), the right to legal assistance- examined above, this provision does not contain any reference to the financial resources of the defendant, therefore the Court was correct when it refused to allow governments to reclaim interpretation costs from convicted persons. Also the elaboration of the obligation to encompass interpretation assistance in respect of appropriate documents and statements outside the trial hearing was a further desirable enhancement of the scope of Article 6(3)(e). Nevertheless, we should note that this aspect of the obligation has some overlap with Article 6(3)(a), the right to be informed in a language the person understands of the accusations against him/her, and the Court adopted a cautious approach to the latter requirement in *Kamasinski*.[75]

The full-time Court has emphasised the pivotal role of trial judges in ensuring that defendants who do not understand the language of the court are provided with effective interpretation assistance. In *Cuscani v United Kingdom*,[76] the applicant was an Italian national with a very limited command of English. He had been the manager of 'The Godfather Restaurant' (!) in Newcastle upon Tyne. The authorities charged him with various offences involving the alleged evasion of hundreds of thousands of pounds of taxes. He was granted legal aid and represented by a Queen's Counsel, junior counsel and solicitors. At his trial Cuscani pleaded guilty, on the advice of his counsel. During that hearing his counsel informed the judge of Cuscani's poor English and asked the court to

---

[75] Above n 50.
[76] Judgment of 24 September 2002.

direct that an interpreter be present at subsequent hearings. The court so ordered. However, when the trial resumed a few weeks later for sentencing no interpreter was present. Cuscasni's counsel accepted that the hearing should proceed without an interpreter. The judge asked if there was anyone in court who knew the defendant and was fluent in Italian and English. Cuscani's counsel, without consulting him, replied that his brother (who was present) could provide translation if required. In fact the brother was never asked to provide any interpretation during the subsequent hearing at which Cuscani was sentenced to four years' imprisonment. The European Court was unanimous in finding that those proceedings violated Article 6(3)(e).

> 38. . . . in the Court's opinion the verification of the applicant's need for interpretation facilities was a matter for the judge to determine in consultation with the applicant, especially since he had been alerted to counsel's own difficulties in communicating with the applicant.

Clearly, we may observe, that the trial judge should have adjourned the hearing on sentencing until a qualified interpreter was present to aid Cuscani.

General conclusions

Our study of the above cases discloses an extensive array of positive obligations under Article 6. These include the obligation on domestic legal systems to determine civil and criminal cases within a reasonable time (Article 6(1)), which has become the most popular source of complaints lodged with the Court. Other express positive obligations elaborated by this Article include the duty on criminal justice authorities to inform charged persons of the detailed nature of the accusations made against them (Article 6(3)(a)), the duty to provide such persons (who are impecunious and facing serious charges) with free legal assistance (Article 6(3)(c) and to provide charged persons with free interpretation assistance if they do not understand the language of the court (Article 6(3)(e)). When interpreting these express positive obligations the Court, in both original and full-time forms, has been greatly influenced by the practical needs of both states and individuals. For example, the Court has refrained from applying a literal meaning to the obligation upon domestic courts to pronounce their judgments publicly (Article 6(1) in *Pretto*),[77] so as to preserve the lawfulness of the well-established practice of many higher courts delivering their determinations via written judgments. Whilst the interests of individuals were safeguarded by the Court's insistence that the obligation upon states to provide criminal legal aid must be satisfied by the provision of actual legal assistance and not by the mere symbolic designation of a lawyer (Article 6(3)(c) in *Artico*).[78]

---

[77] Above n 39.
[78] Above n 57.

The Court has also found several implied positive obligations within the text of Article 6. This aspect of the development of positive obligations under the Convention began quite early in the Court's jurisprudence in *Airey*,[79] regarding the requirement to provide legal aid to civil claimants in complex proceedings as an element of the right to a fair hearing (Article 6(1)). Another example of an implied obligation is the duty upon criminal courts to adopt 'counterbalancing' procedures where they permit the use of anonymous witnesses (Article 6(3)(d) in *Doorson*).[80]

The full-time Court has generally been deepening and widening the scope of positive obligations under this Article. An illustration of the former phenomenon is the greater protection of prisoners' right to public hearings of criminal proceedings conducted in prisons exhibited in *Riepan*.[81] The contemporary Court has also broadened the ambit of the implied obligation to provide civil legal assistance to encompass defendants in *McVicar*[82] and the express obligation to provide criminal legal aid to cover significant pre-trial proceedings in *Berlinski*.[83] These trends should be seen as an acknowledgement of the significance of positive obligations under this crucial Article.

[79] Above n 4.
[80] Above n 70.
[81] Above n 21.
[82] Above n 9.
[83] Above n 68.

6

Article 8: Right to respect for private and family life

T HE TEXT OF this Article adopts a two paragraph form. In the first paragraph the rights are expressed and in the second paragraph permissible interferences with those rights are elaborated.

> (1) Everyone has the right to respect for his private and family life, his home and his correspondence.
>
> (2) There shall be no interference by a public authority with the exercise of this right except such as is in accordance with the law and is necessary in a democratic society in the interests of national security, public safety or the economic well-being of the country, for the prevention of disorder or crime, for the protection of health or morals, or for the protection of the rights and freedoms of others.

Positive obligations have been asserted by applicants in a wide range of contexts under the terms of this Article and many of them have been upheld by the Court. In a number of cases[1] applicants have invoked a combination of the individual rights enshrined in Article 8(1), including the rights to respect for private and family life and a person's home, to support their claims. In our examination of the jurisprudence we shall analyse the cases according to the dominant right being asserted in the particular case.

PRIVATE LIFE

Protection of persons from sexual abuse

A Chamber of the original Court was unanimous in finding that the respondent state had failed to comply with its positive obligation to secure practical and effective protection for a young person from such abuse in *X. and Y. v The Netherlands*.[2] The second applicant was a mentally handicapped sixteen year-old who had been living in a privately operated home for disabled children. One night the son-in-law of the directress forced Y. to go to his room and have

---

[1] For example, in the pollution cases examined below at n 96.
[2] A.91 (1985).

sexual intercourse with him. This event caused her to suffer serious mental disturbance. X., who was Y.'s father, complained on her behalf to the police. Subsequently the public prosecutor decided not to prosecute the son-in-law. X. challenged that decision in the courts, but the Court of Appeal ruled that under Dutch law persons over the age of sixteen who believed themselves to be the victims of crimes had to personally file a complaint with the police. As Y. was unable to do so, due to her disabilities, no criminal charge could be brought against the son-in-law. The Court of Appeal acknowledged that there was a gap in the law. X. complained to the Commission that the impossibility of bringing a criminal prosecution against the son-in-law meant that the Dutch authorities had failed to satisfy Y.'s right to respect for her private life. The Commission unanimously upheld that complaint.

Before the Court it was not disputed that Article 8 was applicable to the facts of the complaint as the concept of 'private life' covered, '. . . the physical and moral integrity of the person, including his or her sexual life.'[3] Furthermore:

> 23. The Court recalls that although the object of Article 8 is essentially that of protecting the individual against arbitrary interference by the public authorities, it does not merely compel the State to abstain from such interference: in addition to this primarily negative undertaking, there may be positive obligations inherent in an effective respect for private or family life (see the *Airey* [*v Ireland*] judgment of 9 October 1979, Series A no. 32, p. 17, para. 32). These obligations may involve the adoption of measures designed to secure respect for private life even in the sphere of the relations of individuals between themselves.

The applicants contended that only the criminal law provided the requisite level of protection for a young person, whilst the respondent state argued that the Convention allowed states to choose the means of securing respect for persons' private lives.

> 24. . . . The Court, which on this point agrees in substance with the opinion of the Commission, observes that the choice of the means calculated to secure compliance with Article 8 in the sphere of the relations of individuals between themselves is in principle a matter that falls within the Contracting States' margin of appreciation. In this connection, there are different ways of ensuring 'respect for private life', and the nature of the State's obligation will depend on the particular aspect of private life that is at issue. Recourse to the criminal law is not necessarily the only answer.

Nevertheless, the Court went on to uphold the applicants' submission that the existence of civil law remedies in respect of the abuse suffered by Y. were inadequate.

> 27. The Court finds that the protection afforded by the civil law in the case of wrongdoing of the kind inflicted on Miss Y is insufficient. This is a case where fundamental values and essential aspects of private life are at stake. Effective deterrence is indispensable in this area and it can be achieved only by criminal-law provisions; indeed, it is by such provisions that the matter is normally regulated.

---

[3] A.91 (1985) para 22.

Moreover, as was pointed out by the Commission, this is in fact an area in which the Netherlands has generally opted for a system of protection based on the criminal law. The only gap, so far as the Commission and the Court have been made aware, is as regards persons in the situation of Miss Y; in such cases, this system meets a procedural obstacle which the Netherlands legislature had apparently not foreseen.

Consequently, there had been a violation of Y.'s right to respect for her private life and the Court awarded her 3,000 Guilders as non-pecuniary damage.

The above judgment is very significant for the Court's willingness to require states to take positive measures to regulate the relationships between individuals. What is required of states clearly depends upon the type of relationship at issue. In Y.'s case there was an abuse of power by an adult over a disabled young person who was not capable of safeguarding her own interests. Hence the Court demanded state intervention through the enactment of criminal law protection for such vulnerable persons. Interestingly, the judgment did not contain an express justification for the recognition of positive obligations under Article 8, other than a reference to the earlier case of *Airey*.[4]

Eleven years later the Court was confronted with a case raising the inverse legal scenario to that in *X. and Y.*. In *Stubbings and Others v United Kingdom*,[5] four women separately alleged that they had suffered serious sexual abuse during their childhood by different persons. The applicants claimed that they did not appreciate the nature of their abuse until many years later when they received psychological therapy. They then sought to bring civil proceedings against their alleged abusers. The House of Lords held in *Stubbings v Webb*,[6] that in accordance with the Limitation Act 1980 these claims had to be brought within six years of the eighteenth birthday (the date of majority) of the alleged victims. As the applicants claims fell outside this time period they were prevented from suing their alleged abusers. Under English law criminal prosecutions for serious offences, such as rape, are not subject to any time bar. The applicants complained to Strasbourg that the interpretation of the Limitation Act given in Ms Stubbings' case by the House of Lords had deprived them of an effective civil remedy against their alleged abusers and consequently the authorities had, *inter alia*, failed to protect their right to respect for their private lives. The Court repeated its judgment in *X. and Y.* that states were subject to positive obligations to respect the private lives of individuals.

64. Sexual abuse is unquestionably an abhorrent type of wrongdoing, with debilitating effects on its victims. Children and other vulnerable individuals are entitled to State protection, in the form of effective deterrence, from such grave types of interference with essential aspects of their private lives (see, *mutatis mutandis*, the above-mentioned *X and Y* judgment, p. 13, para. 27).

65. In the instant case, however, such protection was afforded. The abuse of which the applicants complained is regarded most seriously by the English criminal law and

[4] See below n 72.
[5] 1996-IV.
[6] [1993] AC 498.

subject to severe maximum penalties. . . . Provided sufficient evidence could be secured, a criminal prosecution could have been brought at any time and could still be brought. . . . Indeed, the Court notes that a charge of indecent assault was brought against the applicant D.S.'s father, to which he pleaded guilty in March 1991. . .

66. In principle, civil remedies are also available provided they are sought within the statutory time-limit. It is nonetheless true that under the domestic law it was impossible for the applicants to commence civil proceedings against their alleged assailants after their twenty-fourth birthdays. . . . However . . . Article 8 does not necessarily require that States fulfil their positive obligation to secure respect for private life by the provision of unlimited civil remedies in circumstances where criminal law sanctions are in operation.

67. Accordingly, in view of the protection afforded by the domestic law against the sexual abuse of children and the margin of appreciation allowed to States in these matters, the Court concludes that there has been no violation of Article 8 of the Convention .

In *Stubbings* the Court determined that the availability of extensive criminal law offences prohibiting sexual abuse in England together with circumscribed civil remedies satisfied the positive obligations incumbent upon the UK under Article 8. The judgment indicates that in assessing whether a state has complied with its positive obligations to protect vulnerable persons from sexual abuse the Court will have regard to the totality of criminal and civil remedies available in the particular domestic legal system. But, *X. and* Y. reminds us that civil remedies alone are insufficient.

Official recognition of transsexuals

There have been a number of cases where applicants have argued that public authorities have failed to provide sufficient legal and administrative recognition of their new personalities as post-operative transsexuals.[7] In *Rees v United Kingdom*,[8] the applicant had been born with all the physical and biological characteristics of a girl and had accordingly been registered as a female with feminine names. However, she soon started to demonstrate male behaviour and was of ambiguous appearance. In her late twenties she began hormone treatment followed by surgery (under the National Health Service). He then changed his forenames to male ones and began living as a man. He sought amendments to his official documents, such as his passport, to reflect his new identity. Eventually all these were amended, except for his birth certificate. The Registrar General refused to alter the latter as he considered that there was no evidence

[7] The Court defined the term transsexual as applying 'to those who, whilst belonging physically to one sex, feel convinced that they belong to the other; they often seek to achieve a more integrated, unambiguous identity by undergoing medical treatment and surgical operations to adapt their physical characteristics to their psychological nature.' Below n 8 para 38.

[8] A.106 (1986).

that an error had been made in recording the applicant's sex according to the established criteria of chromosomal sex, gonadal sex and apparent sex (external genitalia and body form). The applicant complained to the Commission that United Kingdom law did not confer on him a legal status corresponding to his actual condition. Unanimously, the Commission considered that there had been a violation of Article 8.

In his submission to the plenary Court, the applicant contended that he was a victim of national laws and practices which breached his right to respect for his private life. He singled out the failure to amend his birth certificate which he claimed caused him to experience embarrassment and humiliation whenever he had to produce his original certificate. The Court acknowledged that it had previously, albeit in other contexts, recognised the existence of positive obligations upon states under Article 8. The basic issues in this case were the existence and scope of those obligations regarding the recognition of transsexuals.

37. As the Court pointed out in its above-mentioned *Abdulaziz, Cabales and Balkandali [v United Kingdom]* judgment [A.94 (1985)] the notion of 'respect' is not clear-cut, especially as far as those positive obligations are concerned: having regard to the diversity of the practices followed and the situations obtaining in the Contracting States, the notion's requirements will vary considerably from case to case.

These observations are particularly relevant here. Several States have, through legislation or by means of legal interpretation or by administrative practice, given transsexuals the option of changing their personal status to fit their newly-gained identity. They have, however, made this option subject to conditions of varying strictness and retained a number of express reservations (for example, as to previously incurred obligations). In other States, such an option does not—or does not yet—exist. It would therefore be true to say that there is at present little common ground between the Contracting States in this area and that, generally speaking, the law appears to be in a transitional stage. Accordingly, this is an area in which the Contracting Parties enjoy a wide margin of appreciation.

In determining whether or not a positive obligation exists, regard must be had to the fair balance that has to be struck between the general interest of the community and the interests of the individual, the search for which balance is inherent in the whole of the Convention (see, *mutatis mutandis*, amongst others, the *James and Others [v United Kingdom]* judgment of 21 February 1986, Series A no. 98, p. 34, para. 50, and the *Sporrong and Lönnroth [v Sweden]* judgment of 23 September 1982, Series A no. 52, p. 26, para. 69). In striking this balance the aims mentioned in the second paragraph of Article 8 (art. 8-2) may be of a certain relevance, although this provision refers in terms only to 'interferences' with the right protected by the first paragraph—in other words is concerned with the negative obligations flowing therefrom (see, *mutatis mutandis*, the *Marckx [v Belgium]* judgment of 13 June 1979, Series A no. 31, p. 15, para. 31).

Rees contended that the British authorities should amend his birth certificate and not inform third parties of that change. The Court, however, did not accept that the positive obligations under Article 8 were that comprehensive.

44. ... there would have to be detailed legislation as to the effects of the change in various contexts and as to the circumstances in which secrecy should yield to the public interest. Having regard to the wide margin of appreciation to be afforded the State in this area and to the requisite balance, the positive obligations arising from Article 8 cannot be held to extend that far.

Taking account of the ability of Rees to change his name and the authorities' willingness to alter most of his official documentation a majority of the Court, twelve votes to three, concluded that there had been no breach of Article 8. But the majority noted that:

47. ... the Court is conscious of the seriousness of the problems affecting these persons and the distress they suffer. The Convention has always to be interpreted and applied in the light of current circumstances (see, *mutatis mutandis*, amongst others, the *Dudgeon* [*v* UK] judgment of 22 October 1981, Series A no. 45, pp.23–24, paragraph 60). The need for appropriate legal measures should therefore be kept under review having regard particularly to scientific and societal developments.

Judges Bindschedler-Robert, Russo and Gersing issued a joint dissenting opinion in which they expressed the view that the British authorities should annotate the birth register to record a change to Rees' sexual identity and provide him with a short certificate which would indicate his new sexual identity.

Although Rees' complaint was not upheld the judgment is important for elaborating the methodology used by the Court to determine the existence and content of positive obligations under Article 8. This is to balance the interests of the society and the individual. The weakness of this process is that it is capable of leading to different conclusions on the same facts as was demonstrated by the divergent views of the majority and the minority. We shall have to bear this possibility in mind when we examine the subsequent jurisprudence.

Four years later another British transsexual made similar complaints to the Strasbourg organs in *Cossey v United Kingdom*.[9] The Commission, by ten votes to six, found no breach of Article 8. The plenary Court did not consider it material that the applicant was a male to female transsexual and in its assessment the facts of her application were not distinguishable from those of *Rees*. The majority of the Court, ten votes to eight, therefore considered that they should follow the previous judgment.

40. ... The Court has been informed of no significant scientific developments that have occurred in the meantime; in particular, it remains the case—as was not contested by the applicant- that gender reassignment surgery does not result in the acquisition of all the biological characteristics of the other sex.

There have been certain developments since 1986 in the law of some of the member States of the Council of Europe. However, the reports accompanying the resolution adopted by the European Parliament on 12 September 1989 (OJ No C 256, 9.10. 1989, p.33) and Recommendation 1117 (1989) adopted by the Parliamentary Assembly of the Council of Europe on 29 September 1989—both of which seek to encourage

[9] A.184 (1990).

harmonisation of laws and practices in this field- reveal, as the Government pointed out, the same diversity of practice as obtained at the time of the *Rees* judgment. Accordingly this is still, having regard to the existence of little common ground between the Contracting States, an area in which they enjoy a wide margin of appreciation (see the Rees judgment, p.15, para. 37). In particular, it cannot at present be said that a departure from the Court's earlier decision is warranted in order to ensure that the interpretation of Article 8 on the point at issue remains in line with present-day conditions.

Judges Bindschedler-Robert and Russo repeated their dissenting view given in *Rees*, whilst judges Macdonald and Spielmann considered that there had been 'clear developments' in the law of 'many' member states since *Rees* and therefore states should no longer be accorded a wide margin of appreciation when the Court evaluated their treatment of transsexuals. Likewise Judge Martens considered that there had been societal developments in the recognition of post-operative transsexuals since *Rees*, he noted that at the time of the former judgment five states provided for the recognition of such persons' new identities but that by the date of the latter case fourteen states facilitated official recognition. The final dissenters were Judges Palm, Foighel and Pekkanen who considered that the existing British birth registration system was not compatible with Article 8.

> The retention of that system cannot, in our opinion, satisfy the requirements of Article 8(2) of the Convention. It is merely a question of administrative procedure which, as the examples from other democratic societies clearly show, can be arranged in several different ways so as not to violate the rights of transsexuals.[10]

Again the Court was divided in its responses to the treatment of transsexuals by public authorities in Britain. But the proportion of judges who considered that those authorities were not complying with their positive obligations under Article 8 had doubled, from approximately twenty percent of the Court in *Rees* to roughly forty percent in *Cossey*.

Another plenary Court found France to be in breach of its obligations towards a transsexual in *B. v France*.[11] The applicant was registered with the civil status registrar as of male sex at birth in 1935. However, from an early age B. adopted female behaviour. In her early thirties B. underwent hormone therapy and began to dress as a woman. A few years later she had surgery to remove her external genital organs. She then sought the permission of the French courts to change here forenames to feminine ones and for an order to amend her birth certificate to reflect her new identity. These requests were rejected. Subsequently, by seventeen votes to one, the Commission upheld the applicant's complaint under Article 8. The Court did not accept B.'s argument that there had been enough new scientific, legal and social developments regarding transsexualism since *Cossey* to justify a new approach. 'On these various points there

[10] *Ibid* Joint Dissenting Opinion, para 4.
[11] A.232-C (1992).

is as yet no sufficiently broad consensus between the member States of the Council of Europe to persuade the Court to reach opposite conclusions to those in its *Rees* and *Cossey* judgments.'[12] However, a very large majority of the Court, fifteen votes to six, distinguished the applicant's circumstances from those of the previous two cases. First, in France birth certificates were intended to be updated throughout the life of the individual (*e.g.* to record marriage or divorce), secondly the French courts had prevented the applicant from changing her forenames to the feminine ones that she wished to adopt and thirdly a number of official documents identified her birth sex (such as her national security number) which caused her serious inconvenience in her life.

> 63. . . . she finds herself daily in a situation which, taken as a whole, is not compatible with the respect due to her private life. Consequently, even having regard to the State's margin of appreciation, the fair balance which has to be struck between the general interest and the interests of the individual has not been attained, and there has thus been a violation of Article 8.

The Court also awarded B. 100,000 Francs compensation for non-pecuniary damage. A common theme amongst the dissentients was the need for the Court to grant individual states freedom to determine their own responses to transsexuals. For example, Judge Pettiti expressed the opinion that, 'if there is a field where States should be allowed the maximum margin of appreciation, having regard to moral attitudes and traditions, it is certainly that of transsexualism . . .'

The judgment in *B.* indicated that where transsexuals could show that the burdens placed upon them by a state's refusal to accord official recognition of their new identities were extensive and that it would not be unduly difficult for the domestic administrative/legal system to provide such recognition, the Court would be willing to find a breach of states' positive obligations applying the fair balance test.

The final judgment of the original Court involving transsexuals revealed a small majority continuing to uphold the legality of the constrained British response to post-operative transsexuals. In *Sheffield and Horsham v United Kingdom*,[13] the two transsexual applicants complained that, *inter alia*, English law continued to treat them according to their registered birth sex in breach of their right to respect for their private lives. Liberty, the non-governmental human rights organisation, supported their applications with a written brief, including a study of the legal treatment of transsexuals in member states which showed that only four states out of thirty-seven refused to amend the birth certificates of such persons. The Commission, by fifteen votes to one, considered that there had been breaches of Article 8. The applicants contended before the Court that there had been developments in the scientific understanding of trans-

---

[12] A.232-C (1992) para 48.
[13] 1998-V.

sexualism and the legal recognition of transsexuals by states since *Cossey*. However, these arguments were rejected by eleven votes to nine.

56. In the view of the Court, the applicants have not shown that since the date of adoption of its *Cossey* judgment in 1990 there have been any findings in the area of medical science which settle conclusively the doubts concerning the causes of the condition of transsexualism. . . .

57. As to legal developments in this area, the Court has examined the comparative study which has been submitted by Liberty. However, the Court is not fully satisfied that the legislative trends outlined by *amicus* suffice to establish the existence of any common European approach to the problems created by the recognition in law of post-operative gender status. In particular, the survey does not indicate that there is as yet any common approach as to how to address the repercussions which the legal recognition of a change of sex may entail for other areas of law such as marriage, filiation, privacy or data protection, or the circumstances in which a transsexual may be compelled to reveal his or her pre-operative gender.

Also the majority did not consider that the applicants had suffered detriment of a serious enough level to override the state's margin of appreciation. Hence there had been no breach of Article 8.

Seven judges issued a joint partly dissenting opinion in which they expressed a contrary analysis of the positive obligation upon states.

. . . It is no longer possible, from the standpoint of Article 8 of the Convention and in a Europe where considerable evolution in the direction of legal recognition is constantly taking place, to justify a system such as that pertaining in the respondent State, which treats gender dysphoria as a medical condition, subsidises gender re-assignment surgery but then withholds recognition of the consequences of that surgery thereby exposing post-operative transsexuals to the likelihood of recurring distress and humiliation.

For the above reason we consider that respect for private life under Article 8 imposes a positive obligation on the respondent State to amend their law in such a way that post-operative transsexuals no longer run the risk of public embarrassment and humiliation by being required to produce a birth certificate which records their original sex. There has therefore been a violation of this provision in the present cases.[14]

Clearly the extent and forms of official recognition of post-operative transsexuals required by Article 8 was a divisive issue for the original Court. In none of the above cases was the Court able to reach a unanimous decision. The Commission was generally more sympathetic to the applicants' claims, for example it found breaches of Article 8 in *Rees* and *Sheffield and Horsham*. The Court appeared to be gradually moving towards a greater recognition of the needs of transsexuals as was illustrated by the increasing size of the minorities who found in the applicants' favour. These cases also illuminated the

---

[14] *Ibid* Joint Partly Dissenting Opinion of Judges Bernhardt, Thor Vilhjalmsson, Spielmann, Palm, Wildhaber, Makarczyk and Voicu. Note, this group included the President of the old Court (Bernhardt) and the future President of the new Court (Wildhaber).

ambiguities inherent in the Court's fair balance test for determining the existence and requirements of positive obligations under Article 8. Both majorities and minorities could utilise the test to produce contrary outcomes. The caution of the majorities was also induced by the scientific uncertainties and diverse state practices, though these seemed to be undergoing a reduction by the time of *Sheffield and Horsham*, regarding transsexuals which resulted in the Court according states a considerable margin of appreciation in their responses to such persons.

In 2002 a Grand Chamber of the full time Court was united in finding that the partial recognition by administrative authorities of post-operative transsexuals' new identities did not satisfy the positive requirements of Article 8. In *Christine Goodwin v United Kingdom*,[15] the applicant had been born a man but underwent gender re-assignment surgery provided by the National Health Service. She had to, *inter alia*, enter into a special arrangement with the Department of Social Security (involving her paying national insurance contributions directly to the Department after her sixtieth birthday) in order to prevent her employer from discovering her original gender, due to the fact that the Department continued to classify her as a male in respect of contributions and pension entitlements. Before the Court she alleged that the British government, despite warnings from the old Court, had failed to take any further measures to reduce the suffering experienced by her, and other post-operative transsexuals, in their daily lives. The Court endorsed the well-established fair balance test to determine the existence of positive obligations under this Article. Whilst noting the earlier British transsexuals judgments the Grand Chamber emphasised the 'crucial importance'[16] of interpreting Convention rights in a practical and dynamic manner. Furthermore:

> 78. . . . The Court is struck by the fact that nonetheless the gender re-assignment which is lawfully provided is not met with full recognition in law, which might be regarded as the final and culminating step in the long and difficult process of transformation which the transsexual has undergone. The coherence of the administrative and legal practices within the domestic system must be regarded as an important factor in the assessment carried out under Article 8 of the Convention. Where a State has authorised the treatment and surgery alleviating the condition of a transsexual, financed or assisted in financing the operations and indeed permits the artificial insemination of a woman living with a female-to-male transsexual (as demonstrated in the case of *X., Y. and Z. v the United Kingdom* [1997-II 619]), it appears illogical to refuse to recognise the legal implications of the result to which the treatment leads.

The Court did not consider that the current state of medical science provided any conclusive argument as to the question of the extent of legal recognition of post-operative transsexuals required by the Convention. Regarding the consen-

---

[15] Judgment of 11 July 2002. The same Grand Chamber also delivered an identical judgment in *I v UK* (11 July 2002).

[16] *Ibid* para 74.

sus amongst member states and in the wider international community the results of a survey, submitted by Liberty, demonstrated a continuing trend towards the legal recognition of the new identities of such persons. Very significantly the Grand Chamber observed that:

85. . . . In the later case of *Sheffield and Horsham*, the Court's judgment laid emphasis on the lack of a common European approach as to how to address the repercussions which the legal recognition of a change of sex may entail for other areas of law such as marriage, filiation, privacy or data protection. While this would appear to remain the case, the lack of such a common approach among forty-three Contracting States with widely diverse legal systems and traditions is hardly surprising. In accordance with the principle of subsidiarity, it is indeed primarily for the Contracting States to decide on the measures necessary to secure Convention rights within their jurisdiction and, in resolving within their domestic legal systems the practical problems created by the legal recognition of post-operative gender status, the Contracting States must enjoy a wide margin of appreciation. The Court accordingly attaches less importance to the lack of evidence of a common European approach to the resolution of the legal and practical problems posed, than to the clear and uncontested evidence of a continuing international trend in favour not only of increased social acceptance of transsexuals but of legal recognition of the new sexual identity of post-operative transsexuals.

At the domestic level the Court noted that an Interdepartmental Working Group had produced a report in the spring of 2000 examining options for resolving the difficulties faced by post-operative transsexuals and in 2001 the Court of Appeal had expressed 'dismay' that no official action had been taken to implement the report.[17] The Court held that:

90. . . . In the twenty first century the right of transsexuals to personal development and to physical and moral security in the full sense enjoyed by others in society cannot be regarded as a matter of controversy requiring the lapse of time to cast clearer light on the issues involved. In short, the unsatisfactory situation in which post-operative transsexuals live in an intermediate zone as not quite one gender or the other is no longer sustainable.

93. . . . Having regard to the above considerations, the Court finds that the respondent Government can no longer claim that the matter falls within their margin of appreciation, save as regards the appropriate means of achieving recognition of the right protected under the Convention. Since there are no significant factors of public interest to weigh against the interest of this individual applicant in obtaining legal recognition of her gender re-assignment, it reaches the conclusion that the fair balance that is inherent in the Convention now tilts decisively in favour of the applicant. There has, accordingly, been a failure to respect her right to private life in breach of Article 8 of the Convention.

The judgment in *Christine Goodwin* represents another milestone in the Court's development of positive obligations under Article 8. The fact that the

---

[17] In *Bellinger v Bellinger* [2001] 3 FCR 1.

Chamber originally convened to hear the case relinquished jurisdiction in favour of the Grand Chamber and the latter body was unanimous in its assessment clearly indicated that the full time Court was seeking to make a major change in the obligations upon states to now provide effective legal recognition of the new identities of post-operative transsexuals. Cleverly, the Grand Chamber characterised the diversity of member states' legal treatment of such persons as an illustration of subsidiarity and not as a reason for limiting the scope of the basic obligation upon states to recognise the new identities of transsexuals. The continual failure of successive British governments to enhance the legal rights of post-operative transsexuals, when compared with the increasing numbers of states (including both member states and non-parties to the Convention) providing legal recognition of new identities, led the Court to finally conclude that a fair balance had not been achieved by the pragmatic limited administrative recognition available in the UK.

Official recognition of the choice of names

The Court first acknowledged that the issue of recognition, or from the perspective of applicants the non-recognition, by domestic authorities of the choice of names by persons could fall within the ambit of Article 8 in *Burghartz v Switzerland*.[18] The applicants were Swiss nationals, resident in Basle, who married in Germany during 1984. In conformity with German law they chose the wife's surname, Burghartz, as their family name and the husband opted to put his own surname in front of the family name and call himself 'Schnyder Burghartz'. On their return to Switzerland the registry office recorded their joint surname as being Schnyder. The applicants challenged that decision and eventually the Federal Court allowed the applicants to be registered under the surname of Burghartz. Nevertheless, the Federal Court refused to grant official recognition to the husband bearing the surname 'Schnyder Burghartz' as it held that under Swiss law only wives were authorised to add their surnames to those of their husbands. The applicants complained to the Commission that the refusal to recognise their choice of surnames violated Articles 8 and 14. By eighteen votes to one the Commission found a violation of Article 14 taken together with Article 8. The Court, by six votes to three, held that Article 8 was applicable even though it made no express reference to names.

> 24. Unlike some other international instruments, such as the International Covenant on Civil and Political Rights (Article 24(2)), the Convention on the Rights of the Child of 20 November 1989 (Articles 7 and 8) or the American Convention on Human Rights (Article 18), Article 8 of the Convention does not contain any explicit provisions on names. As a means of personal identification and of linking to a family, a person's name none the less concerns his or her private and family life. The fact that society and

---

[18] A.280-B (1994).

the State have an interest in regulating the use of names does not exclude this, since these public law aspects are compatible with private life conceived of as including, to a certain degree, the right to establish and develop relationships with other human beings, in professional or business contexts as in others (see, *mutatis mutandis*, the *Niemietz v Germany* judgment of 16 December 1992, A.251-B, para.29).

Furthermore, the Court accepted that the husband's retention of his surname might have a significant effect upon his academic career and therefore Article 8 could be invoked in the circumstances of the present application. The Court, five votes to four, went on to find a breach of that Article when combined with Article 14 (prohibition of discrimination) as the respondent state was not able to provide 'an objective and reasonable justification' for the non-recognition of husbands' right to put their surnames before the family name when compared with their wives' right to add their surnames. This element of sexual discrimination in the recognition of surnames by the Swiss authorities was the key to the Court finding a violation of the Convention.

In their joint dissenting opinion Judges Pettiti and Valticos expressed the belief that Article 8 did not apply to the assignment of family names.

> 1. . . . Not only does this Article not expressly refer to this issue, or even to naming in general, but political, legal, social and religious conceptions still vary so much from one country to another in this field, which is still in the process of change, that to claim to impose in this instance this or that view concerning the rules that should be followed in the matter of married or divorced couples' family names would certainly to be to go beyond the scope of Article 8 and of the undertakings entered into by the States.

They were also concerned that creating a right to choose names could lead to numerous applications in the future.

Another aspect of the recognition of surnames was examined by the Court a few months later in *Stjerna v Finland*.[19] The Finnish applicant sought the permission of his national authorities to change his surname (to 'Tawaststjerna'). He claimed that his ancestors had used the surname he wished to adopt, his current surname (which was of old Swedish form) was frequently mispronounced and misspelt, and had given rise to a pejorative nickname ('churn'). The Advisory Committee on Names recommended that his request be rejected, because the last ancestor to use his proposed surname had died over 200 years ago. Finally, the Supreme Administrative Court upheld the authorities' refusal to allow the change of surname. Before the Commission Stjerna argued that this refusal violated his right to respect for his private life guaranteed by Article 8. A majority of the Commission, twelve votes to nine, considered that provision had not been breached in his case. The Court, including Judge Pettiti, was unanimous in upholding the applicability of that Article to the applicant's complaint. Furthermore, the Court accepted that the refusal of domestic authorities to allow a person to change his/her surname could raise an issue in respect of

[19] A.299-B (1994).

states' positive obligations under Article 8. In determining whether there had been a breach of these obligations the Court invoked the fair balance test. The Court began by observing that:

> 39. Despite the increased use of personal identity numbers in Finland and in other Contracting States, names retain a crucial role in the identification of people. Whilst therefore recognising that there may exist genuine reasons prompting an individual to wish to change his or her name, the Court accepts that legal restrictions on such a possibility may be justified in the public interest; for example in order to ensure accurate population registration or to safeguard the means of personal identification and of linking the bearers of a given name to a family.

As there was little common ground between the member states regarding the circumstances when a change of name would be legally recognised the Court held that states enjoyed a 'wide margin of appreciation' in reaching these decisions. The Court was unwilling to attach any significance to the applicant's claimed ancestral links with his desired surname as it had not been used for over 200 years.

> 41. As to the instances of inconvenience complained of by the applicant, the Court is not satisfied on the evidence adduced before it that the alleged difficulties in the spelling and pronunciation of the name can have been very frequent or any more significant than those experienced by a large number of people in Europe today, where movement of people between countries and language-areas is becoming more and more common-place.
> . . . Finally, although the applicant's current name may have given rise to a pejorative nickname, this was not a specific feature of his name since many names lend themselves to distortion.
> In the light of the foregoing, the Court does not find that the sources of inconvenience the applicant complained of are sufficient to raise an issue of failure to respect private life under paragraph 1.

Consequently, the Court was united in finding no breach of the Convention. This decision indicates that individuals will have to be able to demonstrate a considerable level of inconvenience through the continued usage of their established name (perhaps, for example, by being regularly confused with a notorious criminal of the same name) before the Court will be prepared to find a state in breach of its circumscribed obligation to recognise a change of name.

Judge Wildhaber (subsequently the first President of the full-time Court) issued a concurring opinion in *Stjerna* which proposed an alternative methodology for analysing positive obligations under Article 8. He felt that the established jurisprudence was 'somewhat incoherent'. When applying the fair balance test the Court generally only had regard to Article 8(1) and accorded states a wide margin of appreciation in the implementation of their positive obligations.

> In my view, it would therefore be preferable to construe the notion of 'interference' so as to cover facts capable of breaching an obligation incumbent on the State under

Article 8(1), whether negative or positive. Whenever a so-called positive obligation arises the Court should examine, as in the event of a so-called negative obligation, whether there has been an interference with the right to respect for private and family life under paragraph 1 of Article 8, and whether such interference was 'in accordance with the law', pursued legitimate aims and was 'necessary in a democratic society' within the meaning of paragraph 2.

To be sure, this approach would not lead to a different result in the instant case, nor in all likelihood in the vast majority of cases of this kind. It does, however, have the advantage of making it clear that in substance there is no negative/positive dichotomy as regards the State's obligations to ensure respect for applicable private and family life, but rather a striking similarity between the applicable principles.

Whilst this approach gives a very wide meaning to the term interference, it has the merit that analogous principles are applied when evaluating whether states have complied with their positive/negative obligations under Article 8. When we have examined the subsequent case law it will be possible to determine whether other judges have adopted this approach.

Restrictions on the official recognition of forenames were examined by the Court in *Guillot v France*.[20] The applicants, Mr and Mrs Guillot, sought to register their daughter with the forenames 'Fleur de Marie, Armine, Angele'. However, the registrar would only record the names Armine, Angele as the name 'Fleur de Marie' did not appear in any calendar of saints' days. Ancient French legislation provided that forenames must be chosen from such calendars. On appeal the French courts allowed the additional registration of the forename 'Fleur-Marie'. The applicants complained to the Commission that the authorities' refusal to register their daughter's forenames as including 'Fleur de Marie'[21] violated their right to respect for their private and family life. By thirteen votes to eleven the Commission expressed the view that there had not been a breach of Article 8.

The Court extended its previous rulings on surnames to encompass forenames.

21. The Court notes that Article 8 does not contain any explicit provisions on forenames. However, since they constitute a means of identifying persons within their families and the community, forenames, like surnames (see, *mutatis mutandis*, the *Burghartz v Switzerland* judgment of 22 February 1994, Series A no. 280-B, p. 28, para. 24, and the *Stjerna v Finland* judgment of 25 November 1994, Series A no. 299-B, p. 60, para. 37), do concern private and family life.

22. Furthermore, the choice of a child's forename by its parents is a personal, emotional matter and therefore comes within their private sphere. The subject matter of the complaint thus falls within the ambit of Article 8, and indeed this was not contested.

Following the approach in *Stjerna* the majority (of seven) considered that the degree of inconvenience caused to the applicants by the authorities' refusal to

---

[20] 1996-V 1593.
[21] The name of the heroine in Eugene Sue's 'Mysteres de Paris'.

register their chosen forenames was decisive in determining if the respondent state had failed to comply with its obligations under Article 8.

> 27. The Court can understand that Mr and Mrs Guillot were upset by the refusal to register the forename they had chosen for their daughter. It notes that this forename consequently cannot appear on official documents and deeds. In addition, it finds it probable that the difference between the child's forename in law and the forename which she actually uses—she is called 'Fleur de Marie' by her family and is known by that name socially—entails certain complications for the applicants when acting as her statutory representatives.
>
> However, the Court notes that it is not disputed that the child regularly uses the forename in issue without hindrance and that the French courts—which considered the child's interest—allowed the application made in the alternative by the applicants for registration of the forename 'Fleur-Marie' . . .
>
> In the light of the foregoing, the Court does not find that the inconvenience complained of by the applicants is sufficient to raise an issue of failure to respect their private and family life under Article 8 para. 1. Consequently, there has not been a violation of Article 8.

The two dissentients, Judges Macdonald and De Meyer, utilised Judge Wildhaber's alternative method of analysis propounded above in *Stjerna*. They considered that France had not demonstrated that it was 'necessary in a democratic society' to refuse to recognise the applicants' choice of forenames for their daughter. Particularly, as they did not see how the name 'Fleur de Marie' could harm the applicants' daughter.

The Court's expansion of its previous jurisprudence to include forenames was a welcome development, but the majority of judges were still very deferential to restrictive national laws governing the choice of names. Indeed, new French legislation passed in 1993 recognised the right of parents to chose their children's forenames, subject to the residual power of family–affairs judges to refuse the registration of names which are contrary to the particular child's interests.

Overall, Judges Pettiti and Valticos' fear in *Burghartz* that the acceptance by the Court of a right to official recognition of chosen names could create a deluge of cases has not occurred. In part this may be due to the (overly) cautious manner in which the Court has applied the right. Nevertheless, subsequent cases have examined the choice of names in different contexts, including an adult's desire to change his surname and parents' choice of forenames for their child. These cases have also revealed two different methods of analysing positive obligations under Article 8 being used by various groups of judges in the old Court.

Access to official information

The Court has determined several cases where applicants have asserted a right to be provided with information held by public authorities. In *Gaskin v United*

Kingdom,[22] the applicant had been in the care of Liverpool City Council for most of his childhood. During those years the Council had placed him with various foster parents. Throughout his period of care the Council had maintained a confidential file on him as required by statutory regulations. Contributors to the file included social workers, foster parents, teachers, doctors and police officers. After his care had ceased the applicant sought access to his file as he considered that he had been ill-treated during that time. Subsequently, he decided to sue the Council for alleged negligence in his care and he applied to the High Court for discovery of his case file. The Council objected to disclosure on the grounds of public interest, as it claimed that the contributors to such files would be unwilling to make frank comments if their reports were subsequently made available to the subjects of the file. The High Court, without reading the file, held that it should not be disclosed. A couple of years later the Department of Health and Social Security issued a circular to local authorities setting out a new policy on disclosure of such files. The subjects of existing social services files should have access to them unless the contributors objected. The applicant's file was composed of 352 documents contributed by 46 persons. Applying the new policy the Council provided the applicant with 65 of those documents contributed by 19 persons. The remainder were not disclosed as the authors would not waive confidentiality. The applicant complained to the Commission that the Council's failure to provide him with access to all his file documents violated, *inter alia*, his right to respect for his private and family life under Article 8. The Commission, on the casting vote of the acting President, found a breach of that right.

The plenary Court stated that:

36. In the opinion of the Commission 'the file provided a substitute record for the memories and experience of the parents of the child who is not in care'. It no doubt contained information concerning highly personal aspects of the applicant's childhood, development and history and thus could constitute his principal source of information about his past and formative years. Consequently lack of access thereto did raise issues under Article 8.

37. The Court agrees with the Commission. The records contained in the file undoubtedly do relate to Mr Gaskin's 'private and family life' in such a way that the question of his access thereto falls within the ambit of Article 8.

This finding is reached without expressing any opinion on whether general rights of access to personal data and information may be derived from Article 8 para. 1 of the Convention. The Court is not called upon to decide in *abstracto* on questions of general principle in this field but rather has to deal with the concrete case of Mr Gaskin's application.

---

[22] A.160 (1989). Note also the similar recent case of *MG v UK* (24 September 2002). The full-time Court was unanimous in finding a breach of art 8 in respect of the applicant's inability to appeal against the local authority's refusal to provide him with access to all his childhood care records Since 2000 there has been a statutory right of appeal under the Data Protection Act 1998.

The Court then applied its fair balance test to determine whether the UK was under a positive obligation to facilitate the applicant's access to his social services file.

> 49. In the Court's opinion, persons in the situation of the applicant have a vital interest, protected by the Convention, in receiving the information necessary to know and to understand their childhood and early development. On the other hand, it must be borne in mind that confidentiality of public records is of importance for receiving objective and reliable information, and that such confidentiality can also be necessary for the protection of third persons. Under the latter aspect, a system like the British one, which makes access to records dependent on the consent of the contributor, can in principle be considered to be compatible with the obligations under Article 8, taking into account the State's margin of appreciation. The Court considers, however, that under such a system the interests of the individual seeking access to records relating to his private and family life must be secured when a contributor to the records either is not available or improperly refuses consent. Such a system is only in conformity with the principle of proportionality if it provides that an independent authority finally decides whether access has to be granted in cases where a contributor fails to answer or withholds consent. No such procedure was available to the applicant in the present case.

Therefore, a majority of the Court, eleven votes to six, held that there had been a breach of Article 8 as the British system did not provide sufficient institutional safeguards in respect of the applicant's right of access to his personal file. Five judges, led by President Ryssdal, issued a joint dissenting opinion in which they concluded that the existing British procedure constituted a fair balance between the competing interests. Once again, we see the vagaries of the application of the fair balance test. It is also noteworthy that the Court emphasised that it was not making a ruling on whether Article 8 contained general rights of access to personal information held by public bodies. Consequently, this was another positive obligation which the Court was applying with great circumspection.

A later judgment by a unanimous Grand Chamber found a breach of Article 8 where administrative authorities had failed for many years to provide local residents with safety and environmental information concerning a nearby chemical factory. In *Guerra and Others v Italy*,[23] the applicants were forty women who lived in a southern Italian town one kilometre from a chemical plant which had a dreadful pollution record (including the acute poisoning of 150 persons by an explosion of arsenic in the 1970s and the release of large quantities of other pollutants over several decades). During 1988 a law was enacted in Italy (to comply with an EEC Directive) requiring mayors to inform their residents of hazardous industrial activities occurring in their areas and the procedures to be followed if an emergency situation developed at such a facility. However, the applicants were not provided with any information by 1995. They brought a complaint to the Strasbourg institutions and before the Court the applicants

---

[23] 1998-I 210.

contended that, *inter alia*, the local authorities failure to provide them with relevant information had infringed their right to respect for their private and family life. The Court did not consider that the Italian authorities could be said to have 'interfered'[24] with the applicants' private or family life, but acknowledged that states might be subject to positive obligations under Article 8. Hence, the Court determined whether the local authorities had taken the necessary steps to ensure effective protection of the applicants' rights.

> 60. The Court reiterates that severe environmental pollution may affect individuals' well-being and prevent them from enjoying their homes in such a way as to affect their private and family life adversely (see, *mutatis mutandis*, the *López Ostra* judgment[25] [*v Spain* A303-C (1994)], § 51). In the instant case the applicants waited, right up until the production of fertilisers ceased in 1994, for essential information that would have enabled them to assess the risks they and their families might run if they continued to live at Manfredonia, a town particularly exposed to danger in the event of an accident at the factory.
>
> The Court holds, therefore, that the respondent State did not fulfil its obligation to secure the applicants' right to respect for their private and family life, in breach of Article 8 of the Convention.

This judgment indicates that states may be found in breach of their positive obligations under Article 8 if they fail to provide crucial safety and environmental information to local residents facing serious risks of severe pollution. This is an entirely different category of official information to that considered in *Gaskin*. Furthermore, the logic of *Guerra* suggests that states are under an obligation to take proactive steps to disseminate this type of information to relevant persons.

The Court later held that where governmental authorities undertake dangerous programmes, which create a risk to the health of those persons involved, the authorities must establish effective procedures which allow such persons to obtain information regarding those activities. In *McGinley and Egan v United Kingdom*,[26] the applicants were British ex-servicemen who had been present during several atmospheric nuclear weapons tests conducted by the U.K. at Christmas Island in the Pacific Ocean during the late 1950s. Both applicants subsequently left the armed forces. A number of years later the applicants applied for war pensions claiming that they were suffering health problems attributable to their exposure to radiation from the weapons tests. Ultimately their applications were rejected by the Pensions Appeal Tribunal. The applicants then complained to the Commission alleging, *inter alia*, that they had not had access to official records disclosing the extent and nature of the radiation exposure that they had been subject to during the tests in breach of their rights under Article 8. By 23 votes to 3 the Commission found a violation of that Article.

[24] Note Judge Wildhaber was not a member of the Grand Chamber.
[25] Below n 98.
[26] 1998-III. See also the case of *LCB v UK*, above ch 2 n 24, which concerned the daughter of a serviceman involved in these tests.

Applying *Gaskin* the Court acknowledged that positive obligations could arise under Article 8.

> 101. . . . Where a Government engages in hazardous activities, such as those in issue in the present case, which might have hidden adverse consequences on the health of those involved in such activities, respect for private and family life under Article 8 requires that an effective and accessible procedure be established which enables such persons to seek all relevant and appropriate information.

A bare majority, five votes to four, then concluded that such a procedure had been available to the applicants via the disclosure provisions of the Tribunal Rules governing the Pensions Appeal Tribunal. Rule 6 of those rules enabled appellants to apply, within six weeks of receipt of the government's statement of case, to the President of the tribunal for a direction that the government should disclose any document which the particular appellant has reason to believe is in the possession of a government department. In the Court's assessment this procedure satisfied the respondent state's positive obligations and therefore no breach of Article 8 had occurred. Conversely, the dissentients considered that this procedure was not sufficient to meet the United Kingdom's obligations. In their joint dissent Judges De Meyer, Valticos and Morenilla expressed the opinion that in such circumstances the state had an obligation to inform relevant persons of the risks they were subject to. 'The applicants had the right to be informed of all the consequences that their presence in the test area could have for them, including those it could have on their pensions. They had the right to know what might happen to them, without having to ask.' Judge Pekkanen considered that the availability of a disclosure procedure for a period of only six weeks was not sufficient to satisfy the obligation upon the British government to provide an 'effective and accessible' means of access to relevant information.

Whilst the Court's articulation of a reciprocal obligation upon states to make information accessible to persons involved in hazardous governmental activities is to be commended, the majority was not particularly demanding in its acceptance of the effectiveness and accessibility of the tribunal disclosure regime. Given the potentially lethal effects of radiation exposure, which may only become apparent many years after the event, to allow service personnel participating in atmospheric nuclear weapons test only a six week period during appellate proceedings in which to seek disclosure of relevant official information seems unduly restrictive.

Despite the Court's reluctance to recognise a general right of access to official information under Article 8, the above cases have revealed that the Court is willing to find an obligation upon states to provide means of access to relevant information for defined groups of persons. Where vulnerable persons are, or have been, in a proximate relationship with public bodies (*e.g.* personnel subject to military discipline or children in public care) then the state must establish effective mechanisms for access to appropriate official information. It is to be hoped that in future years the Court will become even more rigorous in its evaluation of the practicality of these access procedures.

Establishing paternity

The Court has unanimously developed the jurisprudence concerning access to official information regarding a person, to establish the separate duty upon states to create legal mechanisms enabling the prompt determination of a person's paternity. In *Mikulic v Croatia*,[27] the applicant was born out of an extra-marital relationship in November 1996. Two months later she and her mother filed a paternity suit against a named man alleged to be her father. On six occasions the Zagreb Municipal Court scheduled appointments for that man to undergo DNA tests, to determine if he was the applicant's father. The man did not attend any of the appointments to provide a specimen of his DNA for analysis. In November 2001, the Municipal Court gave judgment finding that the man was the applicant's father, based upon his repeated avoidance of the DNA tests and the testimony of the applicant's mother. The man then appealed against the judgment. The applicant complained to the Strasbourg Court alleging, *inter alia*, that the Croatian judicial system had been inefficient in determining her paternity claim and thereby left her uncertain as to her personal identity in breach of her right to respect for her private life under Article 8. The Court accepted that her claim fell within the ambit of that right.

> 53. . . . There appears, furthermore, to be no reason of principle why the notion of 'private life' should be taken to exclude the determination of the legal relationship between a child born out of wedlock and her natural father.
>
> 54. The Court has held that respect for private life requires that everyone should be able to establish details of their identity as individual human beings and that an individual's entitlement to such information is of importance because of its formative implications for his or her personality (see the *Gaskin v the United Kingdom* judgment of 7 July 1989, Series A no. 159, p. 16, § 39).

The Court then examined, by reference to the well-established fair balance test, whether Croatia had complied with its positive obligations under Article 8. Having regard to the diversity of paternity procedures and evidential rules in member states the Court concluded that Article 8 did not require states to compel alleged fathers to undergo DNA testing. However, if such testing was not compulsory in a particular state the legal system must provide 'alternative means enabling an independent authority to determine the paternity claim speedily.'[28] That had not happened in the applicant's case therefore Article 8 had been violated.

[27] Judgment of 7 February 2002.
[28] *Ibid* para 64.

The judgment in *Mikulic* again reveals the amorphous nature of the concept of private life in Article 8. Additionally, the Court was according significant weight to the diversity of paternity proceedings in members states when assessing the specific content of the positive obligation upon states to provide an efficient system for resolving these sensitive disputes. As compulsory DNA testing of alleged fathers (scientifically the most reliable and expeditious method of determining paternity) was not a universal feature of states' practices the Court was not willing to impose such a specific requirement upon Croatia.

Provision of facilities for disabled/ill persons

In *Botta v Italy*,[29] the applicant, who was physically disabled, contended that various public authorities in Italy had not taken sufficient measures to ensure that the operators of private beach services near Ravenna complied with statutory requirements to provide facilities for disabled persons (such as access ramps and special toilets). The domestic requirements had been enacted in 1989, but when the applicant visited the area in the summer of 1990 no such facilities were available. He complained to the local mayor in the spring of 1991, however when he returned on holiday in the summer of that year the facilities had not been constructed. By 1997 some of the private beaches had built special changing cubicles and toilets for disabled persons, but no ramps had been constructed. The local authority planned to have all the necessary facilities installed by the summer of 1999. The Commission, by twenty-four votes to six, considered that there had not been a breach of the applicant's rights under Article 8.

Before the Court, Botta argued that the respondent state had failed to comply with its positive obligations under that Article to monitor the implementation of the domestic requirements concerning facilities for disabled persons. The Commission believed that, 'the rights asserted by the applicant were social in character, concerning as they did participation by disabled people in recreational and leisure activities associated with beaches, the scope of which went beyond the concept of legal obligation inherent in the idea of "respect" for "private life" contained in paragraph 1 of Article 8.'[30] The Commission highlighted the financial implications for the state in satisfying the applicant's claims. Furthermore, the 'social nature' of the rights were more suitable for protection under the 'flexible' machinery of the European Social Charter.[31] In the submission of the respondent government for the Court to accept the applicant's claims would be to make the Court the adjudicator of states' social policies, a role not envisaged by the drafters of the Convention.

---

[29] 1998-I 412.

[30] *Ibid* para 28.

[31] This convention does not have a judicial enforcement system, see DJ Harris and J Darcy, *The European Social Charter*, 2nd edn (Ardsley NY, Transnational Publishers Inc, 2001) ch 3.

The Court was unanimous in determining that Article 8 was not applicable to Botta's complaint. Whilst states were subject to positive obligations under this Article, the previous case law, in cases such as *X. & Y. v The Netherlands* and *Guerra v Italy*, had involved situations where there were immediate links between the positive measures sought and the applicants' private lives.

> 35. In the instant case, however, the right asserted by Mr Botta, namely the right to gain access to the beach and the sea at a place distant from his normal place of residence during his holidays, concerns interpersonal relations of such broad and indeterminate scope that there can be no conceivable direct link between the measures the State was urged to take in order to make good the omissions of the private bathing establishments and the applicant's private life.

The above reasoning is not necessarily convincing as a matter of logic because Botta was seeking the enforcement of existing domestic legal duties upon identifiable beach operators and local authorities. He had been on holiday to the area two years in a row and had sought to invoke domestic legal remedies to compel the relevant local authorities to enforce the law. Surely, in those circumstances it was irrelevant how far away the beaches were from his home? There were direct relationships between him, the operators and the mayor. However, the Court's reluctance to find Article 8 applicable in the circumstances is more explicable from the perspective of the policy arguments advocated by the Commission and the Italian government. For the Court to include social rights[32] within the scope of Article 8 could be viewed as a legislative step too far by the judiciary as it would involve the protection of a different class of rights.[33] Nevertheless, as we shall examine below, the Court has been willing to require the protection of persons from serious environmental pollution under the aegis of Article 8 and that type of protection can involve considerable public expenditure and may be characterised as a newer generational

---

[32] From an international perspective see, H Steiner and P Alston, *International Human Rights in Context*, 2nd edn (Oxford, OUP 2000) ch 4 and from a UK viewpoint see, KD Ewing, 'Constitutional Reform and Human Rights: Unfinished Business?' (2000) 5(3) *Edinburgh Law Review* 1.

[33] For an advocate of significant differences between political and civil rights compared to economic and social rights see, E Vierdag, 'The Legal Nature of the Rights Granted by the International Covenant on Economic, Social and Cultural Rights' (1978) 9 *Netherlands Yearbook of International Law* 69–105. Whereas, GJH van Hoof argues against a 'black-and-white distinction' between these forms of rights see, 'The Legal Nature of Economic, Social and Cultural Rights: a Rebuttal of Some Traditional Views' in P Alston and K Tomasevski (eds) *The Right to Food* (Dordrecht, Martinus Nijhoff Publishers, 1984). Van Bueren, citing the UN World Conference on Human Rights, Vienna Declaration and Programme of Action (UN Doc A/CONF/157/23), contends that human rights are indivisible: 'Including the Excluded: the Case for an Economic, Social and Cultural Human Rights Act' [2002] *Public Law* 456. In *Zehnalova v Czech Republic* (14 May 2002) the Court declared inadmissible, *ratione materiae*, a complaint from a physically disabled person that local and central government authorities had not taken sufficient action to enable her to gain access to public buildings in her home town. The Court stated that it had to determine the boundary between art 8 and the social rights guaranteed by European Social Charter. art 8 could only be invoked in the exceptional case where lack of access to public buildings interfered with the applicant's personal development. That had not been established.

right[34] than the civil and political rights underpinning most of the Convention's substantive guarantees.

The full-time Court has tentatively indicated that there may be circumstances where the positive obligations under Article 8 mandate the provision of housing assistance for chronically ill persons by public authorities. In *Marzari v Italy*,[35] the applicant suffered from the unusual and serious illness of metabolic myopathy, which causes physical exhaustion and muscular pain when temperatures change. The authorities recognised him as being 100% disabled and he received a pension. From 1992 the local housing authority was under a duty to provide him with suitable accommodation. The housing authority made a flat available to him, but he considered it unsuitable and stopped paying the rent in 1993 (in 1994 he poured 400 litres of petrol around the building as a protest forcing his fellow occupants to vacate the premises for a week). The housing authority began possession proceedings against him and in 1998 he was evicted. He complained to the Court that the authorities had failed to find a satisfactory solution to his housing needs in breach of their obligations under Article 8. The Court held that:

> . . . although Article 8 does not guarantee the right to have one's housing problem solved by the authorities, a refusal of the authorities to provide assistance in this respect to an individual suffering from a severe disease might in certain circumstances raise an issue under Article 8 of the Convention because of the impact of such refusal on the private life of the individual. . . . there may be positive obligations inherent in effective respect for private life. A State has obligations of this type where there is a direct and immediate link between the measures sought by an applicant and the latter's private life (*Botta v Italy*, paras. 33–34). . . . The Court considers that no positive obligation for the local authorities can be inferred from Article 8 to provide the applicant with a specific apartment.

As the relevant authorities had sought to provide the applicant with an adequate flat and were willing to carry out the remedial work considered necessary, as recommended by a specialist commission, to make it suitable for the applicant, the Court concluded that the respondent state had discharged its positive obligations to respect the applicant's private life. Therefore, the application was declared inadmissible.

This decision suggests that if public authorities failed to provide any housing support for a seriously ill person, who could not afford to pay for their own housing, then that could constitute a breach of Article 8. Hence there may be basic social welfare duties within the positive obligations upon states under this Article. Applicants in future cases will probably seek to contend that these social welfare responsibilities should extend beyond the provision of help with accommodation.

---

[34] See, F Klug, *Values for a Godless Age* (London, Penguin Books, 2000) 9.
[35] Decision of 4 May 1999.

FAMILY LIFE

Legal recognition of the family relationship between parent(s) and illegitimate children

The duty upon states to provide for the legal recognition of the relationship between a parent and her illegitimate child was established by a plenary Court in *Marckx v Belgium*.[36] Under Belgian law unmarried mothers had to take legal proceedings to obtain official recognition of their maternal affiliation with their children. Ms Marckx claimed that this requirement, *inter alia*, breached her right to respect for her family life under Article 8. The Commission upheld her complaint by ten votes to four. The Court accepted that Article 8 did not distinguish between 'legitimate' and 'illegitimate' families. Furthermore, the natural ties between the applicant and her daughter constituted family life for the purposes of Article 8. The next issue for the Court was to consider what the notion of respect under that Article required of the Belgian authorities.

> 31. . . . By proclaiming in paragraph 1 the right to respect for family life, Article 8 signifies firstly that the State cannot interfere with the exercise of that right otherwise than in accordance with the strict conditions set out in paragraph 2. As the Court stated in the '*Belgian Linguistic*' case, the object of the Article is 'essentially' that of protecting the individual against arbitrary interference by the public authorities (judgment of 23 July 1968, Series A no. 6, p. 33, para. 7). Nevertheless it does not merely compel the State to abstain from such interference: in addition to this primarily negative undertaking, there may be positive obligations inherent in an effective 'respect' for family life.
>
> This means, amongst other things, that when the State determines in its domestic legal system the régime applicable to certain family ties such as those between an unmarried mother and her child, it must act in a manner calculated to allow those concerned to lead a normal family life. As envisaged by Article 8, respect for family life implies in particular, in the Court's view, the existence in domestic law of legal safeguards that render possible as from the moment of birth the child's integration in his family. In this connection, the State has a choice of various means, but a law that fails to satisfy this requirement violates paragraph 1 of Article 8 without there being any call to examine it under paragraph 2.

A majority of the Court, ten votes to five, determined that the necessity for the applicant to seek judicial recognition of her affiliation with her daughter violated Article 8, as the Belgian authorities had failed to provide recognition of that relationship from the time of the daughter's birth. Additionally an unmarried parent utilising the judicial recognition procedure forfeited the ability to bequeath certain forms of property to their child.

The judgment in *Marckx* has an historic significance beyond the area of family law because it was the first case where the Court found a breach of a positive

---

[36] A.31 (1979).

obligation under Article 8. Despite the importance of this development the Court merely provided a cursory justification for the existence of these obligations, namely that of securing effective state respect for family life. Practically this meant that in some circumstances domestic authorities have to take proactive measures to satisfy their Convention duties. In this case that involved establishing a family law system which recognised the legal relationship between a parent and her child from the instance of the latter's birth without the former having to initiate a burdensome judicial process.

Subsequently *Marckx* was applied to the relationships between a daughter and her unmarried parents in *Johnston and Others v Ireland*.[37] The first two applicants had been living together since 1971, but had been unable to marry due to the Irish constitutional ban on divorce which prevented the first applicant from divorcing his wife (their marriage had irretrievably broken down in 1965). The applicants' daughter, the third applicant, had been born in 1978. The three applicants complained, *inter alia*, that there had been a failure to respect their family life because of the disadvantaged status of the third applicant in Irish law (e.g the limited recognition of paternal affiliation between the daughter and her father). The Commission, unanimously, found a breach of Article 8. Similarly the plenary Court was united in upholding this violation. After endorsing the existence of states' positive obligations under Article 8, the Court held that:

> 55. . . . However, especially as far as those positive obligations are concerned, the notion of 'respect' is not clear-cut: having regard to the diversity of the practices followed and the situations obtaining in the Contracting States, the notion's requirements will vary considerably from case to case. Accordingly, this is an area in which the Contracting Parties enjoy a wide margin of appreciation in determining the steps to be taken to ensure compliance with the Convention with due regard to the needs and resources of the community and of individuals (see the *Abdulaziz, Cabales and Balkandali* judgment of 28 May 1985, Series A no. 94, pp. 33–34, § 67).

Despite this deference to national authorities' assessments of domestic requirements the Court determined that Ireland had not established a legal structure which adequately recognised the family relationships between the applicants.

> 74. . . . As it observed in its above-mentioned *Marckx* judgment, 'respect' for family life, understood as including the ties between near relatives, implies an obligation for the State to act in a manner calculated to allow these ties to develop normally (Series A no. 31, p. 21, § 45). And in the present case the normal development of the natural family ties between the first and second applicants and their daughter requires, in the Court's opinion, that she should be placed, legally and socially, in a position akin to that of a legitimate child.

> 75. Examination of the third applicant's present legal situation, seen as a whole, reveals, however, that it differs considerably from that of a legitimate child; in addition, it has not been shown that there are any means available to her or her parents to eliminate or reduce the differences. Having regard to the particular circumstances of

[37] A.112 (1986).

this case and notwithstanding the wide margin of appreciation enjoyed by Ireland in this area (see paragraph 55 (c) above), the absence of an appropriate legal regime reflecting the third applicant's natural family ties amounts to a failure to respect her family life.

This decision represented a warning to states that even in areas of positive obligations where they were accorded wide margins of appreciation there were minimum requirements below which states would be found in breach of their Convention duties.

The Dutch birth registration system was challenged in *Kroon and Others v The Netherlands*.[38] The first applicant (Mrs Kroon) had married a Mr M'Hallem-Driss in 1979. However, their marriage broke down the following year and Mrs Kroon lived apart from her husband (his whereabouts since 1986 have been unknown). Mrs Kroon developed a stable relationship with the second applicant (Mr Zerrouk) and in 1987 their son (Samir) was born. The latter was registered as the son of Mrs Kroon and her husband (as Samir M'Hallem-Driss). Mrs Kroon and Mr Zerrouk applied for Samir to be registered as the son of Mr Zerrouk, his biological father. However, this was refused as Dutch law only allowed the husband of a married woman (in this case Mr M'Hallem-Driss) to bring proceedings to deny the paternity of a child born to his wife. The applicants claimed a breach of their right to respect for their family life. By twelve votes to six the Commission agreed with them. The Court ruled that there was, 'a positive obligation on the part of the competent authorities to allow complete legal family ties to be formed between Mr Zerrouk and his son Samir as expeditiously as possible.'[39] Furthermore a majority, of seven to two, determined that:

> 40. In the Court's opinion, 'respect' for 'family life' requires that biological and social reality prevail over a legal presumption which, as in the present case, flies in the face of both established fact and the wishes of those concerned without actually benefiting anyone. Accordingly, the Court concludes that, even having regard to the margin of appreciation left to the State, the Netherlands has failed to secure to the applicants the 'respect' for their family life to which they are entitled under the Convention.

Interestingly, the Court appeared to have reduced the extent of the margin of appreciation to be accorded to states in regard to this positive obligation since the earlier judgment in *Johnston*. The majority in *Kroon* characterised it as a 'certain margin of appreciation,'[40] whilst in *Johnston* it was described as a 'wide margin of appreciation'. No explanation for this change of scrutiny standards was offered by the Court.

The difficulties of applying this positive obligation when biological and social reality conflict were dramatically illustrated in *X., Y. and Z. v United*

---

[38] A.297-C (1994).
[39] *Ibid* para 36.
[40] *Ibid* para 31.

Kingdom.[41] The first applicant was a female to male transsexual who had undergone hormone and surgical treatments in the late 1970s. Since that time he had lived in a stable relationship with Y., a female. Ten years later they were given permission, by a hospital ethics committee, for Y. to undergo Artificial Insemination by Donor (AID). In 1992 Y. gave birth to a daughter, Z.. X. sought to be registered as Z.'s father on her birth certificate. However his request was rejected by the Registrar General as he considered that only a biological man could be regarded as a father for the purpose of registration (legislation provided that the male partners of unmarried women who gave birth to children through the use of AID should be recorded as the fathers of those children). The Commission, by thirteen votes to five, expressed the opinion that there had been a breach of the applicants' right to respect for their family life. However, the Court considered that there was no consensus amongst the parties to the Convention regarding the recognition of parental rights by transsexuals. Therefore, states were to be accorded a 'wide margin of appreciation'[42] when the Court assessed if they had complied with their positive obligation to respect family life in such unusual circumstances. A large majority, fourteen votes to six, of the Grand Chamber determined that the U.K. had not breached Article 8.

> 52. In conclusion, given that transsexuality raises complex scientific, legal, moral and social issues, in respect of which there is no generally shared approach among the Contracting States, the Court is of the opinion that Article 8 cannot, in this context, be taken to imply an obligation for the respondent State formally to recognise as the father of a child a person who is not the biological father. That being so, the fact that the law of the United Kingdom does not allow special legal recognition of the relationship between X and Z does not amount to a failure to respect family life within the meaning of that provision (A.8).

The added, and contentious (note our earlier analysis of the case law on the official recognition of transsexuals), element of transsexuality in the complex family life of the applicants resulted in the Court reverting to a deferential (wide margin of appreciation) standard of review in this case.

Generally the Court's articulation of this positive obligation reflects a progressive trend that has sought to remove discrimination in the legal systems of member states against illegitimate children and ensure that their family relationships with their natural parents are acknowledged by municipal law. The obligation requires states to make the necessary adjustments to domestic legal regimes. The discretion accorded to states to determine the nature and extent of the official recognition of these family relationships was narrowed over time by the Court. However, the limits of this positive obligation were demonstrated in *X. Y & Z.* where the original Court was not willing to mandate the recognition of a non-biological relationship between a father figure and his daughter con-

---

[41] 1997-II 619.
[42] *Ibid* para 44.

ceived by AID. Time will tell if the European consensus moves towards according such social family relationships similar recognition as biological ones.

Taking children into public care

Since the late 1980s the Court has interpreted Article 8 as imposing procedural duties upon domestic governmental authorities when they exercise powers to take children into public care. This type of positive obligation was first articulated by a unanimous plenary Court in *W. v United Kingdom*.[43] The applicant and his wife had a history of marital problems. Their third child (S.) was born in October 1978 and they voluntarily placed him in the care of their local authority in March 1979. A few months later the authority passed resolutions assuming parental rights over S., however the applicant and his wife were not informed about these developments. In the spring of 1980 the authority's adoption committee, without consulting the applicant or his wife, approved the proposal from officials that S. should be placed with long-term foster parents and that W. (and his wife) should be restricted in their access to S.. During the next month the director of social services determined that W. and his wife should not be allowed to visit S. (in order to enable S. to develop a good relationship with his new foster parents). W. and his wife sought to challenge the authority's decisions in the courts but the Court of Appeal (in 1981) held that it would not be in S.'s best interests to be returned to the care of his natural parents. Eventually, in 1984, the High Court approved the foster parents' application to adopt S.

The Commission, by thirteen votes to one, found that the actions of the local authority had violated W.'s right to respect for his family life. Before the Court he repeated his argument that the procedures followed by the authority in reaching its decisions to restrict and then terminate W.'s access to S. violated his rights under Article 8. The Court began by emphasising that:

> 59. The mutual enjoyment by parent and child of each other's company constitutes a fundamental element of family life. Furthermore, the natural family relationship is not terminated by reason of the fact that the child is taken into public care.

The Court then repeated its established jurisprudential view that effective respect for family life could involve positive obligations upon states. The judgment acknowledged that making decisions regarding the taking of children into public care and regulating their natural parents access to them once they were in care were sensitive and extremely difficult. Consequently, the Court would not impose an inflexible procedure upon domestic authorities exercising these powers.

> 62. . . . On the other hand, predominant in any consideration of this aspect of the present case must be the fact that the decisions may well prove to be irreversible: thus,

---

[43] A.121 (1987). Note, similar rulings were given in the parallel cases of *B v UK* A 121-B (1987) and *R v UK* A 121-C (1987).

where a child has been taken away from his parents and placed with alternative carers, he may in the course of time establish with them new bonds which it might not be in his interests to disturb or interrupt by reversing a previous decision to restrict or terminate parental access to him. This is accordingly a domain in which there is an even greater call than usual for protection against arbitrary interferences.

It is true that Article 8 contains no explicit procedural requirements, but this is not conclusive of the matter. The local authority's decision-making process clearly cannot be devoid of influence on the substance of the decision, notably by ensuring that it is based on the relevant considerations and is not one-sided and, hence, neither is nor appears to be arbitrary. Accordingly, the Court is entitled to have regard to that process to determine whether it has been conducted in a manner that, in all the circumstances, is fair and affords due respect to the interests protected by Article 8 . . .

63. The relevant considerations to be weighed by a local authority in reaching decisions on children in its care must perforce include the views and interests of the natural parents. The decision-making process must therefore, in the Court's view, be such as to secure that their views and interests are made known to and duly taken into account by the local authority and that they are able to exercise in due time any remedies available to them.

The Court went on to find that the applicant had not been sufficiently involved in the authority's crucial decision-making processes in the Spring of 1980 when the authority was making fundamental decisions regarding the long-term care of S.. Hence, even having regard to the domestic margin of appreciation in respect of public care decisions, the Court found the procedures followed by the domestic authorities had violated the applicant's right to respect for his family life.

The above ruling was a commendable development of Article 8 by the Court as it sought to provide basic procedural safeguards for parents when public authorities were making care decisions in respect of their children. The judgment did not seek to impose a standard procedure upon domestic authorities, but left them with freedom to tailor their decision-making systems to the needs of individual families. However, to be compatible with Article 8 those procedures had to ensure that the parents' views were adequately considered. This is clearly essential because, as the sad facts of W. graphically illustrate, care decisions may have irreversible consequences for the survival of the natural family relationship.

In subsequent cases the Court has elaborated fundamental elements of the procedural obligations upon public authorities when exercising powers concerning the taking of children into care. Several cases indicate the need for the authorities to provide parents with relevant official documents. In *McMichael v United Kingdom*,[44] the applicants were a couple who had mental health problems. In November 1987 the second applicant gave birth to a son (whom she denied was the son of the first applicant, although she was living with the latter). Her doctor diagnosed a serious reoccurrence of her mental illness and

[44] A.307-B (1995).

the public authorities convened a tribunal of independent experts (the children's hearing) to determine the care of the son. The children's hearing granted an order for the son to be kept in a place of safety by the local authority. In February 1988 the children's hearing held a meeting at which the applicants were present. The hearing had a report on the son, complied by the local social work department. In accordance with statutory rules the applicants were not given copies of the report, but the chairman informed them of the substance of the report. The hearing decided that the applicants' son should be placed in compulsory public care. Five years later the Scottish courts authorised the son's adoption by his foster parents. Before the Strasbourg Court, the British government conceded that the failure of the children's hearing to disclose the report on the applicants' son to them was unfair. Consequently, the Court found that 'the decision-making process determining the custody and access arrangements in regard to [the son] did not afford the requisite protection of the applicants' interests as safeguarded by Article 8.'[45] The provision of the verbatim report to the parents, rather than an oral summary of the contents by the chairperson of the hearing, would potentially better equip the parents to challenge the accuracy of any disputed content. Furthermore, by having access to the whole report the legitimacy of the local authorities actions might have been enhanced in the parents' eyes.

A Grand Chamber of the full-time Court has held, unanimously, that governmental authorities in possession of relevant information concerning a child subject to public care measures must generally make that material available to the parent(s) without the latter having to formally seek its disclosure. In *T.P. and K.M. v United Kingdom*,[46] the first applicant was a young single mother with a daughter (the second applicant) nearly five years old. The local authority became concerned that the daughter was the victim of sexual abuse. An interview, recorded on video, was conducted with the daughter (in the absence of the first applicant) by a consultant child psychiatrist (employed by the local health authority) and a social worker (employed by the local social services) in November 1987. The child revealed that she had been abused by a man named X.. The first applicant's current boyfriend shared the same forename (X.Y.). Later that day, the local authority applied to the magistrates court for a place of safety order in respect of the daughter on the basis that she was being abused at home by X.Y.. The court granted that order and she was taken into public care. During the following year the first applicant was only allowed very limited access to her daughter. In subsequent judicial proceedings the consultant and the health authority objected to the video of the second applicant's interview being disclosed to the first applicant. In November 1988 the first applicant's solicitors were given a transcript of the daughter's interview and it became

---

[45] *Ibid* para 92.

[46] Judgment of 10 May 2001. Note the same Grand Chamber dealt with the inverse situation (where the public authorities had failed to take prompt action to assume care over vulnerable children) in *Z v UK* examined above ch 3 n 2.

apparent that the person she had identified as her abuser was not X.Y.. Subsequently, the High Court granted leave for the second applicant to be returned to live with the first applicant. The applicants complained to Strasbourg that, *inter alia*, the unjustifiable taking into care of the second applicant had violated their right to respect for their family life. Before the Court, the government contended that the first applicant could have applied to the High Court for an order obliging the local authority to disclose the video tape of the interview at any time after the second applicant had been taken into public care. However, the Court considered that this possibility did not satisfy the duties incumbent upon domestic authorities.

> 82. . . . The positive obligation on the Contracting State to protect the interests of the family requires that this material be made available to the parent concerned, even in the absence of any request by the parent. If there were doubts as to whether this posed a risk to the welfare of the child, the matter should have been submitted to the court by the local authority at the earliest stage in the proceedings possible for it to resolve the issue involved.

Hence there had been a breach of Article 8.

The decision in *T.P.* is a further significant strengthening of parental rights under Article 8, as it places the primary burden of disclosure upon those public authorities that possess the relevant materials. Given that many parents experiencing the compulsory taking of their children into care are likely to be in a distressed state at that time, requiring the public authorities to take the initiative in disclosing relevant information will reduce the burdens upon the parents and, perhaps, enable them to gain a fuller understanding of the situation. Compliance with this positive obligation may also enable mistakes and misunderstandings to be clarified at an earlier stage in the proceedings with obvious benefits for all the parties concerned.

A dramatic example of public authorities' failure to provide a parent with basic information about the placement of her children in care occurred in *Scozzari and Giunta v Italy*.[47] The first applicant had been living in Italy with the father of her two young children (the father was wanted by the Belgian authorities, as he had been sentenced to a period of twenty-seven years' forced labour for serious violent crimes). The relationship between the first applicant and her partner deteriorated and the latter used violence against the former. Consequently, the local social welfare authorities convened a meeting of social workers and specialists who had been supervising the first applicant and her children. The meeting decided to recommend the placement of the children in a special agricultural community ('Ill Forteto'). Next day, the Florence Youth Court ordered the children's placement in Ill Forteto and suspended the mother and father's parental rights. Later the mother discovered that twelve years previously two of the current staff members of Ill Forteto, including the president of the community, had been convicted of physical and/or sexual abuse

---

[47] Judgment of 13 July 2000.

of children in the community Before the Strasbourg Court the first applicant alleged, *inter alia*, that the placement of her children in Ill Forteto violated her rights under Article 8. The Grand Chamber was unanimous in upholding that complaint.

> 208. It should also be noted that the authorities have at no point explained to the first applicant why, despite the men's convictions, sending the children to 'Il Forteto' did not pose a problem. In the Court's view, such a failure to communicate is not compatible with the duties incumbent on States to act fairly and to provide information when taking serious measures interfering in a sphere as delicate and sensitive as family life. Unless full and pertinent explanations are given by the authorities concerned, parents should not be forced, as they were in the instant case, merely to stand by while their children are entrusted into the care of a community whose leaders include people with serious previous convictions for ill treatment and sexual abuse.

The decision of the Italian authorities to place vulnerable children in the care of an organisation headed by a person with a criminal record of child abuse seems incomprehensible. In such circumstances the obligation upon the authorities to explain to the parents the reasoning behind their proposed placement should be even more extensive.

A failure by judicial authorities to provide a parent with pertinent information concerning the decision to take her children into care occurred in *Buchberger v Austria*.[48] The applicant was a single mother who had two young children. Her job was delivering papers in the morning. One day she was forty-five minutes late back from work (because she claimed she had been unwell) and a neighbour had contacted the local authority as she had seen the applicant's two-year old son wandering around in his garden wearing only pyjamas despite the freezing temperature. The local Youth Welfare Office took the applicant's two young sons into provisional care and applied to the District Court for the transfer of custody of the boys to the Office. After a hearing, at which the applicant was assisted by counsel, the District Court ordered the the prompt return of the boys to the applicant. In subsequent appellate proceedings the Office submitted a report to the Regional Court. The Regional Court also obtained several court files concerning other civil and criminal proceedings against the applicant. She was not informed of this further evidence. Custody of the boys was transferred to the Office by the Regional Court as it found that their living conditions with the applicant were desolate and chaotic. The Strasbourg Court was unanimous in determining that the procedure followed by the Regional Court violated the applicant's right to respect for her family life.

> 43. . . . It is not in dispute that this additional evidence has not been brought to the applicant's attention. However, in the circumstances of the case the Regional Court should not have decided without having given the applicant an opportunity to react thereto. The additional evidence was of particular importance to the proceedings as the Regional Court considered it sufficiently strong to overturn the first instance

---

[48] Judgment of 20 December 2001.

decision. The Regional Court did not merely rely on the outcome of previous court proceedings but considered the further contents of the case-file. Moreover, it relied on a recent report by the Youth Welfare Office, a document which the applicant had never seen.

44. In the Court's opinion, the failure of the Regional Court to inform the applicant of the additional evidence obtained during the appeal proceedings which deprived her of the possibility to react thereto reveals an insufficient involvement of her in the decision-making process.

This judgment reminds domestic judicial authorities of the obvious necessity to ensure that parents, or their legal representatives, are fully apprised of all relevant information in order to enable the parents to have a fair opportunity to rebut adverse evidence against their suitability to retain custody of their children.

Limitations on the rights of parents to participate in official decision-making processes concerning the custody and care of their children were articulated by a Grand Chamber in *K. and T. v Finland*.[49] K. was expecting T.'s child when her mother reported K. to the local social welfare authorities because of a decline in K.'s mental health (she had a history of serious mental illness). K. underwent voluntary psychiatric care and the social welfare authorities decided to place M. (K.'s five-year old son) in a children's home for three months (K. and T. did not object to this placement). When K. went into hospital to give birth, the local Social Director issued an emergency care order taking K.'s new daughter (J.) into public care. The order was served on the hospital and as soon as K. gave birth J. was removed from her to be cared for in another ward. Three days later the Social Director made another emergency care order in respect of M.. A few weeks later the local Social Welfare Board made 'normal' care orders in respect of both M. and J.. K. and T. were able to participate in the process leading up to the making of the latter orders. Soon afterwards the County Administrative Court confirmed the 'normal' care orders in respect of both children. The Grand Chamber considered that it was necessary to examine separately the making of the emergency and 'normal' care orders (for each child) as they were different powers (procedurally and substantively). In regard to the first type of power:

166. The Court accepts that when an emergency care order has to be made, it may not always be possible, because of the urgency of the situation, to associate in the decision-making process those having custody of the child. Nor, as the Government point out, may it even be desirable, even if possible, to do so if those having custody of the child are seen as the source of an immediate threat to the child, since giving them prior warning would be liable to deprive the measure of its effectiveness. The Court must however be satisfied that in the present case the national authorities were entitled to

---

[49] Judgment of 12 July 2001. Note, this was the first judgment of the Grand Chamber when rehearing a case after referral from a Chamber under the controversial art 43 of the Convention. For an examination of that aspect of the decision see: A Mowbray, 'ECHR: Institutional Developments and Recent Cases' [2001] 1 *Human Rights Law Review* 333, 335.

consider that in relation to both J. and M. there existed circumstances justifying the abrupt removal of the children from the care of the applicants without any prior contact or consultation. In particular, it is for the respondent State to establish that a careful assessment of the impact of the proposed care measure on the applicants and the children, as well as of the possible alternatives to taking the children into public care, was carried out prior to the implementation of a care measure.

A majority of the Grand Chamber (fourteen votes to three) concluded that the emergency order in respect of J. was not necessary in a democratic society, because there had to be 'extraordinarily compelling reasons'[50] to justify the physical removal of a new born child, immediately after birth, from her/his mother where the parents have not been involved in the care order process. However, the making of the emergency care order in regard to M. was found to be compatible with Article 8 by a majority of eleven judges (he was already separated from his parents and there was the risk that his family could remove him from voluntary care at any time). The Court was united in finding the making of both the 'normal' care orders were in accordance with Article 8.

The judgment in *K. and T.* represents a sensible balance between the interests of parents and their children. Where leaving children in the care of their parents raises an immediate serious risk to the children's welfare, the authorities can take unilateral emergency care measures to safeguard the children. However, those authorities will have to be able to demonstrate that such an extreme decision, and the procedures by which it was reached, were compatible with parental rights under Article 8. Furthermore, the majority was particularly strict in its evaluation of the legality of the emergency order removing J. from her mother immediately after birth. This was because of the traumatic nature of such an intervention for the mother (and her child) and the limited opportunities for K. to harm J. whilst under medical supervision.

The Court has produced a significant body of case law on the positive obligations of domestic authorities making decisions regarding the public care of children. These procedural requirements apply to both administrative bodies (*e.g.* the local authority in *W. v United Kingdom*) and domestic courts (*e.g.* the Regional Court in *Buchberger*). The Strasbourg jurisprudence reveals a sensitivity to the different contexts within which public care decisions have to be taken (*e.g.* urgent family crises which necessitate emergency public intervention and circumstances where there is time for greater deliberation before a decision is taken to remove children from the care of their parents, *e.g. K. and T. v Finland*). Nevertheless, the cases indicate that in general domestic authorities must devise and follow procedures that enable parents to have an adequate opportunity to express their views regarding the care of their children.

---

[50] *Ibid* para 168.

Reuniting children with their natural parents

Both the part-time and full-time Courts have recognised that states are under an obligation to take measures to facilitate the reuniting of children taken into pub-lic care with their natural parents. In *Eriksson v Sweden*,[51] the applicant's daughter was taken into care by the local Social Council, in 1978, when she was one month old because the conditions in her home were unsatisfactory (the applicant had been sentenced to a period of imprisonment for possession of nar-cotics). The daughter was placed in a foster home. Whilst in prison the appli-cant underwent a religious conversion. After leaving prison the applicant made a number of attempts to gain access to her daughter and to have the care order terminated. In 1983 the Social Council ended the care order but prohibited the applicant (and her husband) from removing her daughter from the foster home (because experts had expressed the view that it would jeopardise the daughter's mental health/development). Despite the fact that the applicant was at this time a municipal child-minder the domestic courts upheld the ban on her removing her daughter from the foster home. Before the Court the applicant complained, *inter alia*, that the Social Council's failure to reunite her with her daughter violated their right to respect for family life. The plenary Court endorsed the established jurisprudential view that:

> 58. The mutual enjoyment by parent and child of each other's company constitutes a fundamental element of family life; furthermore, the natural family relationship is not terminated by reason of the fact that the child has been taken into public care (see *Olsson v Sweden*, A.130 (1988), para. 59).

Therefore, the relationship between the applicant and her daughter fell within the scope of Article 8. The Court then articulated the positive obligation upon states to take steps to aid the reunification of natural parents and their children who are in public care.

> 71. In cases like the present a mother's right to respect for family life under Article 8 includes a right to the taking of measures with a view to her being reunited with her child. The care order had been lifted, and there was no doubt as to the suitability of Mrs Eriksson to take care of children or of the conditions in her home. . . .
>
> The Court recognises that difficulties may arise in consequence of the termination of public care of young children, especially where the child has been taken into care at a very young age and has spent many years away from his natural parents' home. However, the unsatisfactory situation that has ensued in the present case seems to a large extent to stem from the failure to ensure any meaningful access between mother and daughter with a view to reuniting them.

Consequently, the Court was unanimous in finding a violation of Article 8. The fact that the care order in respect of the applicant's daughter had been termi-nated, the ability of the applicant to offer a supportive and safe home for her

---

[51] A.156 (1989).

daughter and the restrictions on the applicant's contacts with her daughter over a period of years were significant elements in the Court finding a breach of the state's positive obligation in *Eriksson*.

The Court subsequently elaborated upon the nature of this obligation in *Olsson v Sweden (No. 2)*.[52] This was the second case[53] that the applicants had brought against the Swedish authorities in respect of the taking into public care and restrictions upon the applicants' access to their children. In the present case the applicants complained about orders from the local Social Council prohibiting them from removing two of their children from foster homes (where they had been for several years) after the formal ending of public care for the children. The Court held that:

> 90. . . . both under Swedish law and under Article 8 of the Convention, the lifting of the care order implied that the children should, in principle, be reunited with their natural parents. In cases like the present, Article 8 includes a right for the natural parents to have measures taken with a view to their being reunited with their children (see, as the most recent authority, the *Rieme v Sweden* judgment of 22 April 1992, Series A no. 226-B, p. 71, para. 69) and an obligation for the national authorities to take such measures.
>
> However, neither the right of the parents nor its counterpart, the obligation of the national authorities, is absolute, since the reunion of natural parents with children who have lived for some time in a foster family needs preparation. The nature and extent of such preparation may depend on the circumstances of each case, but it always requires the active and understanding co-operation of all concerned. Whilst national authorities must do their utmost to bring about such co-operation, their possibilities of applying coercion in this respect are limited since the interests as well as the rights and freedoms of all concerned must be taken into account, notably the children's interests and their rights under Article 8 of the Convention. Where contacts with the natural parents would harm those interests or interfere with those rights, it is for the national authorities to strike a fair balance (see, *mutatis mutandis*, the *Powell and Rayner v the United Kingdom* judgment of 21 February 1990, Series A no. 172, p. 18, para. 41).
>
> In sum, what will be decisive is whether the national authorities have made such efforts to arrange the necessary preparations for reunion as can reasonably be demanded under the special circumstances of each case.
>
> It is for the Court to review whether the national authorities have fulfilled this obligation. In doing so, it will leave room for a margin of appreciation, if only because it has to base itself on the case-file, whereas the domestic authorities had the benefit of direct contact with all those concerned.

Taking account of the social welfare authorities offers to fund the costs of the applicants visiting the foster homes where their children were staying and the authorities creation of an access plan for the applicants to visit their children a majority of the Court, six votes to three, concluded that the Swedish authorities

---

[52] A.250 (1992).

[53] For the first case see *Olsson v Sweden* A.130 (1988) examined in A Mowbray, *Cases & Materials on the European Convention on Human Rights* (London, Butterworths, 2001) 376–77.

had satisfied their positive obligation under Article 8. Hence we learn that the essence of this obligation is for domestic authorities to take reasonable steps to facilitate such reunions. Given the almost limitless variations in family relationships and circumstances the Court could not realistically be more prescriptive in its general definition of this obligation.

The full-time Court addressed this positive obligation in *K. and T. v Finland*.[54]

> 178. The Grand Chamber, like the Chamber, would first recall the guiding principle whereby a care order should in principle be regarded as a temporary measure, to be discontinued as soon as circumstances permit, and that any measures implementing temporary care should be consistent with the ultimate aim of reuniting the natural parents and the child (see, in particular, the above-mentioned *Olsson (no. 1)* judgment, § 81). The positive duty to take measures to facilitate family reunification as soon as reasonably feasible will begin to weigh on the responsible authorities with progressively increasing force as from the commencement of the period of care, subject always to its being balanced against the duty to consider the best interests of the child.

As the Finnish authorities had only made a few enquiries as to whether the applicants would be able to bond with their children during the seven years in which the latter were in public care, the Court was unanimous in finding a breach of Article 8. The Court expressed the view that, 'the minimum to be expected of the authorities is to examine the situation anew from time to time to see whether there has been any improvement in the family's situation.'[55] This judgment is very significant as it reveals that this positive duty does not only exist when public care has been terminated (as in *Eriksson* and *Olsson (No.2)*), but begins as soon as children are taken into public care. The relevant authorities must regularly review whether the children can be safely returned to their natural parents and take reasonable steps to facilitate the reunion between them where that is feasible. Furthermore, the positive obligation places an increasing burden on domestic authorities to take appropriate action as the duration of individual care orders lengthen. This is because the Court appreciates the danger that the longer a particular care order persists, especially in respect of young children, the greater the difficulties (*e.g.* in breaking the emotional bonds children may have developed with their foster parents) of successfully reuniting children with their natural parents.

The Court has also held that this positive obligation applies in respect of private agreements relating to the care of children. In *Hokkanen v Finland*,[56] the applicant's wife died in 1985. Whilst he was dealing with the consequences of her death the applicant agreed that his parents-in-law could provisionally look after his daughter (who was nearly two years' old). A few months later the

---

[54] Above n 49.
[55] *Ibid* para 179.
[56] A.299-A (1994).

grandparents told him that they would not return his daughter to him. In 1986 the District Court ordered that temporarily the daughter should remain with the grandparents, but the applicant was granted defined access rights. The grandparents did not comply with the access order and despite numerous court proceedings the last time the applicant saw his daughter was in early 1987. In 1991 the Court of Appeal transferred custody of the daughter to the grandparents, because she had lived with them for six years. The applicant complained to the Commission alleging, *inter alia*, that the Finnish authorities had failed to take appropriate measures to facilitate the speedy reunion of his daughter and himself in breach of his right to respect for his family life. By nineteen votes to two, the Commission expressed the opinion that there had been a violation of Article 8. The Court held that:

> 55. . . . In previous cases dealing with issues relating to the compulsory taking of children into public care and the implementation of care measures, the Court has consistently held that Article 8 includes a right for the parent to have measures taken with a view to his or her being reunited with the child and an obligation for the national authorities to take such action. . . . In the opinion of the Court, this principle must be taken as also applying to cases such as the present where the origin of the provisional transfer of care is a private agreement.

The Court then applied its reasonable steps test to determine if the authorities had discharged their positive obligation to facilitate the applicant's access to his daughter. Noting '. . . the inaction of the authorities placed the burden on the applicant to have constant recourse to a succession of time-consuming and ultimately ineffectual remedies to enforce his rights,'[57] the Court was united in finding a breach of Article 8. However a majority, by six votes to three, upheld the lawfulness of the transfer of custody to the grandparents. This was due to the Court according the national authorities a margin of appreciation,[58] in recognition of their better position to evaluate the evidence concerning complex family relationships. It seems rather harsh on the applicant that the grandparents' consistent illegal behaviour, in denying him access to his daughter, resulted in them being awarded custody over her. Indeed, the dissentients observed:

> Over many years the Finnish authorities were faced with and tolerated the prolongation of a situation which they had on many occasions noted to be unlawful and which they were accordingly under a duty to bring to an end. On each occasion they yielded in the face of the grandparents' persistent obstination [sic.] and thus enabled them to create a fait accompli which the authorities eventually resigned themselves to endorsing as regards both custody and access.[59]

Nevertheless, the Court's extension of states' positive obligation to take reasonable measures to facilitate the reunion of natural parents with their children

---

[57] *Ibid* para 61.
[58] On this concept see H Yourow, *The Margin of Appreciation Doctrine in the Dynamics of European Human Rights Jurisprudence* (Dordrecht, Matinus Nijhoff, 1996).
[59] Above n 56, Partly Dissenting Opinion of Judge De Meyer, joined by Judges Russo and Jungwiert.

to private custody arrangements[60] is to be welcomed as the tragic facts in *Hokkanen* demonstrate such personal agreements may degenerate into highly acrimonious disputes. Domestic authorities with expertise in family relationships must be available to provide effective solutions in such circumstances.

Another context in which this positive obligation applies is following the divorce or separation of parents. The Court applied the obligation to this type of situation in *Ignaccolo-Zenide v Romania*.[61] The applicant was a French national who married a Romanian national (D.Z.) in 1980. They had two daughters (born in 1981 and 1984). A divorce was granted to the applicant and D.Z. by a French court in 1989. The court approved an agreement between the former spouses that parental responsibility was given to D.Z. and the applicant received access and staying rights. During the next year D.Z. moved to the United States and the applicant complained to the French courts that D.Z. was denying her access to her daughters. In May 1991 the Metz Court of Appeal gave parental responsibility to both parents and ordered that the children should live with the applicant. She subsequently brought a number of actions in different courts in the United States, but D.Z. did not comply with those judgments requiring him to return his daughters to the applicant. In 1994 D.Z. and his daughters went to live in Romania. Both the United States and French governments requested the Romanian government to return the children to the applicant in accordance with the 1980 Hague Convention on the Civil Aspects of International Child Abduction. The applicant also made an urgent application under Article 2 of the Hague Convention to the Romanian courts for an order requiring D.Z. to comply with the 1991 judgment of the Metz Court of Appeal. In December 1994 the Bucharest Court of First Instance issued such an order. The applicant subsequently visited Romania eight times for the purpose of meeting her daughters but, despite several attempts by the Romanian authorities to enforce the Bucharest Court order, the applicant was only able to see her daughters once (for a few minutes at their school in 1997, where D.Z. was a teacher!). The meeting did not go well and the daughters' expressed the wish never to see the applicant again.

The Commission was of the unanimous view that there had been a breach of Article 8. Before the Court the applicant claimed that the Romanian authorities had not taken sufficient steps to facilitate the return of her daughters. In the judgment of the Chamber:

> 94. . . . As to the State's obligation to take positive measures, the Court has repeatedly held that Article 8 includes a parent's right to the taking of measures with a view to his or her being reunited with his or her child and an obligation on the national authorities to take such action (see, for example, the following judgments: *Eriksson v Sweden*, 22 June 1989, Series A no. 156, pp. 26–27, . . .).

---

[60] On 1 March 2002, BBC Radio 4 reported that there were approximately 10,000 children in private foster care throughout the UK.

[61] Judgment of 25 January 2000. See, N Mole, 'The Hague Convention and art 8 of the European Convention on Human Rights' [2000] *International Family Law* 121.

However, the national authorities' obligation to take measures to facilitate reunion is not absolute, since the reunion of a parent with children who have lived for some time with the other parent may not be able to take place immediately and may require preparatory measures to be taken. The nature and extent of such preparation will depend on the circumstances of each case, but the understanding and cooperation of all concerned are always an important ingredient. Whilst national authorities must do their utmost to facilitate such cooperation, any obligation to apply coercion in this area must be limited since the interests as well as the rights and freedoms of all concerned must be taken into account, and more particularly the best interests of the child and his or her rights under Article 8 of the Convention. Where contacts with the parent might appear to threaten those interests or interfere with those rights, it is for the national authorities to strike a fair balance between them (see the *Hokkanen* judgment cited above, p. 22, § 58).

95. Lastly, the Court considers that the positive obligations that Article 8 of the Convention lays on the Contracting States in the matter of reuniting a parent with his or her children must be interpreted in the light of the Hague Convention of 25 October 1980 on the Civil Aspects of International Child Abduction ('the Hague Convention'). This is all the more so in the instant case as the respondent State is also a party to that instrument, Article 7 of which contains a list of measures to be taken by States to secure the prompt return of children.

96. What is decisive in the present case is therefore whether the national authorities did take all steps to facilitate execution of the order of 14 December 1994 that could reasonably be demanded (ibid.).

An overwhelming majority of the Court, six votes to one, concluded that the Romanian authorities had failed to make 'adequate and effective'[62] efforts to enforce the applicant's right to the return of her daughters. The Court emphasised that in abduction cases 'the adequacy of a measure is to be judged by the swiftness of its implementation,'[63] because of the danger that the passage of time will undermine the relationship between the abducted children and the parent lawfully entitled to their custody. Here there had been several delays in bailiffs visiting D.Z.'s home to look for the children in 1995 and total inaction by the authorities between December 1995–January 1997. Consequently, these deficiencies meant that there had been a breach of Article 8.

The judgment in *Ignaccolo-Zenide* marked another significant step in the expansion of this positive obligation. Although encompassing a different type of separation of a natural parent from her child, compared to the earlier public and private care cases, the basic rationale of the obligation was the same- to try and restore healthy relationships between parents and their children. The Court also demonstrated a sensitive awareness of the potentially destructive effect of the elapse of time upon the durability of the relationship between a separated child and his/her parent(s). This may in part be explained by the requirements of the Hague Convention which mandate state parties to 'secure the prompt return of

---

[62] *Ibid* para 113.
[63] *Ibid* para 102.

children.'[64] Hence we see another international treaty influencing the content of positive obligation under the Convention.

Subsequently, in *Nuutinen v Finland*,[65] the Court applied this positive obligation in the context of separated parents who had not been married. The applicant had a history of convictions for serious offences of violence. In late 1991 he assaulted his pregnant girlfriend (H.) when their relationship was ending. Several months later H. gave birth to their daughter (I.). H. and I. then moved to another part of Finland. In 1993 the applicant applied to the local City Court for custody of I. to be shared between him and H. and for rights of access to his daughter. H. objected and in 1994 she married another man. Despite numerous court orders for H. to allow the applicant controlled access to his daughter H. never complied. Eventually, in 1998, the District Court determined that the applicant should only have access to I. when she reached the age of fourteen. The applicant complained to Strasbourg that the Finnish authorities had failed to make sufficient efforts to enforce his rights of access to his daughter. The Court was split on the vital issue of whether the domestic authorities had complied with their Convention duty to take reasonable steps to facilitate access to I.. The majority, of four, taking account of the applicant's lack of co-operation with the social welfare authorities and his 'aggressive manner'[66] concluded that, having regard to the state's margin of appreciation, the Finnish agencies had taken adequate measures to try an obtain a reunion between the applicant and his daughter. The three dissentients observed that:

> It may be true that the father in the present case is not an ideal person, but since when is personal perfection a precondition to becoming a father or, consequently, to exercise parental rights? To say that he was aggressive and that the mother was afraid of him, insofar as his aggressiveness was a logical consequence of the fact that he has been brutally denied access to his own daughter, is part of the same circular absurdity.
> . . .
>
> The ancient formula *Nemo auditur propriam turpitudinen allegans*. ('Nobody should profit from his or her own wrongdoing.') explains even better this recurrent possibility of perversion of justice. It is, therefore, to be regretted that the European Court of Human Rights, especially in view of some of its own precedents, refused to see this issue and, in effect, legalised the obstinate parent's disregard for the rule of law.[67]

The division within the Court emphasised the difficulty of determining what are reasonable measures by public authorities towards family reunions within fractured and antagonistic parental relationships. However, at least the Court in *Nuutinen* was united in extending this positive obligation to unmarried parents who have separated.

---

[64]   Art 7 of the 1980 Hague Convention.
[65]   Judgment of 27 June 2000.
[66]   *Ibid* para 135.
[67]   Dissenting Opinion of Judge Zupancic, joined by Judges Pantiru and Turmen.

The generally cautious approach of the Court when scrutinising the legality of the measures taken by domestic authorities to try and reunite children with their parents following acrimonious family break-ups was demonstrated by the unanimous judgment in *Glaser v United Kingdom*.[68] Divorce proceedings between the applicant and his wife were initiated in 1991. Their three children went to live with the mother and the applicant had agreed contact with them. In 1992 the mother ended the applicant's contact with his children. He obtained a contact order from Kingston-Upon-Thames County Court. However, the mother did not comply with the order and in 1993 she and the children moved to Scotland. The applicant brought numerous actions in both the English and Scottish courts but the mother continued to refuse him access to the children. Eventually, a contact meeting was arranged in early 2000. The applicant complained, *inter alia,* that the English and Scottish authorities had failed to comply with their obligations under Article 8. The Court held that:

> 64. Where the measures in issue concern parental disputes over their children, however, it is not for the Court to substitute itself for the competent domestic authorities in regulating contact questions, but rather to review under the Convention the decisions that those authorities have taken in the exercise of their power of appreciation.

Overall, the Court determined that 'in this very difficult situation'[69] the various courts and administrative agencies in England and Scotland had struck a fair balance between the competing interests of the applicant, his ex-wife and their children. Inevitably the nature of the judicial processes at Strasbourg,[70] which frequently take place years after the domestic actions/inaction have occurred and essentially rely upon written evidence (rather than the hearing and questioning of witnesses), means that the judges of the Court are likely to accord considerable weight to the decisions of family welfare experts who have had professional involvement with the family members at the local level.[71] Of course, if the application discloses clear failings in the authorities' measures to reunite parents and their children, as in *Ignaccolo-Zenide*, then a breach of this positive obligation will be found.

Marital separation

The Court has found that states' duty to respect family life can encompass the positive obligation to facilitate the separation of married couples when their

---

[68] Judgment of 19 September 2000.

[69] *Ibid* para 87.

[70] In this case the Chamber decided, after consulting the parties, that no hearing on the merits was necessary.

[71] For a similar view in the context of the Court's review of authorities' decisions to take children into public care see, RA Lawson and HG Schermers, *Leading Cases of the European Court of Human Rights* (Nijmegen, Ars Aequi Libri, 1997) 255–56.

relationships have irretrievably broken down. In *Airey v Ireland*,[72] the applicant wished to obtain a decree of judicial separation from her husband, who had been convicted of assaulting her. Under Irish law such decrees were only available from the High Court and the costs of legal representation before that court were beyond her means (amounting to between twelve and thirty times her net weekly wage). Before the Strasbourg institutions, Mrs Airey contended that by failing to provide an accessible legal procedure for obtaining judicial separations Ireland had violated Article 8.[73] Following its earlier judgment in *Marckx* the Court acknowledged that positive obligations arose in the context of respecting family life. A majority of the Court, four votes to three, found a breach of that right.

> 33. In Ireland, many aspects of private or family life are regulated by law. As regards marriage, husband and wife are in principle under a duty to cohabit but are entitled, in certain cases, to petition for a decree of judicial separation; this amounts to recognition of the fact that the protection of their private or family life may sometimes necessitate their being relieved from the duty to live together.
>
> Effective respect for private or family life obliges Ireland to make this means of protection effectively accessible, when appropriate, to anyone who may wish to have recourse thereto. However, it was not effectively accessible to the applicant: not having been put in a position in which she could apply to the High Court . . . she was unable to seek recognition in law of her *de facto* separation from her husband. She has therefore been the victim of a violation of Article 8.

Once again, the Court was utilising the goal of the practical effectiveness of Convention rights to justify the imposition of a positive obligation. Mrs Airey's dire circumstances, involving physical abuse by her husband combined with her inability to obtain legal representation for seven years because of her impecuniosity, emphasised the need for the domestic authorities to provide her with the means to gain a judicial decree of separation. The state could comply with this obligation by either funding legal representation for such persons or by simplifying the procedures in domestic courts to enable ordinary lay persons to adequately represent themselves.

In the subsequent case of *Johnston and Others v Ireland*,[74] the applicants sought to argue that the judgment in *Airey* should be extended to impose a positive obligation upon states to enable couples to obtain a divorce when their marriages have collapsed. However, an overwhelming majority of the Court, sixteen votes to one, was unwilling to expand the obligation that far. Taking account of the *travaux preparatoires* revelation that the drafters deliberately limited Article 12 to include only the right to marry, the Court held that:

> 57. It is true that, on this question, Article 8, with its reference to the somewhat vague notion of 'respect' for family life, might appear to lend itself more readily to an

---

[72] A.32 (1979).

[73] For an examination of her complaint under art 6 see above ch 5 n 4.

[74] Above n 37.

evolutive [*sic.*] interpretation than does Article 12. Nevertheless, the Convention must be read as a whole and the Court does not consider that a right to divorce, which it has found to be excluded from Article 12 can, with consistency, be derived from Article 8, a provision of more general purpose and scope . . . although the protection of private or family life may sometimes necessitate means whereby spouses can be relieved from the duty to live together (see the *Airey* judgment, para. 33), the engagements under-taken by Ireland under Article 8 cannot be regarded as extending to an obligation on its part to introduce measures permitting the divorce and the re-marriage which the applicants seek.

This is a vivid example of the Court's inability to use the concept of a positive obligation to create a right under the Convention which states excluded when drafting the Convention. The continuing sensitivity of some states to the recognition of a right to divorce was reflected in its further exclusion from Protocol 7 (guaranteeing *inter alia*, equality between spouses), which was opened for signature in 1984. The Irish electorate in 1995, by a 0.6% majority of the vote, decided to remove the constitutional ban on divorce.

Immigration decisions concerning the admission of non-national family members

There have been several cases where applicants have complained that states have refused to authorise the entry of non-national (alien) family members and thereby breached the applicants' right to respect for their family life. In *Abdulaziz, Cabales and Balkandali v United Kingdom*,[75] the three foreign appli-cants were lawfully resident in the United Kingdom, however the British immi-gration authorities refused permission for the applicants' alien husbands to join them for permanent residence in the UK. The applicants, *inter alia*, alleged a breach of Article 8. A plenary Court was convened to determine their innovative claim. After citing its earlier judgment in *Marckx* as recognising the existence of positive obligations under this Article the Court held:

> 67. . . . . However, especially as far as those positive obligations are concerned, the notion of 'respect' is not clear-cut: having regard to the diversity of the practices fol-lowed and the situations obtaining in the Contracting States, the notion's require-ments will vary considerably from case to case. Accordingly, this is an area in which the Contracting Parties enjoy a wide margin of appreciation in determining the steps to be taken to ensure compliance with the Convention with due regard to the needs and resources of the community and of individuals. . . . In particular, in the area now under consideration, the extent of a State's obligation to admit to its territory relatives of settled immigrants will vary according to the particular circumstances of the per-sons involved. Moreover, the Court cannot ignore that the present case is concerned not only with family life but also with immigration and that, as a matter of well-

---

[75] A.94 (1985).

established international law and subject to its treaty obligations, a State has the right to control the entry of non-nationals into its territory.

68. The Court observes that the present proceedings do not relate to immigrants who already had a family which they left behind in another country until they had achieved settled status in the United Kingdom. It was only after becoming settled in the United Kingdom, as single persons, that the applicants contracted marriage. . . . The duty imposed by Article 8 cannot be considered as extending to a general obligation on the part of a Contracting State to respect the choice by married couples of the country of their matrimonial residence and to accept the non-national spouses for settlement in that country.

   In the present case, the applicants have not shown that there were obstacles to establishing family life in their own or their husbands' home countries or that there were special reasons why that could not be expected of them.

Therefore, the Court was unanimous in concluding that there had been no breach of Article 8.[76]

The cautious attitude of the Court towards the scope of states' positive obligation regarding the immigration of non-national family members can be explained on a number of grounds. First, this case was determined during the initial stage of the Court's development of positive obligations under Article 8, hence the judicial emphasis upon the 'wide' margin of appreciation to be accorded to national authorities' decisions. Secondly, the Court acknowledged the traditional right in international law of states to regulate immigration into their territories. This has been a key element of the sovereignty of states and remains an extremely sensitive political issue in many member states. Although the judgment in *Abdulaziz* ruled that there was not a general obligation upon states to allow the settlement of alien spouses, it did leave open the possibility (depending upon particular circumstances) of states being under some Convention obligation to accept the entry of relatives of settled immigrants.

   The existence, or not, of an obligation upon a state to admit (for settlement) the child of alien parents holding residence permits granted on humanitarian grounds was examined in *Gul v Switzerland*.[77] The applicant, a Turkish national, had sought political asylum in Switzerland during 1983. His wife joined him in that country five years later. She received emergency medical care on her arrival for serious burns caused by an accident in Turkey. Later that year she gave birth to the applicant's daughter in Switzerland. In 1989 the Swiss authorities rejected Mr Gul's asylum application, but he, Mrs Gul and their daughter were given humanitarian residency permits. Subsequently, the applicant applied for permission for his two sons, aged nineteen and seven, living in Turkey to be allowed to join him and his wife. The Swiss authorities refused (by this time Mr Gul was ill and in receipt of a Swiss partial-invalidity pension and

---

[76] Note, the Court went on to find a breach of art 14 in combination with art 8 due to sexual discrimination against the applicants (at that time males lawfully resident in the UK had greater rights to bring their foreign wives into the country for settlement): see Mowbray above n 53 pp 607–13.
[77] 1996-I 165.

his wife's injuries prevented her from looking after their daughter, she was being cared for in a Swiss home). The Commission, by fourteen votes to ten, considered that the Swiss authorities' refusal to permit the applicant's younger son to reside with him in Switzerland violated Article 8. The Court articulated the test for determining the Convention obligations of Switzerland in the following manner:

> 38. . . . the boundaries between the State's positive and negative obligations under this provision (Article 8) do not lend themselves to precise definition. The applicable principles are, nonetheless, similar. In both context regard must be had to the fair balance that has to be struck between the competing interests of the individual and of the community as a whole; and in both contexts the State enjoys a certain margin of appreciation . . .

Following *Abdulaziz* the Court broadened the breadth of the immunity of states, 'where immigration is concerned, Article 8 cannot be considered to impose upon a State a general obligation to respect the choice by married couples of the country of their matrimonial residence and to authorise family reunion in its territory.'[78] The Court then considered whether allowing the applicant's younger son to settle in Switzerland would be the only way for the applicant to develop family life with him. A majority, seven votes to two, concluded that it was not as Mr Gul had been able to visit him in Turkey on several occasions in recent years, there was no evidence that Mrs Gul could not receive appropriate medical care in Turkey and the son had spent all his life in that country. Therefore, Switzerland had not breached its obligations under Article 8.

In his dissenting opinion Judge Martens, with the approval of Judge Russo, traced the evolution in the Court's 'doctrine' on positive obligations. He noted that in *Abdulaziz* the Court took account of the existence (or not) of a consensus between member states as to the occurrence of such an obligation in the particular circumstances of the case and accorded a wide margin of appreciation to the respondent state when determining if a positive obligation existed.

> 8. . . . This approach has been rightly criticised both outside and inside the Court. One of the main objections was that under this doctrine, in the context of positive obligations, the margin of appreciation might already come into play at the stage of determining the existence of the obligation, whilst in the context of negative obligations it only plays a role, if at all, at the stage of determining whether a breach of the obligation is justified.[79]

Now the Court's doctrine had 'evolved considerably' to the position where:

> . . . the difference in treatment between positive and negative obligations has gradually dwindled away. . . . The present doctrine notably implies that the distinction

---

[78] *Ibid* para 38.
[79] *Ibid* Dissenting Opinion of Judge Martens

between the two types of obligation has no bearing on either the burden of proof or the standards for assessing whether a fair balance has been struck.[80]

Having regard to the medical difficulties of the applicant and his wife, the needs of their son and daughter and uncertainties as to how the Turkish authorities would treat the applicant if he were to return to that country for settlement, Judge Martens concluded that the Swiss refusal to admit the applicant's young son was a disproportionate act which was 'not necessary in a democratic society'.

Judge Martens' chronology of the development of the Court's analysis of positive obligations under this Article is a valuable examination of the rapid progress made in the decade between *Abdulaziz* and *Gul*. However, as we have already discovered earlier in this chapter, in our study of official recognition of transsexuals, the fair balance test is so flexible that it can be applied by both majorities and minorities to justify their opposing determinations. Even where the settled immigrant parents had suffered from a number of misfortunes the Court in *Gul* was not willing to impose a positive obligation upon the host country to accept further dependent members of the family for settlement.

The Court was more narrowly divided in its application of the fair balance test in *Ahmut v The Netherlands*.[81] Mr Ahmut was a trader of Moroccan nationality who moved to the Netherlands in 1986. Prior to that event he had established a family in Morocco by marrying in the 1960s and his wife subsequently bore five children. He divorced her in 1984 and she died in 1987. Mr Ahmut married a Dutch national two months after migrating to that country, but they separated in February 1990 (he acquired joint Dutch nationality in that month) and were divorced in December 1990. Three months later he married a Moroccan national and she was given a residence permit by the Dutch authorities to live with him. In the spring of 1990 the applicant's youngest son (who was nine years' old) arrived in the Netherlands (his elderly grandmother was unable to care for him any longer in Morocco) and sought a residence permit. This was refused by the Dutch authorities (they considered that his brothers and uncles could look after him in Morocco). The applicant contended that the refusal violated Article 8 and the Commission, by nine votes to four, found a breach of that provision. Applying *Gul* the Court examined whether the Netherlands was under a positive obligation to grant a residence permit to the applicant's son. By a majority of one (five votes to four) the Court determined that there had not been a violation of Article 8. The majority was influenced by a number of factors including the son's strong linguistic/cultural links with Morocco (he had lived in that country for most of his life), the presence of family members in Morroco who could care for him and (of great significance) the fact that Mr Ahmut had consciously decided to move to the Netherlands. Therefore, the Court concluded that in refusing to grant a residence permit to the son the

---

[80] 1996-I 165 paras 8–9.
[81] 1996-VI.

Dutch authorities could not be said to have failed to strike a fair balance between the applicant's interests and those of the government in regulating immigration into its territory.

In their dissents Judges Valticos and Morenilla considered that the decisive fact in the applicant's favour was that he had acquired Dutch nationality. The former expressed the belief that, '. . . in any country, a national is entitled to have his son join him, even if the son does not have the same nationality.'[82] Judge Martens, joined by Judge Lohmus, stated his fear that the Court's judgment '. . . marks a growing tendency to relax control, if not an increased preparedness to condone harsh decisions, in the field of immigration.'[83] He considered that the applicant's case fell within dicta from *Abdulaziz*:

> . . . that where the issue of family reunification arises in a case of 'immigrants who already had a family which they left behind', the State of settlement is in principle bound to respect the choice of immigrants who have achieved settled status there and, accordingly, must as a rule admit members of the family left behind by such settlers. There may, perhaps, be exceptions to this rule. However, in my opinion, where reunion with the immigrant's little children is at stake it is very difficult to admit that the rule should not be followed.[84]

Overall we can conclude that the Court has been extremely reluctant to find states in breach of a positive obligation to accept non-national family members for settlement in their territories. Whilst the former Commission considered such breaches to have occurred in *Gul* and *Ahmut*, the Court did not endorse those opinions. Applications in respect of various categories of family members, including wives and dependent young children, have been unsuccessful. Consequently, the facts of a particular application will have to demonstrate a very serious need for admission (perhaps involving an immediate risk to the life of the family member in his/her country of origin) to persuade the Court to find that a member state has failed to correctly weigh the balance between the applicant family and the interests of the population already living in the member state's territory. From a jurisprudential perspective these cases demonstrate the maturation of the Court's conception of positive obligations under Article 8. This is particularly evident in the downgrading of the role of the margin of appreciation doctrine in determining the existence of specific positive obligations. The harmonisation of the Court's doctrinal approach to positive and negative[85] obligations identified by Judge Martens in *Gul* is to be welcomed as recognition of the importance of positive obligations in the Convention system.

---

[82] Dissenting Opinion of Judge Valticos
[83] Dissenting Opinion of Judge Martens, joined by Judge Lohmus, para 2.
[84] *Ibid* para 5.
[85] Note, however, the Court's greater willingness to find breaches of art 8 where resident non-national family members have been deported: see Mowbray above n 53 pp 371–74.

Facilitating the traditional lifestyles of minorities

In the context of the traditional nomadic lifestyle followed by gypsies (also known as Roma) the full-time Court has recognised the emergence of a positive obligation upon states to facilitate the maintenance of the cultural traditions of national minorities who wish to preserve their historical lifestyles. A Grand Chamber examined the nature and content of this obligation in *Chapman v United Kingdom*.[86] The applicant was born a gypsy and travelled constantly in caravans with her family in search of work (predominately in Hertfordshire). She and her husband, together with their children, stopped in various temporary and unofficial camp sites whilst they were on a waiting list for a permanent site. The police and local authority officials repeatedly moved them from their unofficial camps. This disrupted the education of her children. Consequently, in 1985, the applicant bought a piece of land (in the area of Three Rivers District Council, Hertfordshire) with the intention of residing in a mobile home on the plot. She applied for planning permission to use her land for residential purposes but this was refused by the Council, as the land was within the Green Belt (an area protected from residential development). Subsequently, after a number of unsuccessful appeals, she was fined several hundreds of pounds by the magistrates' court for continuing to live on her land without planning permission. The applicant complained to the Commission alleging that the enforcement actions interfered with her rights to respect for her home, private and family life as a gypsy with a traditional lifestyle of living in mobile homes, which allowed for travelling, as protected by Article 8. The Commission, by eighteen votes to nine, found no breach of that Article.

Before the Court, the British government accepted that the applicant's complaints concerned her right to respect for her home, but contended that it was not necessary for the Court to also examine whether the national measures had affected her private and family life.[87] Very significantly the Court rejected this submission.

> 73. The Court considers that the applicant's occupation of her caravan is an integral part of her ethnic identity as a gypsy, reflecting the long tradition of that minority of following a travelling lifestyle. This is the case even though, under the pressure of development and diverse policies or from their own volition, many gypsies no longer live a wholly nomadic existence and increasingly settle for long periods in one place in order to facilitate, for example, the education of their children. Measures which affect the applicant's stationing of her caravans have therefore a wider impact than on the

---

[86] Judgment of 18 January 2001. The same Grand Chamber gave similar rulings in four other gypsy cases raising analogous issues: *Coster v UK, Beard v UK, Lee v UK,* and *Jane Smith v UK* (judgments also given on 18 January 2001).

[87] Note, in the earlier comparable gypsy case of *Buckley v UK* 1996-II 483, the original Court had focused upon the home limb of art 8(1) and declined to consider whether the case concerned the rights to respect for private and family life (para 55 of the judgment).

right to respect for home. They also affect her ability to maintain her identity as a gypsy and to lead her private and family life in accordance with that tradition.

Therefore, the refusals of planning permission and later enforcement proceedings against the applicant interfered with her rights to respect for her home, private and family life. Those interferences were 'in accordance with the law' and pursued the legitimate aim of protecting the 'rights of others'. Hence the essential question for the Court was whether the domestic measures were 'necessary in a democratic society'? Taking account of a number of developments at the European level to enhance the protection of the lifestyles of minorities (including the 1995 Framework Convention for the Protection of National Minorities,[88] a 1993 Recommendation from the Parliamentary Assembly of the Council of Europe and a 1994 Resolution of the European Parliament (European Union) calling upon governments to improve the protection of gypsies), the majority of ten judges observed that:

> 93. . . . there may be said to be an emerging international consensus amongst the Contracting States of the Council of Europe recognising the special needs of minorities and an obligation to protect their security, identity and lifestyle . . . not only for the purpose of safeguarding the interests of the minorities themselves but to preserve a cultural diversity of value to the whole community.

> 94. However, the Court is not persuaded that the consensus is sufficiently concrete for it to derive any guidance as to the conduct or standards which Contracting States consider desirable in any particular situation. The Framework Convention, for example, sets out general principles and goals but signatory states were unable to agree on means or implementation. This reinforces the Court's view that the complexity and sensitivity of the issues involved in policies balancing the interests of the general population, in particular with regard to environmental protection and the interests of a minority with possibly conflicting requirements, renders the Court's role a strictly supervisory one.

> 95. Nonetheless, although the fact of being a member of a minority with a traditional lifestyle different from that of the majority of a society does not confer an immunity from general laws intended to safeguard assets common to the whole society such as the environment, it may have an incidence on the manner in which such laws are to be implemented. As intimated in the *Buckley* judgment, the vulnerable position of gypsies as a minority means that some special consideration should be given to their needs and their different lifestyle both in the relevant regulatory planning framework and in arriving at the decisions in particular cases (*loc. cit.*, paras. 76, 80, 84). To this extent there is thus a positive obligation imposed on the Contracting States by virtue of Article 8 to facilitate the gypsy way of life . . .

However, the majority were not willing to accept the applicant's contention that because the number of gypsies in the UK was greater than the number of spaces available in authorised gypsy sites the actions taken against her were automatically a breach of Article 8. According to the Court:

[88] The UK had ratified this Convention in 1998 and by February 2000 twenty-seven other Council of Europe states had also ratified it.

98. . . . This would be tantamount to imposing on the United Kingdom, as on all the other Contracting States, an obligation by virtue of Article 8 to make available to the gypsy community an adequate number of suitably equipped sites. The Court is not convinced, despite the undoubted evolution that has taken place in both international law, as evidenced by the Framework Convention, and domestic legislations in regard to protection of minorities, that Article 8 can be interpreted to involve such a far-reaching positive obligation of general social policy being imposed on States (see paragraphs 93–94 above).

Furthermore, the Court considered that:

99. It is important to recall that Article 8 does not in terms give a right to be provided with a home. Nor does any of the jurisprudence of the Court acknowledge such a right. While it is clearly desirable that every human being has a place where he or she can live in dignity and which he or she can call home, there are unfortunately in the Contracting States many persons who have no home. Whether the State provides funds to enable everyone to have a home is a matter for political not judicial decision.

Hence the Court's task was to determine whether the respondent state had 'relevant and sufficient' reasons for the measures taken against the applicant. The majority found that test was satisfied having regard to, *inter alia*, the Planning Inspectors' hearing the applicant's submissions and visiting the site, the extension of time given to the applicant to comply with planning requirements and the applicant's freedom to seek lawful places for her mobile home on authorised sites outside Hertfordshire. Consequently no violation of Article 8 had occurred.

The dissentients issued an opinion[89] in which they disagreed with the majority's assessment that the planning proceedings taken against the applicant were necessary in a democratic society. In the belief of the dissentients, the developing European consensus 'recognising the special needs of minorities and an obligation to protect their security, identity and lifestyle,'[90] demanded a greater degree of protection for the applicant than that accorded to her by the majority.

3. . . . This consensus includes a recognition that the protection of the rights of minorities, such as gypsies, requires not only that Contracting States refrain from policies or practices which discriminate against them but that also, where necessary, they should take positive steps to improve their situation through, for example, legislation or specific programmes. We cannot therefore agree with the majority's assertion that the consensus is not sufficiently concrete or with their conclusion that the complexity of the competing interests renders the Court's role a strictly supervisory one (see paragraphs 93-94). This does not reflect in our view the clearly recognised need of gypsies to protection of their effective enjoyment of their rights and perpetuates their vulnerability as a minority with differing needs and values from the general community. The impact of planning and enforcement measures on the enjoyment by a gypsy of the right to respect for home, private and family life therefore has a dimension beyond

[89] Joint Dissenting Opinion of Judges Pastor Ridruejo, Bonello, Tulkens, Straznicka, Lorenzen, Fischbach and Casadevall.

[90] *Ibid* para 3.

environmental concerns. Having regard to the potential seriousness of an interference which prohibits a gypsy from pursuing his or her lifestyle at a particular location, we consider that, where the planning authorities have not made any finding that there is available to the gypsy any alternative, lawful site to which he or she can reasonably be expected to move, there must exist compelling reasons for the measures concerned.

Also, the dissentients disputed the accuracy of the majority's view that Article 8 excluded any obligation upon states to provide homes to specific persons.

> 7. . . . Furthermore, it is not the Court's case-law that a right to be provided with a home is totally outside the ambit of Article 8. The Court has accepted that there may be circumstances where the authorities' refusal to take steps to assist in housing problems could disclose a problem under Article 8—see for example the case of *Marzari v Italy*,[91] where the Court held a refusal of the authorities to provide housing assistance to an individual suffering from a severe disease might in certain circumstances raise an issue because of the impact of such refusal on the private life of the individual (no. 3644/97, decision of 4 May 1999). Obligations on the State arise therefore where there is a direct and immediate link between the measures sought by an applicant and the latter's private life (*Botta v Italy*[92] judgment of 24 February 1998, *Reports* 1998-I, p. 422, §§ 33–34).

Taking notice of the fact that the local authority had been found to be in breach of its duty to make adequate provision for gypsies in 1985 and no improvement had been made in subsequent years, the dissentients found that the enforcement action taken against the applicant exceeded the domestic margin of appreciation, was disproportionate and therefore could not be regarded as 'necessary in a democratic society'. They concluded by stating that, 'our view that Article 8 of the Convention imposes a positive obligation on the authorities to ensure that gypsies have a practical and effective opportunity to enjoy their rights to home, private and family life, in accordance with their traditional lifestyle, is not a startling innovation.'[93]

Although the majority in *Chapman* did not find a breach of the applicant's right to respect for her family life, they did go further than the original Court in accepting that planning decisions could have an impact on the ethnic identity and traditional way of life of gypsies that fell within Article 8's conception of 'family life'. This represents the tentative beginnings of a positive obligation upon states to take measures to encourage the protection of the cultural lifestyles of minority groups within their societies. The disagreement between the majority and minority in *Chapman* concerned the stage of development of that obligation in the context of gypsies. The dissentients believed that the European consensus required more practical measures of support for persons like the applicant from governments than the majority were willing to demand under the Convention at that time. The relatively large size of the group of

---

[91] Examined previously, above n 35.
[92] Examined previously, above n 29.
[93] Above n 89 para 9.

dissentients (seven) in *Chapman* suggests that future cases may require even greater practical measures of support for minorities from governments. The views of the two groups of judges also revealed an important difference of opinion as to the extent to which Article 8 could be invoked to require states to provide individuals with homes. The majority did not accept that such a right existed under the Article, whilst the minority would not rule out the existence of a positive obligation upon states to provide housing to particular individuals who are in dire need for accommodation. This divergence of judicial views is significant for demonstrating the uncertain outer boundaries of positive obligations under Article 8, especially the degree to which they can be applied to require the provision of social welfare facilities under the Convention.

Provision of family welfare payments

The original Court was united in holding that Article 8 did not impose a positive obligation on states to pay parental leave allowances enabling working parents to take paid leave to look after their newly-born children. Under legislation passed in 1977 Austria had provided for working mothers to receive a state parental leave allowance for up to one year after the birth of their children. In *Petrovic v Austria*,[94] Mr Petrovic challenged the refusal of the authorities to pay him a parental allowance when he gave up employment to look after his new-born child, whilst his wife continued to work. Before the Court he argued that refusal violated his right to respect for his family life under Article 8 combined with unlawful sex discrimination contrary to Article 14. The Court stated that:

> 26. In this connection the Court, like the Commission, considers that the refusal to grant Mr Petrovic a parental leave allowance cannot amount to a failure to respect family life, since Article 8 does not impose any positive obligation on States to provide the financial assistance in question.

However, the Court determined that the Austrian allowance fell within the scope of Article 8 as it demonstrated respect for family life by the government. A majority, seven votes to two, concluded that there had not been a breach of Article 14 together with Article 8 because:

> 42. There still remains a very great disparity between the legal systems of the Contracting States in this field. While measures to give fathers an entitlement to parental leave have now been taken by a large number of States, the same is not true of the parental leave allowance, which only a very few States grant to fathers.

> 43. The Austrian authorities' refusal to grant the applicant a parental leave allowance has not, therefore, exceeded the margin of appreciation allowed to them. Consequently, the difference in treatment complained of was not discriminatory within the meaning of Article 14.

[94] 1998-II 579.

Judges Bernhardt and Spielmann issued a joint dissenting opinion in which they expressed the view that whilst member states had freedom to choose their own types of social welfare systems, Article 14 prohibited them from granting benefits in a sexually discriminatory manner.

The judgment in *Petrovic* is noteworthy as another demonstration of the Court's historical reluctance to find that the positive obligations inherent in Article 8 mandate the provision of social welfare benefits to particular individuals. Nevertheless, it appears that in more recent times states have increasingly come to accept the validity of the dissentients' view that social security schemes must not embody sexual discrimination. For example, the Court struck out the case of *Fielding v United Kingdom*,[95] after the government agreed a friendly settlement in which over £14,000 was paid to the male applicant because under previous social security legislation only females were entitled to receive bereavement benefits on the death of their spouses.

HOME

Protection from pollution

There have been several cases where applicants have claimed that governments have breached their right to respect for their homes, through failing to provide adequate protection against environmental pollution affecting those homes. The Court accepted that local residents affected by noise pollution from aircraft using a major civil airport could in principle invoke Article 8 in *Powell and Rayner v United Kingdom*.[96] The first applicant lived under a flight departure route several miles from Heathrow airport, whilst the second applicant lived directly under flight paths just over one mile from the airport's northern runway. The former Commission determined that their applications were only admissible in respect of Article 13 (right to an effective remedy), therefore the Court had to consider the requirements of Article 8 in the context of the applicants' claims that they had been denied an effective domestic remedy to challenge the alleged failure to protect their homes from aircraft noise pollution. The Court held that Article 8 applied to both applicants as the quality of their private lives and abilities to enjoy the amenities of their homes had been adversely affected, to different degrees, by noise from aircraft using Heathrow. This airport had been privatised in 1986, therefore the government submitted that their only obligations under Article 8 in regard to the applicants' homes were positive ones. In the Court's opinion:

> 41. Whether the present case be analysed in terms of a positive duty on the State to take reasonable and appropriate measures to secure the applicants' rights under

---

[95] Judgment of 29 January 2002. The British government has subsequently agreed other friendly settlements in respect of similar complaints.

[96] A.172 (1990).

paragraph 1 of Article 8 or in terms of an 'interference by a public authority' to be justified in accordance with paragraph 2, the applicable principles are broadly similar. In both contexts regard must be had to the fair balance that has to be struck between the competing interests of the individual and of the community as a whole; and in both contexts the State enjoys a certain margin of appreciation in determining the steps to be taken to ensure compliance with the Convention (see, for example, the Rees judgment of 17 October 1986, Series A no. 106, p. 15, § 37, as concerns paragraph 1 (art. 8-1), and the *Leander* judgment of 26 March 1987, Series A no. 116, p. 25, § 59, as concerns paragraph 2) (art. 8-2). Furthermore, even in relation to the positive obligations flowing from the first paragraph of Article 8 (art. 8-1), 'in striking [the required] balance the aims mentioned in the second paragraph (art. 8-2) may be of a certain relevance' (see the *Rees* judgment previously cited, loc. cit.).

The Court noted the, uncontested, data produced by the government demonstrating the economic importance of Heathrow (it is the UK's largest port in terms of visible trade, handling cargo of £26.3 billion and 44 million passengers in 1988), and 'as the Commission pointed out in its admissibility decisions, the existence of large international airports, even in densely populated urban areas, and the increasing use of jet aircraft have without question become necessary in the interests of a country's economic well-being.'[97] Many measures, including restrictions on night flights, aircraft noise monitoring, a £19 million scheme for the sound insulation of 16,000 homes and the purchase of homes very close to the runways, had been undertaken to reduce the noise pollution from Heathrow. Consequently, the Court determined that:

> 45. In view of the foregoing, there is no serious ground for maintaining that either the policy approach to the problem or the content of the particular regulatory measures adopted by the United Kingdom authorities gives rise to violation of Article 8, whether under its positive or negative head. In forming a judgment as to the proper scope of the noise abatement measures for aircraft arriving at and departing from Heathrow Airport, the United Kingdom Government cannot arguably be said to have exceeded the margin of appreciation afforded to them or upset the fair balance required to be struck under Article 8. This conclusion applies to Mr Rayner as much as to Mr Powell, even though Mr Rayner has suffered a much higher level of disturbance and even though careful consideration was given to his complaint by the Commission at the admissibility stage.

Therefore, neither applicant had an arguable claim that they had suffered a violation of their rights under Article 8 and hence no domestic remedy was required under Article 13.

The judgment in *Powell and Rayner* demonstrated that the Court was willing to accept that complaints concerning environmental pollution could be brought within the ambit of Article 8. Furthermore, states could be liable if they failed to take adequate measures, such as through enacting and enforcing appropriate regulatory regimes, to ameliorate the effects of significant forms of pollution

---

[97] A.172 (1990) para 42.

caused by private sector businesses that affected persons' enjoyment of their homes. The utilisation of the concept of positive obligations to require governments to take suitable measures in regard to private sector pollution was of great significance in an era of widespread privatisations of former publicly owned and controlled industries across many member states. In contemporary times the majority of industrial pollution is likely to originate from the private sector. Furthermore, *Powell and Rayner* also establishes the potential liability, under Article 8, of states for the effects of significant pollution derived from major infrastructure facilities (such as airports and railway stations) even if these too are in the private sector. But, acknowledging the necessity of many possible sources of pollution in modern developed societies, the Court also accorded states a margin of appreciation in their difficult task of balancing the conflicting interests of society as a whole and the needs of residents near unavoidable sources of pollution.

The first case where the Court upheld an environmental complaint was in *Lopez Ostra v Spain*.[98] Mrs Lopez Ostra contented that the Spanish authorities had failed to adequately protect her home and family life from the noxious gases (hydrogen sulphide, with a smell like rotten eggs) emitted by a tannery waste reprocessing plant that was built, by a company, twelve metres from her home. The discharges from the plant continued for five years and the applicant together with her family had to leave their home after three years (they were rehoused at public expenses in rented accommodation) because of the continuing pollution. The Court elaborated the threshold for pollution to fall within the ambit of Article 8; 'naturally, severe environmental pollution may affect individuals' well-being and prevent them from enjoying their homes in such a way as to affect their private and family life adversely, without, however, seriously endangering their health.'[99] The Court found that the discharges from the reprocessing plant were sufficiently serious in their effects on the applicant and her family to meet this standard. Whilst the plant was necessary for the economic well-being of the town and its leather industry, the judges were united in concluding that a fair balance had not been struck by the authorities in seeking to protect the applicant from the effects of severe pollution. A major factor in this conclusion was the opposition of local and national public authorities to Mrs Lopez Ostra's legal attempts to have the plant closed.

It is somewhat ironic that it was a reprocessing plant, designed to solve local industrial pollution concerns, that was itself the source of the problem in the above case. Nevertheless, the judgment clearly demonstrated that if governmental authorities allowed the persistence of severe pollution from industrial facilities to adversely affect local residents, the state was liable to breach its positive obligations to respect those persons' homes and family/private lives. This valuable decision means that it is not sufficient for states to simply create

---

[98] A.303-C (1994).
[99] *Ibid* para 51.

pollution control regimes, they must also take adequate steps to enforce those rules.[100]

Controversially a Chamber majority found the post 1993 regime governing night flights from Heathrow to be in breach of Article 8 in *Hatton and Others v United Kingdom*.[101] The eight applicants lived near the airport or under the flight paths of planes using it. They contended that the regulation of night flights, involving noise quotas and maximum numbers of aircraft movements, by the Department of Transport had not been preceded by adequate investigations into the incidents of sleep prevention caused by night flights or the precise economic benefits of allowing night flights. The Chamber, five votes to two, distinguished the current case from the earlier Heathrow cases by reference to the different factual circumstances, namely the present action was concerned with night flights under the post 1993 regime. After citing the established fair balance test the majority held that:

> 97. The Court would, however, underline that in striking the required balance, States must have regard to the whole range of material considerations. Further, in the particularly sensitive field of environmental protection, mere reference to the economic well-being of the country is not sufficient to outweigh the rights of others. The Court recalls that in the above-mentioned *Lopez Ostra v Spain* case, and notwithstanding the undoubted economic interest for the national economy of the tanneries concerned, the Court looked in considerable detail at 'whether the national authorities took the measures necessary for protecting the applicant's right to respect for her home and for her private and family life . . .' (judgment of 9 December 1994, p. 55, § 55). It considers that States are required to minimise, as far as possible, the interference with these rights, by trying to find alternative solutions and by generally seeking to achieve their aims in the least onerous way as regards human rights. In order to do that, a proper and complete investigation and study with the aim of finding the best possible solution which will, in reality, strike the right balance should precede the relevant project.

The majority noted that the government had not undertaken any research into the economic importance of night flights prior to introducing the 1993 scheme, nor had there been any serious attempt to evaluate the effect of night flights on the applicant's sleep patterns. Therefore, the government had breached its positive obligations under Article 8 to take 'reasonable and appropriate measures'[102] regarding the applicants' rights to respect for their homes and private/family lives.

Judge Costa issued a separate opinion in which he acknowledged that the Court had become more protective of environmental rights:

> Since the beginning of the 1970s, the world has become increasingly aware of the importance of environmental issues and of their influence on people's lives. Our Court's case-law has, moreover, not been alone in developing along those lines. For example, Article 37 of the Charter of Fundamental Rights of the European Union of

---

[100] See also *Guerra v Italy*, above n 23.
[101] Judgment of 2 October 2001.
[102] *Ibid* para 95.

18 December 2000 is devoted to the protection of the environment. I would find it regrettable if the constructive efforts made by our Court were to suffer a setback.

That is why I have finally subscribed, in the main, to the reasoning of the majority of my colleagues, and fully to their conclusion.[103]

Judge Greve did not consider that there had been a breach of Article 8. She believed that the majority had impermissibly narrowed the margin of appreciation accorded to states in environmental matters by the established case law.

> The amount and complexity of the factual information needed to strike a fair balance in these respects is more often than not of such a nature that the European Court will be at a marked disadvantage compared to the national authorities in terms of acquiring the necessary level of understanding for appropriate decision-making. Moreover, environmental rights represent a new generation of human rights. How the balance is to be struck will therefore affect the rights not only of those close enough to the source of the environmental problem to invoke Article 8, but also the rights of those members of the wider public affected by the problem and who must be considered to have a stake in the balancing exercise.[104]

Sir Brian Kerr[105] was the other dissenter. He also criticised the majority's 'wholly new test' for environmental complaints as being contrary to the existing margin of appreciation given to states in this area of decision-making. Furthermore:

> If Convention standards are not met in an individual case, it is the role of the Court to say so, regardless of how many others are in the same position. But when, as here, a substantial proportion of the population of south London is in a similar position to the applicants, the Court must consider whether the proper place for a discussion of the particular policy is in Strasbourg, or whether the issue should be left to the domestic political sphere.[106]

The Chamber judgment in *Hatton* imposed more onerous obligations upon states to conduct thorough prior investigations into the environmental effects of planned major projects and activities which present a risk to the Article 8 rights of individuals. In practical terms the majority were requiring states to undertake comprehensive environmental and economic cost/benefit analyses before approving significant developments/activities likely to cause serious pollution. The British government considered that this judgment was not compatible with the earlier jurisprudence of the Court and requested the Grand Chamber to re-hear the case under Article 43. A panel of the Grand Chamber agreed to this exceptional request in March 2002.[107] Therefore the most authoritative body of the full-time Court will now have the opportunity to determine the nature of

---

[103] Separate Opinion of Judge Costa.

[104] Partly Dissenting Opinion of Judge Greve.

[105] The British ad hoc judge. Judge Bratza had withdrawn from the case, he had acted as counsel for the British Government in *Powell & Rayner*.

[106] Dissenting Opinion of Sir Brian Kerr.

[107] Decision of 27 March 2002.

states positive obligations to protect persons' homes from environmental pollution.

The predominant jurisprudence concerning this right is directed at interferences with persons' written and electronic communications by public authorities.[108] However, in *A.B. v The Netherlands*,[109] a British prisoner being held in a jail in the Netherlands Antilles complained, *inter alia*, that his inability to make telephone calls to persons outside the prison violated his rights under Article 8. The Court was unanimous in holding that states were not under a positive obligation to make such a form of communication available to prisoners.

> 92. In respect of the telephone facilities, the Court considers that Article 8 of the Convention cannot be interpreted as guaranteeing prisoners the right to make telephone calls, in particular where the facilities for contact by way of correspondence are available and adequate.

As the authorities allowed prisoners to send up to three letters per week (the costs of writing materials and postage were born by the prison authorities), the Court rejected this element of the applicant's complaints.

General conclusions

We have seen that the textual basis for the positive obligations enforced by the Court under Article 8 is the duty upon states to 'respect' the rights elaborated in paragraph one of that provision. Whilst the Court's justification for developing these obligations has been to seek to ensure that the guaranteed rights are effectively safeguarded by states.[110] In the early jurisprudence the Court declared that the notion of respect was ill-defined in the context of positive obligations and therefore states would be accorded a wide margin of appreciation when determining if they had complied with their Convention responsibilities.[111] However, over time the Court limited the use of the margin of appreciation in deciding whether a specific positive obligation existed.[112] The fair balance test emerged as the common judicial method for determining both the existence of individual positive obligations[113] and compliance with the requirements of an established positive obligation.[114] Judge Wildhaber, as he then was,

---

[108] See, Mowbray above n 53 pp 387–99.
[109] Judgment of 29 January 2002.
[110] See, *Marckx* above n 36.
[111] For example in *Abdulaziz* above n 75.
[112] As explained by Judge Martens in *Gul* above n 77.
[113] For example in *Rees* above n 8.
[114] Such as the obligation to provide protection against severe environmental pollution applied in *Lopez Ostra* above n 98.

proposed[115] an alternative method of analysing whether states had complied with their positive obligations that was similar to the technique used by the Court when dealing with negative obligation cases. However, his proposal has not been adopted by a number of Chambers in both the original and full-time Courts.[116] Furthermore, he has presided over a Grand Chamber which unanimously applied the fair balance test.[117]

Whilst the Court has recognised the existence of positive obligations under Article 8 in a diverse range of circumstances, from official recognition of the personality of post-operative transsexuals[118] to the facilitation of the maintenance of minority lifestyles,[119] many of the cases have been concerned with alleged defects in legal regimes and procedures devised by public authorities. Examples of failings in criminal and civil legal systems include *X. and Y. v Netherlands*[120] (absence of criminal law protection for disabled juvenile victim of sexual abuse) and *Johnston*[121] (insufficient recognition of the family relationship between unmarried parents and their daughter by the civil law). Flawed procedures have been found in cases concerning access to official information[122] and the taking of children into public care.[123] The outer boundaries of Article 8 have been demonstrated by the Court's reluctance to find the existence of positive obligations which require the provision of social facilities and welfare benefits by states, such as recreational facilities for physically disabled persons[124] or the payment of family allowances.[125] However, some of the judges are more willing to countenance the recognition of these obligations, at least in particular cases of dire need.[126] Also the jurisprudence reveals that the positive obligations derived from this Article can extend into the realm of newer generational rights, like environmental ones.[127]

---

[115] In *Stjerna* above n 19.

[116] Examples of the fair balance test being utilised to determine states compliance with positive obligations in subsequent cases include *Gul* (above n 77), *Ahmut* (above n 81) and *Mikulic* (above n 27).

[117] In *Christine Goodwin* above n 15.

[118] As in *B v France* above n 11.

[119] As in *Chapman* above n 86.

[120] Above n 2.

[121] Above n 37.

[122] For example, *Gaskin* above n 22.

[123] For example, *W v UK* above n 43.

[124] As in *Botta* above n 29.

[125] As in *Petrovic* above n 94.

[126] For example the provision of state assistance towards the housing needs of chronically ill persons, see *Marzari* above n 35 and the dissenters in *Chapman* above n 89.

[127] From *Powell and Rayner*, above n 96, onwards

7

Articles 9, 10, 11 and 14

———»·•·«———

Articles 9, 10 and 11 have two paragraph structures like that of Article 8.

ARTICLE 9: FREEDOM OF THOUGHT, CONSCIENCE AND RELIGION

Provides that:

(1) Everyone has the right to freedom of thought, conscience and religion; this right includes freedom to change his religion or belief and freedom, either alone or in community with others and in public or private, to manifest his religion or belief, in worship, teaching, practice and observance.

(2) Freedom to manifest one's religion or beliefs shall be subject only to such limitations as are prescribed by law and are necessary in a democratic society in the interests of public safety, for the protection of public order, health or morals, or for the protection of the rights and freedoms of others.

Protection of freedom of thought, conscience and religion

Dicta in *Otto-Preminger-Institut v Austria*,[1] indicated that the original Court envisaged the potential for situations where states were obliged to take measures to safeguard the Article 9 rights of specific persons from hostile attacks by other private individuals or groups. The applicant operated, in Innsbruck, an 'art-house' cinema and proposed to show a film called *Das Liebeskonzil* ('Council in Heaven') which contained a production of a controversial nineteenth-century play[2] of the same title. The play portrayed many leading figures of the Christian religion in an extremely negative manner. When the applicant advertised the film, only paying customers over the age of seventeen would have been admitted, the local diocese of the Roman Catholic church, on behalf of the 87% of Tyrolleans stated to be believers in that church, requested the Public Prosecutor to bring criminal proceedings against the applicant. The Prosecutor

---

[1] A.295-A (1994).
[2] Written by Oskar Panizza, who had been imprisoned by the German courts for publishing the play.

sought, *inter alia*, seizure of the film and the Regional Court ordered its seizure and forfeiture.

The applicant complained that the domestic authorities' actions violated the organisation's freedom of expression as guaranteed by Article 10. Before the Court, the government contended that the interference with the applicant's freedom of expression was necessary, under Article 10(2), to protect the right to respect for their religious beliefs of the local Roman Catholic population. Thereby linking constraints on Article 10 with the protection of religious beliefs under Article 9. The Court observed that:

> 47. .... Those who choose to exercise the freedom to manifest their religion, irrespective of whether they do so as members of a religious majority or a minority, cannot reasonably expect to be exempt from all criticism. They must tolerate and accept the denial by others of their religious beliefs and even the propagation by others of doctrines hostile to their faith. However, the manner in which religious beliefs and doctrines are opposed or denied is a matter which may engage the responsibility of the State, notably its responsibility to ensure the peaceful enjoyment of the right guaranteed under Article 9 to the holders of those beliefs and doctrines. Indeed, in extreme cases the effect of particular methods of opposing or denying religious beliefs can be such as to inhibit those who hold such beliefs from exercising their freedom to hold and express them.

Taking account of the lack of a European consensus, or even a common view within one state, on the significance of religion within modern societies the Court accorded the respondent a 'certain'[3] margin of appreciation in determining the measures that were necessary to protect the religious beliefs of the Tyrolleans. A majority of the Court, six votes to three, concluded that the seizure and forfeiture of the film could be justified under Article 10(2) and no breach of applicant's Convention right had occurred.

Whilst the above case concerned an applicant whose freedom of expression had been curtailed to protect the religious beliefs of others, the judgment revealed the Court expressing the view that states must take action to guarantee Article 9 rights to persons within their jurisdiction. However, the difficult issues are determining the threshold of unacceptable anti-religious (or anti-other Article 9 protected beliefs) expression and the extent of permitted state interference with such forms of expression. Obviously, anti-religious expression involving violence requires state suppression, but peaceful (artistic) expression, as in *Otto-Preminger Institut*, was much more problematic for the Court. The majority responded by allowing a considerable deference to the assessments of national authorities via the invocation of the margin of appreciation doctrine.[4] Whereas, the dissentients[5] considered that:

---

[3] Above n 1 para 50.

[4] Regarding this judicial creation see, A Mowbray, *Cases and Materials on the European Convention on Human Rights* (London, Butterworths, 2001) 449–53 and Y Arai-Takahashi, *The Margin of Appreciation Doctrine and the Principle of Proportionality in the Jurisprudence of the ECHR* (Antwerp, Intersentia, 2002).

[5] Judges Palm, Pekkanen and Makarczyk.

7. The duty and the responsibility of a person seeking to avail himself of his freedom of expression should be to limit, as far as he can reasonably be expected to, the offence that his statement may cause to others. Only if he fails to take necessary action, or if such action is shown to be insufficient, may the State step in.[6]

In their evaluation the fact that the applicant warned potential viewers of the nature of the film was a reasonable limitation of the potential offence of the film to Roman Catholics. Therefore, the seizure and forfeiture of the film by the domestic courts was not a proportionate measure. The dissentients' approach has much to commend it and the national authorities were, arguably, overprotective of the religious sensitivities of the people living in the Tyrol.

In the subsequent case of *Wingrove v United Kingdom*,[7] the Court, by seven votes to two, followed the majority's approach in *Otto-Preminger Institut* and upheld the legality of the British authorities refusal to licence the distribution of the applicant's allegedly blasphemous video film. The Court held that:

58. . . . Moreover, as in the field of morals, and perhaps to an even greater degree, there is no uniform European conception of the requirements of 'the protection of the rights of others' in relation to attacks on their religious convictions. What is likely to cause substantial offence to persons of a particular religious persuasion will vary significantly from time to time and from place to place, especially in an era characterised by an ever growing array of faiths and denominations. By reason of their direct and continuous contact with the vital forces of their countries, State authorities are in principle in a better position than the international judge to give an opinion on the exact content of these requirements with regard to the rights of others as well as on the 'necessity' of a 'restriction' intended to protect from such material those whose deepest feelings and convictions would be seriously offended.

Hence, domestic agencies are accorded considerable latitude by the Court in determining what measures are necessary to protect the Article 9 beliefs of persons within their societies.[8]

ARTICLE 10: FREEDOM OF EXPRESSION

Guarantees that:

(1) Everyone has the right to freedom of expression. This right shall include freedom to hold opinions and to receive and impart information and ideas without interference by public authority and regardless of frontiers. This article shall not prevent States from requiring the licensing of broadcasting, television or cinema enterprises.

(2) The exercise of these freedoms, since it carries with it duties and responsibilities, may be subject to such formalities, conditions, restrictions or penalties as are

[6] Joint Dissenting Opinion above n 1.

[7] 1996-V 1937.

[8] Note, Lord Lester QC has criticised the Court's reluctance to protect controversial artistic works: see, Lord Lester QC 'Universality versus Subsidiarity: A Reply' [1998] *European Human Rights Law Review* 73.

prescribed by law and are necessary in a democratic society, in the interests of national security, territorial integrity or public safety, for the prevention of disorder or crime, for the protection of health or morals, for the protection of the reputation or rights of others, for preventing the disclosure of information received in confidence, or for maintaining the authority and impartiality of the judiciary.

State provision of information

The Court has been reluctant to recognise the existence, under this Article, of a positive obligation upon states to provide information to persons. Applicants have sought to persuade the Court to find such an obligation in different contexts, but so far most judges have not been willing to uphold those claims. In *Gaskin v United Kingdom*,[9] the Court was united in rejecting the applicant's contention that the '. . . right . . .to receive and impart information . . .' guaranteed by Article 10(1) required the government to provide the applicant with official files concerning his childhood in the care of a public authority.

> 52. The Court holds, as it did in the aforementioned *Leander [v Sweden]*[10] judgment, that 'the right to freedom to receive information basically prohibits a Government from restricting a person from receiving information that others wish or may be willing to impart to him.'[11] Also in the circumstances of the present case, Article 10 does not embody an obligation on the State concerned to impart the information in question to the individual.

Intriguingly, the latter sentence raised the possibility that the Court might accept the possibility of an official information disclosure obligation arising in a different context. However, the judgment provided no clues as to the factual elements necessary for a positive obligation to be recognised.

The Court was faced with a later assertion of this obligation in the different context of official information concerning industrial pollution in *Guerra and Others v Italy*.[12] The Commission, by twenty-one votes to eight, had expressed the opinion that Article 10 imposed a positive obligation upon public authorities to '. . . collect, process and disseminate such information, which by its nature could not otherwise come to the knowledge of the public.'[13] In that body's view the provision of environmental information by governments to their peoples was an essential method of health protection. The failure of the Italian authorities to provide information on the known pollution record and risks of a particular chemical factory to local residents breached Article 10. However, after citing the above quotation from *Leander*, the Court held, by eighteen votes to two, that Article 10 was not applicable. The guaranteed free-

---

[9] Above ch 6 n 22.
[10] A.116 (1987).
[11] *Ibid* para 74.
[12] Above ch 6 n 23.
[13] *Leander v Sweden*, above n 10 para 52.

dom to receive information, . . . cannot be construed as imposing on a State, in circumstances such as those of the present case, positive obligations to collect and disseminate information of its own motion.[14] Although that conclusion might appear to be a decisive rejection of a governmental information obligation by the Grand Chamber, a number of judges expressed varying degrees of support for such a duty in separate opinions. Judge Palm, joined by Judges Bernhardt, Russo, Macdonald, Makarczyk and Van Dijk, issued a concurring opinion in which she stated that, '. . . under different circumstances the State may have a positive obligation to make available information to the public and to disseminate such information which by its nature could not otherwise come to the knowledge of the public.'[15] Judge Jambrek was much more specific as to when he considered this duty arose.

> In my view, the wording of Article 10, and the natural meaning of the words used, does not allow the inference to be drawn that a State has positive obligations to provide information, save when a person of his/her own will demands/requests information which is at the disposal of the government at the material time.
>
> I am therefore of the opinion that such a positive obligation should be considered as dependent upon the following condition: that those who are potential victims of the industrial hazard have requested that specific information, evidence, tests, etc., be made public and be communicated to them by a specific government agency. If a government did not comply with such a request, and gave no good reasons for not complying, then such a failure should be considered equivalent to an act of interference by the government, proscribed by Article 10 of the Convention.[16]

Judge Thor Vilhjalmsson, in his partly concurring/dissenting opinion, supported the Commission's interpretation of Article 10. Therefore, eight judges in fact countenanced the potential existence of this form of positive obligation.

The full-time Court may enforce a governmental information obligation under Article 10 in future times.[17] But, it seems that it will require dramatic circumstances to induce the necessary judicial creativity. Both *Gaskin* and *Guerra* involved relatively limited numbers of applicants seeking access to defined categories of pre-existing official information and yet the Court was not willing to impose a positive obligation of disclosure upon states. If the Court was to develop this obligation, Judge Jambrek's concurring opinion in *Guerra* would provide a good analytical basis for the application of this obligation in many situations as it encompassed a reasonable balance between the interests of directly affected individuals and the correlative burdens on public authorities.

[14] *Ibid* para 53.
[15] *Ibid* Concurring Opinion of Judge Palm.
[16] *Ibid* Concurring Opinion of Judge Jambrek.
[17] For a consideration of the case law under art 8 see the section on 'Access to Official Information' in ch 6 above.

Protection of freedom of expression

A broad positive obligation requiring governmental bodies to take protective security measures to safeguard journalists and media organisations from unlawful violence has been developed and applied by a unanimous Chamber of the full-time Court in *Ozgur Gundem v Turkey*.[18] The applicants were the former editors and owners of the newspaper 'Ozgur Gundem' which was published in Turkey between 1992 and 1994. The paper was estimated to have a national circulation of about 45,000 copies. The government considered that the paper and its staff supported the PKK (terrorist/political organisation). The applicants asserted that journalists, distributors and others associated with the paper were subject to a series of attacks (it was uncontested that seven journalists/employees of the paper had been violently killed in separate incidents together with six attacks on distributors/newsagents) and, despite repeated requests by the applicants, the authorities had failed to take measures to protect the freedom of expression of the paper and its staff/distributors. The Court held that:

> 42. . . . although the essential object of many provisions of the Convention is to protect the individual against arbitrary interference by public authorities, there may in addition be positive obligations inherent in an effective respect of the rights concerned. It has found that such obligations may arise under Article 8 (see, amongst others, the *Gaskin v the United Kingdom* judgment of 7 July 1989, Series A no. 160, §§ 42-49) and Article 11 (the *Plattform 'Ärzte für das Leben' v Austria* judgment of 21 June 1988, Series A no. 139, § 32). Obligations to take steps to undertake effective investigations have also been found to accrue in the context of Article 2 (e.g. *the McCann and Others v the United Kingdom* judgment of 27 September 1995, Series A no. 324, § 161) and Article 3 (the *Assenov and Others v Bulgaria* judgment of 28 October 1998, *Reports* 1998-VIII, p. 3265, at § 102), while a positive obligation to take steps to protect life may also exist under Article 2 (the *Osman v the United Kingdom* judgment of 28 October 1998, Reports 1998-VIII, pp. 3159–3161, §§ 115–117).

> 43. The Court recalls the key importance of freedom of expression as one of the preconditions for a functioning democracy. Genuine, effective exercise of this freedom does not depend merely on the State's duty not to interfere, but may require positive measures of protection, even in the sphere of relations between individuals (*mutatis mutandis*, the *X and Y v the Netherlands* judgment of 26 March 1985, Series A no. 91, § 23). In determining whether or not a positive obligation exists, regard must be had to the fair balance that has to be struck between the general interest of the community and the interests of the individual, the search for which is called for throughout the Convention. The scope of this obligation will inevitably vary, having regard to the diversity of situations obtaining in Contracting States, the difficulties involved in policing modern societies and the choices which must be made in terms of priorities and resources. Nor must such an obligation be interpreted in such a way as to impose an impossible or disproportionate burden on the authorities (see, amongst other authorities, the *Rees v the United Kingdom judgment* of 17 October 1986, Series A no. 106, § 37, the *Osman v the United Kingdom* judgment, cited above, § 116).

---

[18] Judgment of 16 March 2000.

The Court found that the Turkish authorities had been made aware of the series of violent attacks upon the newspaper and its staff/distributors. However, only one protective measure had been taken (a police escort was provided for the distribution of the paper in one province on a single occasion). The Court also ruled that the government's belief that the newspaper was a propaganda instrument of the PKK did not, even if it was in fact true, justify the state's failure to provide necessary protection against unlawful violent attacks. Consequently, the Turkish authorities had breached Article 10 by failing '. . . to comply with their positive obligation to protect Ozgur Gundem in the exercise of its freedom of expression.'[19]

The judgment in *Ozgur Gundem* is very significant for creating a new positive obligation under Article 10. The justification for the Court's recognition of this obligation is identical to that invoked for many of the other positive obligations under the Convention,[20] namely states' responsibility to ensure effective respect for the rights guaranteed by the treaty. Furthermore, the test adopted by the Court in *Ozgur Gundem* to determine the existence of the relevant positive obligation was the fair balance methodology which, as we have seen,[21] has frequently been utilised by the Court when reaching analogous decisions under Article 8. Also, the forms of state action required by the positive obligation in *Ozgur Gundem* were similar to those required under the protective policing measures obligation found within Article 2.[22] Hence there were substantial connections between this new positive obligation and previous jurisprudence derived from other Articles. Over time we shall be able to gauge whether the circumstances of *Ozgur Gundem* were, hopefully, an isolated occurrence or whether other publishers and journalists have similar valid complaints that member states are failing to adequately protect their vital freedom of expression.

ARTICLE 11: FREEDOM OF ASSEMBLY AND ASSOCIATION

Affirms that:

(1) Everyone has the right to freedom of peaceful assembly and to freedom of association with others, including the right to form and to join trade unions for the protection of his interests.

(2) No restrictions shall be placed on the exercise of these rights other than such as are prescribed by law and are necessary in a democratic society in the interests of national security or public safety, for the prevention of disorder or crime, for the protection of health or morals or for the protection of the rights and freedoms of others. This

---

[19] *Ibid* para 46.
[20] See, for example, those enforced under art 8, above ch 6.
[21] *Ibid* General Conclusions section.
[22] See ch 2 above.

article shall not prevent the imposition of lawful restrictions on the exercise of these rights by members of the armed forces, of the police or of the administration of the State.

Protection of peaceful assembly

The case of *Plattform 'Arzte fur das Leben'*[23] *v Austria*[24] raised the important question whether states had positive obligations under this Article to safeguard the freedom of peaceful assembly. The applicant was an association of doctors that campaigned against abortion. The association gave notice to the local police authority that it planned to hold a religious service at a particular church followed by a march to the surgery of a doctor who carried out abortions. The police granted permission for the association to use the public highway and, subsequently, banned two counter-demonstrations. On the day of the march police officers were deployed beside the route. However, the association feared incidents along the route so the march was re-arranged to proceed from the church to an altar on a hillside. The police warned that the new route was not suited to crowd control. During the church service a large number of counter-demonstrators gathered outside the church, they had not given the required notice of their assembly, but the police did not seek to disperse them. The counter-demonstrators sought to disrupt the later march (some counter-demonstrators threw clumps of earth and eggs at the association's members). When the public order situation had further deteriorated, to near physical violence between the two groups, riot-control police formed a physical barrier between the groups to allow the association's members to retrace their route. Eighteen months later the association obtained permission from the police to organise another demonstration in the cathedral square of Salzburg. A short while before the applicant's protest was due to begin about 350 counter-demonstrators also gathered in the square. One hundred police officers were deployed to form a protective cordon around the association's members. When another group of protestors (supporters of the applicant) began to cause trouble the police cleared the square. The applicant complained that the police had failed to protect its demonstrations but the Austrian Constitutional Court held that it had no jurisdiction to deal with the complaint.

The Commission, unanimously, found a breach of the applicant's right to an effective domestic remedy (Article 13). Because of the Commission's admissibility decision the Court was limited to examining whether the applicant had an arguable claim that its right to peaceful assembly had not been secured by the Austrian authorities, due to the alleged failures of the police to provide adequate protection for the applicant's members. The government contended that Article

---

[23] Translated as Campaign "Doctors for the right to life".
[24] A.139 (1988).

11 did not impose a positive obligation upon states to protect demonstrators. A unanimous Chamber rejected that submission.

31. The Court does not have to develop a general theory of the positive obligations which may flow from the Convention, but before ruling on the arguability of the applicant association's claim it has to give an interpretation of Article 11.

32. A demonstration may annoy or give offence to persons opposed to the ideas or claims that it is seeking to promote. The participants must, however, be able to hold the demonstration without having to fear that they will be subjected to physical violence by their opponents; such a fear would be liable to deter associations or other groups supporting common ideas or interests from openly expressing their opinions on highly controversial issues affecting the community. In a democracy the right to counter-demonstrate cannot extend to inhibiting the exercise of the right to demonstrate.

Genuine, effective freedom of peaceful assembly cannot, therefore, be reduced to a mere duty on the part of the State not to interfere: a purely negative conception would not be compatible with the object and purpose of Article 11. Like Article 8, Article 11 sometimes requires positive measures to be taken, even in the sphere of relations between individuals, if need be (see, *mutatis mutandis*, the *X and Y v the Netherlands* judgment of 26 March 1985, Series A no. 91, p. 11, § 23).

The scope of this obligation was defined in the following terms:

34. While it is the duty of Contracting States to take reasonable and appropriate measures to enable lawful demonstrations to proceed peacefully, they cannot guarantee this absolutely and they have a wide discretion in the choice of the means to be used (see, *mutatis mutandis*, the *Abdulaziz, Cabales and Balkandali [v UK]* judgment of 28 May 1985, Series A no. 94, pp. 33–34, § 67, and the Rees [*v UK*] judgment of 17 October 1986, Series A no. 106, pp. 14–15, §§ 35–37). In this area the obligation they enter into under Article 11 of the Convention is an obligation as to measures to be taken and not as to results to be achieved.

Noting the numbers and types of police officers deployed at the two demonstrations, together with the actions they took to protect the applicant's members, the Court held that it was clear that reasonable and appropriate measures had been taken to safeguard the applicant's right to demonstrate peacefully. Therefore, the applicant had no arguable claim that Article 11 had been violated and Article 13 did not apply.

This was one of the relatively early judgments of the original Court finding a positive obligation implied in the language of a substantive right. Although the Court did not consider it necessary to attempt to provide a general theoretical explanation for positive obligations, the judgment did seek to justify this specific obligation in terms of the purpose of Article 11 and securing the effective enjoyment of those rights by peaceful protestors. Later jurisprudence[25] concerning other positive obligations involving police action has also adopted the reasonable measures standard to assess whether these domestic authorities have

[25] For example, *Osman v UK*, above ch 2 n 12.

satisfied the demands of the Convention. There is additionally symmetry in the Court's rulings that states must take positive actions to protect freedom of expression by peaceful protestors in *Plattform* and by the media (in *Ozgur Gundem,*)[26] as both forms of expression are inextricably linked to the Court's underlying conception of democratic society.[27] Indeed, reports in the media of peaceful protests may help to foster a wider public debate upon the merits of the protestors' views, whilst media reports of matters of public policy (for example, government proposals for new legislation) may be the inspiration for peaceful protests supporting or opposing those policies which in turn may influence the content of the policies ultimately implemented.

Protection of freedom of association

Building upon the jurisprudential foundation of *Plattform* the Court has recognised that states can also be subject to positive obligations regarding individuals' freedom of association. The case of *Gustafsson v Sweden,*[28] concerned the implied negative right to freedom of association (*i.e.* the right not to be forced to join an association which the individual does not wish to be a member of).[29] The applicant was a restaurateur who objected to collective bargaining between employers and employees. Therefore, he refused to join the relevant employers' association or sign a collective bargaining agreement with the Hotel and Restaurant Workers' Union. Instead, he claimed that he paid his employees higher rates than those established by the collective bargaining system. The Union placed his restaurant under a blockade in 1987 and sympathetic industrial action was taken against the applicant by other unions. Transport unions boycotted deliveries to his restaurant in 1988. The applicant, relying upon the Convention, asked the government to prohibit the unions' industrial action against his business. The Ministry of Justice dismissed his request and the applicant's subsequent judicial review action against the government was rejected by the Swedish courts. In 1991 the applicant sold his restaurant. The Commission, by thirteen votes to four, upheld his complaint that the government had breached Article 11 by failing to protect his negative right not to be a party to collective bargaining with the Union.

Before the Court, the government argued that the negative right under Article 11 was not in issue as the applicant had not been forced to join an association against his will. However, the Court, following the approach of the Commission, found that right was applicable as the unions' actions were

---

[26] Above n 18.

[27] See, A Mowbray, 'The Role of the European Court of Human Rights in the Promotion of Democracy' [1999] *Public Law* 703.

[28] 1996-II 637.

[29] For an examination of this contentious judicial creation see A Mowbray, above n 4 pp 563–74.

directed at forcing Gustafsson to become a party to the collective bargaining system. Regarding the duties of governmental bodies, the Court held that:

45. . . . Although the essential object of Article 11 is to protect the individual against arbitrary interferences by the public authorities with his or her exercise of the rights protected, there may in addition be positive obligations to secure the effective enjoyment of these rights. . . . It follows that national authorities may, in certain circumstances, be obliged to intervene in the relationships between private individuals by taking reasonable and appropriate measures to secure the effective enjoyment of the negative right to freedom of association (see, *mutatis mutandis, Plattform 'Arzte fur das Leben' v Austria*, paras. 32–34).

But, the Court also acknowledged that Article 11 safeguarded the freedom of trade unions to protect their members' interests by action. Consequently:

45. . . . In view of the sensitive character of the social and political issues involved in achieving a proper balance between the competing interests and, in particular, in assessing the appropriateness of State intervention to restrict union action aimed at extending a system of collective bargaining, and the wide degree of divergence between the domestic systems in the particular area under consideration, the Contracting States should enjoy a wide margin of appreciation in their choice of the means to be employed.

52. . . . The positive obligation incumbent on the State under Article 11, including the aspect of protection of personal opinion, may well extend to treatment connected with the operation of a collective bargaining system, but only where such treatment impinges on freedom of association. Compulsion which, as here, does not significantly affect the enjoyment of that freedom, even if it causes economic damage, cannot give rise to any positive obligation under Article 11.

A majority of the Court, twelve votes to seven, concluded that the Swedish government had not failed to secure the applicant's right under Article 11.

In his dissenting opinion Judge Martens, joined by Judge Matscher, elaborated the nature of the positive obligation he believed this aspect of Article 11 imposed on states.

10. It follows that the High Contracting Parties, being bound to secure every individual's negative freedom of association, have a positive obligation to protect that freedom against abuse or disproportionate use of collective action by trade unions. The necessary inference is that Article 11—just like Article 8 and Article 1 of Protocol No. 1—implies a procedural requirement: individuals claiming to be victims of abuse or disproportionate use of collective action by trade unions should be able to seek legal protection before an independent and impartial tribunal. I note that this conclusion is consistent with the Committee of Independent Experts' case-law as to a positive obligation for Contracting States to provide legal remedies with respect to practices which unduly obstruct negative freedom of association under Article 5 of the European Social Charter (see Conclusions VIII, p. 77, and XI-1, p. 78).

Similarly, Judge Morenilla's dissent found Sweden to be in breach of its positive obligation, derived from a combination of Articles 1 and 11, to provide 'legal and procedural means . . .to protect the individual against measures taken by the trade unions considered by employers or employees to be "unreasonable or inappropriate".'[30] Likewise Judge Jambrek expressed the view that:

> 1. According to the Court's case-law, Sweden had a positive obligation under Article 11 of the Convention to secure to everyone within its jurisdiction the effective enjoyment of his or her right to freedom of association with others, including the right not to join or to withdraw from an association. The Convention being a living instrument which must be interpreted in the light of present-day conditions, that obligation entailed a duty for the respondent State to prevent abuse of a dominant position by a trade union aimed at compelling anyone to join an association or to adhere to a system of collective bargaining.[31]

The judgment of the Court in *Gustafsson* accords states an extensive margin of appreciation in determining how they should intervene in conflicts between trade unions and businesses. Just because trade union action causes economic damage to a business involved in a collective bargaining dispute that of itself is not sufficient to require positive intervention by public authorities. Hence, this decision may be seen as cautious indirect support for legitimate trade union action by the Court.[32] Indeed, when the Grand Chamber subsequently dismissed Gustafsson's request for a revision of the above judgment (on the ground that he had evidence to dispute the government's assertion, before the Court, that he could not establish that his salaries were better than those of the relevant collective agreement) it held:

> 31. . . . In fact, rather than determining the disagreement between the applicant and the Government as to the terms and conditions of employment, the Court had regard to the general interest sought to be achieved through the union action, in particular the special role and importance of collective agreements in the regulation of labour relations in Sweden.[33]

The full-time Court has found a state to be in breach of its positive obligations towards trade unions and their members in the joined cases of *Wilson and The National Union of Journalists; Palmer, Wyeth and The National Union of Rail, Maritime and Transport Workers; Doolan and Others v United Kingdom*.[34] During the early 1990s two employers, the publisher of the *Daily Mail* newspaper and a dock company, sought to terminate collective bargaining arrangements with the applicant trade unions. The employers offered financial incentives, including higher rates of pay, to their employees who signed new personal contracts of employment relinquishing trade union rights. The individual applicants refused the new contracts and sought to challenge the legality of the

---

[30]   Above n 28, Dissenting Opinion of Judge Morenilla, para 4.

[31]   *Ibid* Partly Dissenting Opinion of Judge Jambrek.

[32]   For criticism of the Court's failure to protect trade union activities under art 11 see KD Ewing, 'The Human Rights Act and Labour Law' (1998) 27 *Industrial Law Journal* 275.

[33]   *Gustafsson v Sweden (Revision)* (30 July 1998).

[34]   Judgment of 2 July 2002. More generally see, KD Ewing, 'The Implications of Wilson and Palmer' (2003) 32 *Industrial Law Journal* 1.

employers' actions. Eventually, the House of Lords[35] found in favour of the employers. In addition the Conservative government sought changes to employment law which prevented employees from challenging action taken by employers to alter their relationship with all/any class of their employees unless the employer had acted in a manner which no reasonable employer would take. Parliament approved that amendment in section 13 of the Trade Union Reform and Employment Rights Act 1993. Subsequently, the Committee of Independent Experts found that section 13 was not compatible with Article 5 (the right to organise) of the Social Charter.[36] The Committee on Freedom of Association of the International Labour Organisation also called upon the British government to amend section 13 to provide workers' organisations with adequate protection from interferences by employers.[37]

Before the Court the applicants contended that the domestic law at the relevant time failed to protect their rights under Article 11. Perhaps surprisingly, the incumbent Labour government sought to defend the case, by emphasising the voluntary nature of the system of collective bargaining and recognition operating in the United Kingdom. Following *Gustafsson* the Court repeated that states had positive obligations to protect Article 11 rights.

> 46. . . . Furthermore, it is of the essence of the right to join a trade union for the protection of their interests that employees should be free to instruct or permit the union to make representations to their employer or to take action in support of their interests on their behalf. If workers are prevented from so doing, their freedom to belong to a trade union, for the protection of their interests, becomes illusory. It is the role of the State to ensure that trade union members are not prevented or restrained from using their union to represent them in attempts to regulate their relations with their employers.

Noting the House of Lords' judgment against the applicants, the Court unanimously concluded that:

> 48. Under United Kingdom law at the relevant time it was, therefore, possible for an employer effectively to undermine or frustrate a trade union's ability to strive for the protection of its members' interests. The Court notes that this aspect of domestic law has been the subject of criticism by [the] Social Charter's Committee of Independent Experts and the ILO's Committee on Freedom of Association. It considers that, by permitting employers to use financial incentives to induce employees to surrender important union rights, the respondent State failed in its positive obligation to secure the enjoyment of the rights under Article 11 of the Convention. This failure amounted to a violation of Article 11, as regards both the applicant unions and the individual applicants.

Whilst the above judgment did not accord the trade unions all the protection that they sought, for example the Court declined to find a duty upon employers

---

[35] *Associated British Ports v Palmer; Associated Newspapers v Wilson* [1995] 2 AC 454.

[36] Conclusions XIII-3, Council of Europe, 1996.

[37] Case No 1852, 309th Report of the Freedom of Association Committee, Vol LXXXI, 1998, Series B, No 1.

to recognise particular trade unions within Article 11,[38] it demonstrated that the full-time Court was responsive to the needs of a healthy trade union system within a free-market economy. Significantly, even allowing for the 'wide'[39] margin of appreciation accorded to states in securing the Article 11 rights of trade unions, the Court was united in determining that the British government had failed to comply with its positive obligations under that Article. Indeed, by securing the passage of legislation undermining the ability of trade unions to represent their members the previous government could be viewed as having unduly favoured one side in the delicate balance of collective bargaining within the United Kingdom. The Court's willingness to find in favour of the applicants may also have been bolstered by the condemnation of the relevant domestic legal provisions by other international bodies.

ARTICLE 14: PROHIBITION OF DISCRIMINATION

The text provides that:

> The enjoyment of the rights and freedoms set forth in this Convention shall be secured without discrimination on any ground such as sex, race, colour, language, religion, political or other opinion, national or social origin, association with a national minority, property, birth or other status.

To treat persons differently according to their relevant individual circumstances

Although the original Court established, in its very early case law,[40] that this Article does not have an independent existence but is to be read in conjunction with the rights guaranteed by the other Articles, the full-time Court has developed an interpretation of Article 14 that can place a positive obligation upon states to treat persons differently. In *Thlimmenos v Greece*,[41] the applicant was a member of the Jehovah's Witnesses. Because of the pacifist beliefs of that religion he refused to wear military uniform (during his period of national service) and was consequently convicted of insubordination by a military tribunal and sentenced to four years' imprisonment in 1983. During 1988 he sat a public examination for entry to the profession of chartered accountancy. Although he passed the examination the Greek Institute of Chartered Accountants refused him admission to the profession due to his earlier military conviction. Thlimmenos complainted to the Commission alleging a breach of Article 14 in

---

[38] Above n 34 para 44.
[39] *Ibid*
[40] *"Belgian Linguistic"* case No 2 A.6 (1968).
[41] Judgment of 6 April 2000.

combination with Article 9. A large majority, twenty-two votes to six, of the Commission upheld his complaint.

The essence of the applicant's argument before the Grand Chamber was that he had been subject to discriminatory treatment by the Greek authorities as they had failed to distinguish between persons with convictions due to their religious beliefs and those with convictions for other motives. The Grand Chamber was unanimous in holding that Thlimmenos' complaint fell within the ambit of Article 9 (freedom of religion). As to whether Article 14 was applicable:

> 44. The Court has so far considered that the right under Article 14 not to be discriminated against in the enjoyment of the rights guaranteed under the Convention is violated when States treat differently persons in analogous situations without providing an objective and reasonable justification (see the *Inze* [*v Austria* A.126 (1987)] judgment, p. 18, § 41). However, the Court considers that this is not the only facet of the prohibition of discrimination in Article 14. The right not to be discriminated against in the enjoyment of the rights guaranteed under the Convention is also violated when States without an objective and reasonable justification fail to treat differently persons whose situations are significantly different.

The judges were united in determining that a criminal conviction for refusing, on religious or philosophical grounds, to wear a military uniform did not involve any form of dishonesty or moral weakness that justified exclusion from the accountancy profession. Hence the authorities failure to distinguish the applicant's criminal history from that of other felons was not justifiable and breached Article 14 in conjunction with Article 9.

The expansion of the concept of discriminatory treatment in *Thlimmenos* means that states are now under a Convention obligation to treat persons differently according to their varied circumstances when applying Convention rights. Only where the government can establish an 'objective and reasonable' explanation for ignoring material differences in an individual's situation will such a failure be compatible with Article 14. An example of a state being able to successfully provide this form of explanation occurred in the tragic case of *Pretty v United Kingdom*.[42] Mrs Pretty contended, *inter alia*, that the domestic criminal prohibition on assisted suicide discriminated against terminally ill persons who were physically unable to commit suicide without the help of others (persons who had the physical capacity were able to commit suicide and their behaviour was not *per se* unlawful). However, the Court accepted the government's submission that the complete ban on assisted suicide was to protect vulnerable persons from any form of pressure to end their lives.

> 89. Even if the principle derived from the *Thlimmenos* case is applied to the applicant's situation however, there is, in the Court's view, objective and reasonable justification for not distinguishing in law between those who are and those who are not physically capable of committing suicide. Under Article 8 of the Convention, the Court has found that there are sound reasons for not introducing in to the law

---

[42] Above ch 3 n 4.

exceptions to cater for those who are deemed not to be vulnerable. . . . The borderline between the two categories will often be a very fine one and to seek to build into the law an exemption for those judged to be incapable of committing suicide would seriously undermine the protection of life which the 1961 Act was intended to safeguard and greatly increase the risk of abuse.

Therefore, the Court was unanimous in finding no breach of Article 14 in combination with Article 8.

General conclusions

Whilst there have not been large numbers of positive obligation cases under these Articles, the jurisprudence discloses the actual or potential existence of such duties within each provision of the Convention. Furthermore, the full-time Court has identified new positive obligation under Articles 10 (*Ozgur Gundem*)[43] and 14 (*Thlimmenos*).[44] Both of these obligations on state authorities, to protect media organisations and their associates from unlawful violence and to have regard to the distinct circumstances of particular individuals when applying/observing Convention rights, are wide-ranging and may be invoked by future applicants in different contexts. Given that Articles 9, 10 and 11 overlap in their protection of beliefs and ideas it is not surprising that their respective positive obligations contain shared elements. For example, the provision of police protection may be required under positive obligations to safeguard persons' freedom of religion under Article 9 (*Otto-Preminger-Institut*), the work of the media in respect of freedom of expression under Article 10 (*Ozgur Gundem*) and the right of persons to assemble for peaceful protest under Article 11 (*Plattform*). The original Court was also rather, some might argue overly, deferential to state assessments of local needs when determining if positive obligations had been satisfied, for example in protecting Christians' religious feelings in *Wingrove* or in maintaining labour relations in *Gustafsson*. However, these Articles do not guarantee unlimited substantive rights (each allows exceptions within their second paragraphs) and they can generate complex cases where the Convention rights of different groups clash (*e.g.* the asserted artistic freedom of expression of the cinema operator and the freedom of religion of Roman Catholic believers in *Otto-Preminger-Institut*). Perhaps, it is therefore not surprising that the Court was cautious when developing and applying positive obligations in these sensitive fields of human behaviour.

[43] Above n 18.
[44] Above n 41.

8

Article 13: Right to an effective remedy

The text of this concise provision requires that:

Everyone whose rights and freedoms as set forth in this Convention are violated shall have an effective remedy before a national authority notwithstanding that the violation has been committed by persons acting in an official capacity.

To provide effective domestic remedies

Under this Article states are required to provide effective remedies before national authorities in respect of complaints made by persons that their Convention rights have been violated. The original Court explained the major principles governing this positive obligation in *Silver and Others v United Kingdom*.[1] The applicants were six prisoners and a person at liberty who contended that the stopping and delaying of their mail by prison officials, following departmental instructions, violated their right to respect for their correspondence guaranteed by Article 8. In addition they claimed that they did not have an effective domestic remedy as mandated by Article 13. The Court was united in stating that:

113. The principles that emerge from the Court's jurisprudence on the interpretation of Article 13 include the following:

    (a) where an individual has an arguable claim to be the victim of a violation of the rights set forth in the Convention, he should have a remedy before a national authority in order both to have his claim decided and, if appropriate, to obtain redress (see the above-mentioned *Klass and others* [*v* Germany] judgment, Series A no. 28, p. 29, § 64);

    (b) the authority referred to in Article 13 may not necessarily be a judicial authority but, if it is not, its powers and the guarantees which it affords are relevant in determining whether the remedy before it is effective (ibid., p. 30, § 67);

    (c) although no single remedy may itself entirely satisfy the requirements of Article 13, the aggregate of remedies provided for under domestic law may do so (see,

[1] A.61. (1983).

> *mutatis mutandis*, the above-mentioned *X v the United Kingdom* judgment,
> Series A no. 46,p. 26, § 60, and the *Van Droogenbroeck* [*v* Belgium] judgment
> of 24 June 1982, Series A no. 50, p. 32, § 56);
>
> (d) neither Article 13 nor the Convention in general lays down for the Contracting
> States any given manner for ensuring within their internal law the effective
> implementation of any of the provisions of the Convention—for example, by
> incorporating the Convention into domestic law (see the *Swedish Engine
> Drivers' Union* [*v Sweden*] judgment of 6 February 1976, Series A no. 20, p. 18,
> § 50).

It follows from the last-mentioned principle that the application of Article 13 in a
given case will depend upon the manner in which the Contracting State concerned has
chosen to discharge its obligation under Article 1 directly to secure to anyone within
its jurisdiction the rights and freedoms set out in section I (see the above-mentioned
Ireland v the United Kingdom judgment, Series A no. 25, p. 91, § 239).

Applying those norms the Court went on to conclude that there had been a
breach of Article 13 where the interferences with the applicants' mail had been
authorised by administrative rules which were incompatible with Article 8,
because they did not satisfy the condition of being 'in accordance with the law'
under Article 8(2), as neither the English courts or other non-judicial agencies
provided an effective remedy to review the operation of such rules. Of wider
importance, the principles governing the application of Article 13 articulated by
the Court in *Silver* have been followed in subsequent cases and endorsed by the
full-time Court.[2] We shall now examine how they have been developed in a
number of leading decisions.

The first principle identified in *Silver* disclosed that states are obliged to provide an effective domestic remedy where persons have an 'arguable claim' to be
the victim of a violation of Convention rights. The meaning to be ascribed to
this concept was considered by a plenary Court in another case involving prisoners' correspondence (this time concerning the Scottish prison system); *Boyle
and Rice v United Kingdom*.[3]

> 55. The Court does not think that it should give an abstract definition of the notion
> of arguability. Rather it must be determined, in the light of the particular facts and the
> nature of the legal issue or issues raised, whether each individual claim of violation
> forming the basis of a complaint under Article 13 was arguable and, if so, whether the
> requirements of Article 13 were met in relation thereto.

Consequently, the Court will make an assessment of whether specific applicant's claims have satisfied this requirement according to the circumstances of
each case. Obviously, the stronger the legal and evidential elements of the claim
are the greater the likelihood that it will meet the arguable claim standard. In
practical terms applicants need to ensure that they have at least a *prima facie*
case of a violation of Convention rights.[4]

[2] For example, in *Kudla v Poland* (26 October 2000) para 157.
[3] A.131 (1988).
[4] *Ibid* para 54.

The second principle in *Silver* revealed that states could satisfy their obligation to provide an effective domestic remedy through the availability of suitable non-judicial agencies. However, the powers and institutional features of non-judicial bodies were crucial in determining whether particular agencies provided an effective remedy. Regarding the powers of non-judicial bodies the judgment in *Silver* noted that the Parliamentary Commissioner for Administration (Parliamentary Ombudsman) did not have the power to make legally binding decisions granting redress to successful complainants, therefore the Court determined that the Ombudsman was not an 'effective remedy' for the purposes of Article 13.[5] Hence, non-judicial bodies that only possess advisory powers are very unlikely to be classified as an effective remedy by the Court, even when they are accorded great respect in the national administrative system.[6] Also, the further the procedures followed by a non-judicial body depart from those of ordinary courts the more likely the Court is to conclude that the particular body is not an effective remedy. For example, in *Chahal v United Kingdom*,[7] the failure of the advisory panel (a body, set up by the Home Secretary, to which prospective national security deportees could make representations) to allow Chahal legal representation and to only provide him with an outline of the grounds for his deportation led the Court to determine that the panel offered insufficient procedural safeguards for applicants and therefore did not constitute an effective remedy.[8] The full-time Court has ruled that if a non-judicial body lacks independence from the government it will not satisfy this element of Article 13. So the numerous influences of the Home Secretary over the Police Complaints Authority (a body responsible for overseeing serious complaints against the police in England and Wales) including appointing, remunerating and dismissing the members of the Authority and promulgating formal guidance to the Authority concerning the preferring of disciplinary or criminal charges against police officers resulted in the Court finding that the Authority did not provide an effective remedy.[9] These cases show that the Court has strictly examined the powers, procedures and independence of non-judicial bodies when evaluating if they provide effective remedies under Article 13.

The third principle articulated in *Silver* enables states to comply with their obligation to provide an effective domestic remedy via a combination of distinct methods of redress. The British authorities successfully invoked the principle in that case to satisfy the Court that prisoners' ability to petition the Home Secretary alleging prison officials were misapplying departmental instructions

---

[5] Above n 1 para 115. The full-time Court reached a similar conclusion in respect of the former Commissioner for Local Administration in Scotland (Local Ombudsman) in *E v UK* (26 November 2002) para 112.

[6] On the Parliamentary Ombudsman see, S Bailey, B Jones and A Mowbray, *Cases and Materials on Administrative Law*, 3rd edn (London, Sweet & Maxwell, 1997) ch 4.

[7] 1996-V.

[8] *Ibid* para 154.

[9] In *Khan v UK* (12 May 2000). Note, that Part 2 of the Police Reform Act 2002 provides for the establishment of a new Independent Police Complaints Commission.

(that were compatible with the Convention) coupled with the supervisory powers of the domestic courts amounted to an effective remedy.[10] In contemporary times the full-time Court has displayed a more rigorous scrutiny of aggregations of remedies. For example, in *Paul and Audrey Edwards v United Kingdom*,[11] the applicants complained, *inter alia*, that they had suffered a breach of Article 13 in respect of their inability to secure domestic redress concerning the killing of their son by a fellow prisoner. The government responded that it had complied with its obligations under Article 13 by providing a combination of remedies including an inquiry into the killing and the possibility of the applicants suing the prison authorities for negligence. The Court, unanimously, found that this combination of remedies did not satisfy Article 13, because of major procedural defects in the inquiry (it lacked the power to compel the attendance of witnesses and the applicants were not allowed to participate adequately in its proceedings) and the courts would not have been able to order the payment of compensation for the non-pecuniary damage suffered by the son.

Both the original and full-time Court have consistently emphasised that the requirement for domestic remedies to be effective does not mean that they have to guarantee complainants a favourable outcome.[12] A more challenging issue for the Court has been in assessing the effectiveness of domestic remedies in cases involving matters of national security. The original Court applied a tolerant form of scrutiny to domestic remedies in respect of complaints concerning secret checks on the background of persons having access to military facilities in *Leander v Sweden*.[13] The Court held that:

> 78. . . . For the purposes of the present proceedings, an 'effective remedy' under Article 13 must mean a remedy that is as effective as can be having regard to the restricted scope for recourse inherent in any system of secret checks on candidates for employment in posts of importance from a national security point of view.

A bare majority of the judges, four votes to three, concluded that the aggregate of remedies available to Leander, including complaints to the Chancellor of Justice and the Parliamentary Ombudsman, satisfied this modified standard of effectiveness. However, in the later case of *Chahal*,[14] a united Grand Chamber declined to apply the *Leander* test to domestic remedies concerning alleged breaches of Article 3 occurring in the context of national security considerations.

> 150. . . . The requirement of a remedy which is 'as effective as can be' is not appropriate in respect of a complaint that a person's deportation will expose him or her to a real risk of treatment in breach of Article 3, where the issues concerning national security are immaterial.

[10] Above n 1 para 118.
[11] Judgment of 14 March 2002 and for the art 2 aspects of the case see above ch 2 n 20.
[12] See eg *Kudla* above n 2 para 157.
[13] A.116 (1987).
[14] Above n 7.

151. In such cases, given the irreversible nature of the harm that might occur if the risk of ill-treatment materialised and the importance the Court attaches to Article 3, the notion of an effective remedy under Article 13 requires independent scrutiny of the claim that there exist substantial grounds for fearing a real risk of treatment contrary to Article 3. This scrutiny must be carried out without regard to what the person may have done to warrant expulsion or to any perceived threat to the national security of the expelling State.

As we have seen above, the Court determined, *inter alia*, that the applicant's right to make representations to the advisory panel did not constitute an effective remedy. This judgment demonstrated that the Court would utilise differential standards when evaluating the effectiveness of domestic remedies in national security cases according to the specific Convention right(s) alleged to have been violated.

The full-time Court did not invoke the *Leander* standard to assess the efficacy of domestic remedies in respect of breaches of military personnel's right to privacy, under Article 8, in *Smith and Grady v United Kingdom*.[15] The judges were unanimous in finding that the high threshold of judicial review, under the principle of 'irrationality' governing decisions involving matters of national security, applied by the English courts to determine the applicants' complaints denied them an 'effective remedy' for the purposes of Article 13.[16]

In the more recent case of *Al-Nashif v Bulgaria*,[17] the Court accepted that limitations on the types of domestic remedies available to individuals may be justified in complaints concerning secret surveillance and security checks on applicants for sensitive forms of employment. However, Article 13 required that there must be remedies which are practically effective.

137. The Court considers that in cases of the expulsion of aliens on grounds of national security—as here—reconciling the interest of preserving sensitive information with the individual's right to an effective remedy is obviously less difficult than in the above-mentioned cases where the system of secret surveillance or secret checks could only function if the individual remained unaware of the measures affecting him.

While procedural restrictions may be necessary to ensure that no leakage detrimental to national security would occur and while any independent authority dealing with an appeal against a deportation decision may need to afford a wide margin of appreciation to the executive in matters of national security, that can by no means justify doing away with remedies altogether whenever the executive has chosen to invoke the term 'national security' (see the above cited *Chahal* judgment and paragraph 96 above on possible ways of reconciling the relevant interests involved).

Even where an allegation of a threat to national security is made, the guarantee of an effective remedy requires as a minimum that the competent independent appeals authority must be informed of the reasons grounding the deportation decision, even if such reasons are not publicly available. The authority must be competent to reject the executive's assertion that there is a threat to national security where it finds it arbitrary

---

[15] Judgment of 27 September 1999.
[16] *Ibid* para 138.
[17] Judgment of 20 June 2002.

or unreasonable. There must be some form of adversarial proceedings, if need be through a special representative after a security clearance. Furthermore, the question whether the impugned measure would interfere with the individual's right to respect for family life and, if so, whether a fair balance is struck between the public interest involved and the individual's rights must be examined.

Because the Bulgarian courts had refused to subject the decision to deport Mr Al-Nashif to judicial review, as the Passport Department had certified that he had committed acts against national security, the Court, by four votes to three,[18] concluded that there had been a breach of Article 13. This judgment shows that the contemporary Court is now defining the basic elements of effective remedies in national security cases more elaborately.

An effective domestic remedy to determine complaints regarding unreasonable delays in civil and criminal proceedings

As we have examined in a previous chapter[19] one of the major problems facing the Court in recent years has been the vast number of cases involving allegations of breaches of the right to the determination of civil and criminal proceedings within a reasonable time by national legal systems (Article 6(1)). The full-time Court responded[20] to this challenge by establishing a new obligation upon states to provide an effective means of domestic redress for these complaints in *Kudla v Poland*.[21] The applicant contended that the determination of fraud charges against him were still continuing after nine years. The Grand Chamber unanimously decided that he had suffered a violation of Article 6(1). Although the original Court had previously held that where a breach of the reasonable time obligation under Article 6(1) had been found it was not necessary to also consider an alleged violation of Article 13,[22] the Grand Chamber, by sixteen votes to one, decided that it was appropriate to 'review'[23] the existing case law. In the assessment of the overwhelming majority:

> 155. If Article 13 is, as the Government argued, to be interpreted as having no application to the right to a hearing within a reasonable time as safeguarded by Article 6 § 1, individuals will systematically be forced to refer to the Court in Strasbourg complaints that would otherwise, and in the Court's opinion more appropriately, have to be addressed in the first place within the national legal system. In the long term the

---

[18] Note, the dissenters considered that Mr Al-Nashif did not have an arguable claim that his deportation violated art 8 and therefore art 13 was not applicable.

[19] Above ch 5.

[20] The member states are also engaged in an ongoing programme to consider revisions to the Convention in order to maintain the effectiveness of the Court, see eg The Committee of Ministers' Declaration on 'The European Court of Human Rights' at the 111th Session of the Committee of Ministers (Strasbourg, 6–7 November 2002).

[21] Above n 2.

[22] For example in *Pizzetti v Italy* A.257-C (1993).

[23] Above n 2 para 148.

effective functioning, on both the national and international level, of the scheme of human rights protection set up by the Convention is liable to be weakened.

Therefore, Article 13 was to be interpreted as obliging states to provide effective remedies for unreasonable delay complaints. The Polish legal system did not offer such a remedy, consequently Kudla's rights under Article 13 had been breached.

Judge Casadevall dissented in *Kudla* as he considered that the Court's new interpretation of Article 13 smacked 'more of expediency than of law.'[24] He also feared that complainants would suffer further delays and complications in seeking to have their civil or criminal proceedings determined speedily, as they would now be obliged to invoke Article 13 before their domestic courts, prior to taking their complaints of delay to Strasbourg. Despite these reservations later Chambers have followed the approach of the majority in *Kudla*. Examples include *Nuvoli v Italy*,[25] where the Court found that the applicant had no domestic remedy to complain about delays of nearly three and a half years in criminal proceedings against him resulting in the Court, unanimously, finding a breach of Article 13 (and of Article 6(1)); and *Rados and Others v Croatia*,[26] where the Court (unanimously) concluded that some of the applicants had suffered breaches of Article 13 as they had not had access to an effective domestic remedy in respect of delays of three to four years in civil proceedings that they had initiated.

The decision of the Court in *Kudla,* to reverse the jurisprudence of its predecessor and recognise this new duty upon states, is a fascinating example of a positive obligation being developed, in part, because of the practical needs of the Strasbourg Court. Although this re-interpretation of Article 13 can be justified in terms of the principle of subsidiarity,[27] namely that the primary responsibility for safeguarding Convention rights rests with the member states, it was also motivated by the case-load crisis facing the Court. So far, it appears that the application of this new obligation has not produced a noticeable reduction in the number of complaints alleging breaches of the reasonable time guarantee within Article 6(1). Though we should note that in both the *Nuvoli* and *Rados* judgments the Court made references to subsequent domestic legislation establishing new remedies to deal with complaints of delay in the Italian and Croatian legal systems.

Obligations of effective investigations

Paralleling the duties upon member states to undertake prompt and effective investigations into killings, serious ill-treatment of persons by state agents and

---

[24] *Ibid* Partly Dissenting Opinion of Judge Casadevall para 3.
[25] Judgment of 16 May 2002.
[26] Judgment of 7 November 2002.
[27] Above n 2 para 152.

allegations regarding the disappearances of detainees under Articles 2, 3, and 5;[28] the Court has also created analogous forms of positive obligations under Article 13. We shall, therefore, examine the scope and content of the duties arising under Article 13 and their relationships with the obligations under the substantive Articles.

First, in respect of Article 13 complaints concerning alleged unlawful killings in breach of Article 2 a Chamber, by eight votes to one, established such a positive obligation in *Kaya v Turkey*.[29] The Court held that:

> 107. In the instant case the applicant is complaining that he and the next-of-kin have been denied an 'effective' remedy which would have brought to light the true circumstances surrounding the killing of Abdülmenaf Kaya. In the view of the Court the nature of the right which the authorities are alleged to have violated in the instant case, one of the most fundamental in the scheme of the Convention, must have implications for the nature of the remedies which must be guaranteed for the benefit of the relatives of the victim. In particular, where those relatives have an arguable claim that the victim has been unlawfully killed by agents of the State, the notion of an effective remedy for the purposes of Article 13 entails, in addition to the payment of compensation where appropriate, a thorough and effective investigation capable of leading to the identification and punishment of those responsible and including effective access for the relatives to the investigatory procedure . . . Seen in these terms the requirements of Article 13 are broader than a Contracting State's procedural obligation under Article 2 to conduct an effective investigation.

Hence according to the majority where persons have an arguable claim, even if that contention is not ultimately upheld by the Court, that a relative has been killed in breach of Article 2 by state agents there is an obligation under Article 13 for the state to undertake a rigorous investigation. This duty of investigation is distinct from that under Article 2. Indeed, the Court went on to find that the inquiries into the death of the applicant's brother failed to comply with the requirements of both Articles 2 and 13. The Chamber also indicated that the Article 13 obligations were 'broader' than the procedural duties derived from Article 2. Presumably this is because the former Article may demand that the state pay compensation to be victim's family in addition to conducting an effective investigation into the circumstances of the killing. Judge Golcuklu, the Turkish judge, dissented as he did not consider that the applicant's complaints raised a separate issue under Article 13.

The relationship between inquiry obligations under Articles 2 and 13 was considered further in *Ergi v Turkey*.[30] The Commission decided that as it had found that there had been a violation of Article 2, due to the inadequate investigation into the killing of the applicant's sister, it was unnecessary to examine whether there had also been a breach of Article 13. Before the Court, the applicant argued that the two obligations were 'not conterminous'. In his opinion,

---

[28] Above chs 2–4.
[29] 1998-I.
[30] 1998-IV.

'[t]he scope of the Article 2 obligation was limited to what had occurred whereas that under Article 13 required not only an effective investigation but also that the system of securing the remedy be effective.'[31] A majority of the Chamber, eight votes to one, agreed with the applicant:

> . . . [t]he Court recalls its findings . . . that the authorities failed to carry out an effective investigation into the circumstances surrounding the death of Havva Ergi. In the view of the Court, this failure undermined the exercise of any remedies the applicant and his niece had at their disposal under Turkish law. Accordingly, it finds that there has been a violation of Article 13 of the Convention.[32]

Under this approach the duty of effective investigation under Article 13 is to be seen as an integral element of the general obligation of member states to provide effective domestic remedies for alleged breaches of the Convention. However, Judge Golcuklu maintained his dissenting belief that where a breach of an obligation of effective investigation had been found under another Convention Article a separate claim under Article 13 did not arise.

A few months later another Chamber[33] held that the inquiry duty under Article 13 was more onerous than the obligation under Article 2, in *Yasa v Turkey*.[34] A majority of the Chamber, Judge Golcuklu again being the dissentient, determined that after five years there had been 'no concrete and credible progress' made by the Turkish authorities in their inquiries into the shooting of the applicant and the killing of his uncle. Consequently, Turkey was in breach of its procedural duty under Article 2. Also, '. . . the respondent State cannot be considered to have conducted an effective criminal investigation as required by Article 13, the requirements of which are stricter still than the investigatory obligation under Article 2 . . .'[35] Sadly, the Court did not expand on the ways in which the Article 13 demands were more stringent.

A united Chamber of the full-time Court found separate breaches of the investigation obligations under Articles 2 and 13 in *Velikova v Bulgaria*.[36] Regarding the latter duty:

> 89. The Court recalls that Article 13 of the Convention guarantees the availability at the national level of a remedy to enforce the substance of the Convention rights and freedoms in whatever form they might happen to be secured in the domestic legal order. The scope of the obligation under Article 13 also varies depending on the nature of the applicant's complaint under the Convention. Nevertheless, the remedy required by Article 13 must be 'effective' in practice as well as in law, in particular in the sense that its exercise must not be unjustifiably hindered by the acts or omissions of the authorities of the respondent State.

---

[31] *Ibid* para 94.
[32] *Ibid* para 98.
[33] Presided over by Judge Bernhardt accompanied by Judges Golcuklu and Wildhaber from the Chamber that determined Ergi.
[34] 1998-VI.
[35] *Ibid* para 115.
[36] Judgment of 18 May 2000.

A violation of Article 2 cannot be remedied exclusively through an award of damages (see the *Kaya v Turkey* judgment of 19 February 1998, *Reports* 1998-I, p. 329, § 105). Given the fundamental importance of the right to protection of life, Article 13 imposes, without prejudice to any other remedy available under the domestic system, an obligation on States to carry out a thorough and effective investigation likely to lead to those responsible being identified and punished and in which the complainant has effective access to the investigation proceedings . . .

In the light of the Court's finding of basic failings in the Bulgarian investigations, including the lack of questioning of key witnesses, the judges determined that those defects had undermined the effectiveness of the applicant's domestic remedies and constituted a violation of Article 13.

Another Chamber sought to distinguish between states' investigation and compensation obligations under Article 13 in *Kelly and Others v The United Kingdom*.[37] The applicants contended, *inter alia*, that they had suffered violations of Article 13 in respect of their complaints that their relatives had been killed by the security forces during a counter-terrorist operation at Loughgall in Northern Ireland. The judges were unanimous in holding that:

154. In cases of the use of lethal force or suspicious deaths, the Court has also stated that, given the fundamental importance of the right to the protection of life, Article 13 requires, in addition to the payment of compensation where appropriate, a thorough and effective investigation capable of leading to the identification and punishment of those responsible for the deprivation of life, including effective access for the complainant to the investigation procedure (see the *Kaya v Turkey* judgment cited above, pp. 330–31, § 107). In a number of cases it has found that there has been a violation of Article 13 where no effective criminal investigation had been carried out, noting that the requirements of Article 13 were broader than the obligation to investigate imposed by Article 2 of the Convention (see also *Ergi v Turkey* . . .).

155. It must be observed that these cases derived from the situation pertaining in south-east Turkey, where applicants were in a vulnerable position due to the ongoing conflict between the security forces and the PKK and where the most accessible means of redress open to applicants was to complain to the public prosecutor, who was under a duty to investigate alleged crimes. In the Turkish system, the complainant was able to join any criminal proceedings as an intervenor and apply for damages at the conclusion of any successful prosecution. The public prosecutor's fact-finding function was also essential to any attempt to take civil proceedings. In those cases, therefore, it was sufficient for the purposes of former Article 26 (now Article 35 § 1) of the Convention, that an applicant complaining of unlawful killing raised the matter with the public prosecutor. There was accordingly a close procedural and practical relationship between the criminal investigation and the remedies available to the applicant in the legal system as a whole.

156. The legal system pertaining in Northern Ireland is different and any application of Article 13 to the factual circumstances of any case from that jurisdiction must take this into account. An applicant who claims the unlawful use of force by soldiers or

---

[37] Judgment of 4 May 2001. The same Chamber gave identical rulings in the simultaneous cases of *McKerr v UK*, *Hugh Jordan v UK* and *Shanaghan v UK*.

police officers in the United Kingdom must as a general rule exhaust the domestic remedies open to him or her by taking civil proceedings by which the courts will examine the facts, determine liability and if appropriate award compensation. These civil proceedings are wholly independent of any criminal investigation and their efficacy has not been shown to rely on the proper conduct of criminal investigations or prosecutions (see e.g. *Caraher v the United Kingdom*, no. 24520/94, decision of inadmissibility [Section 3] 11.01.00).

157. In the present case, seven of the applicants lodged civil proceedings, of which five are still pending, the Hughes family having settled their claims and another family having ceased to pursue their claims. Two families did not consider that it was worthwhile bringing such proceedings. The Court has found no elements which would prevent civil proceedings providing the redress identified above in respect of the alleged excessive use of force . . .

158. As regards the applicants' complaints concerning the investigation into the death carried out by the authorities, these have been examined above under the procedural aspect of Article 2. . . . The Court finds that no separate issue arises in the present case.

159. The Court concludes that there has been no violation of Article 13 of the Convention.

The above judgment indicates that the Court's assessment of the efficacy of domestic compensation proceedings will take account of the institutional arrangements of the respondent state's legal system. Where civil actions, separate from criminal investigations, are available to victims' families then normally the latter must avail themselves of these remedies before seeking to bring a case at Strasbourg.[38] However, the Court's unwillingness to consider if the investigations into the killings of the applicants' relatives were effective for the purposes of Article 13 was not adequately explained. As we have already discovered in the earlier case law the Court (with the exception of Judge Golcuklu) continually emphasised that in respect of killings Article 13 requires both compensation and effective investigations by domestic authorities. Furthermore, the Court stated in *Yasa* that the investigation obligations under Article 13 were more strict than those arising under Article 2. Hence, it could have been expected that the Court would have found the actual investigations to have failed to meet the requirements of Article 13, as they had already been determined to be inadequate under Article 2.

Secondly, regarding Article 13 complaints involving alleged breaches of Article 3 the Court found a duty of investigation in *Aksoy v Turkey*.[39]

98. The nature of the right safeguarded under Article 3 of the Convention has implications for Article 13. Given the fundamental importance of the prohibition of torture . . . and the especially vulnerable position of torture victims, Article 13 imposes, without prejudice to any other remedy available under the domestic system, an obligation on States to carry out a thorough and effective investigation of incidents of torture.

---

[38] Note, a similar ruling was applied in the later case of *McShane v UK* (28 May 2002).
[39] 1996-VI 2287.

Accordingly, as regards Article 13, where an individual has an arguable claim that he has been tortured by agents of the State, the notion of an effective remedy entails, in addition to the payment of compensation where appropriate, a thorough and effective investigation capable of leading to the identification and punishment of those responsible and including effective access for the complainant to the investigatory procedure. It is true that no express provision exists in the Convention such as can be found in Article 12 of the 1984 United Nations Convention against Torture and Other Cruel, Inhuman or Degrading Treatment or Punishment, which imposes a duty to proceed to a 'prompt and impartial' investigation whenever there is a reasonable ground to believe that an act of torture has been committed. However, in the Court's view, such a requirement is implicit in the notion of an 'effective remedy' under Article 13 . . .

Taking note of the public prosecutor's failure to enquire into the paralysis of Aksoy's arms when he was brought from police detention, the Chamber, by eight votes to one,[40] concluded that the lack of investigation by the Turkish authorities into Aksoy's injuries violated the Article 13 effective investigation obligation.

A Grand Chamber of the Court approved the *Aksoy* reasoning and definition of the nature of the investigation duty in *Aydin v Turkey*.[41] The Court, by sixteen votes to five,[42] determined that there had not been a thorough investigation of the applicant's allegations of rape and other forms of torture by state agents. The majority was particularly critical of the public prosecutor's deferential attitude towards members of the security forces and the conduct of the medical examinations he arranged.

107. It would appear that his primary concern in ordering three medical examinations in a rapid succession was to establish whether the applicant had lost her virginity. The focus of the examinations should really have been on whether the applicant was a rape victim, which was the very essence of her complaint. In this respect it is to be noted that neither [of the doctors who performed the examinations] had any particular experience of dealing with rape victims . . .

The Court notes that the requirements of a thorough and effective investigation into an allegation of rape in custody at the hands of a State official also implies that the victim be examined, with all appropriate sensitivity, by medical professionals with particular competence in this area and whose independence is not circumscribed by instructions given by the prosecuting authority as to the scope of the examination. It cannot be concluded that the medical examinations ordered by the public prosecutor fulfilled this requirement.

Consequently, these defects undermined any domestic remedies available to the applicant and a violation of Article 13 had occurred.

---

[40] Note, Judge Golcuklu dissented as he considered that domestic remedies had not been exhausted

[41] 1997-VI 1889.

[42] Judges Golcuklu, Pettiti, De Meyer, Lopes Rocha and Gotchev dissented as they considered that although there were 'manifest shortcomings' in the prosecutor's investigations, the applicant's conduct, such as disappearing from the region where the events had allegedly taken place, meant that she had not exhausted domestic remedies.

The circumstances in which an obligation of investigation arises under Article 13 were broadened by a unanimous Chamber in *Assenov and Others v Bulgaria*.[43]

> 117. . . . Where an individual has an arguable claim that he has been ill-treated in breach of Article 3, the notion of an effective remedy entails, in addition to a thorough and effective investigation of the kind also required by Article 3. . . . effective access for the complainant to the investigatory procedure and the payment of compensation where appropriate . . .

The Court found that, *inter alia*, the initial military prosecution investigations into Assenov's treatment by the police were 'cursory' and therefore a violation of Article 13 had occurred. This widening of the duty to undertake effective inquiries where an arguable claim of any type of Article 3 maltreatment (*i.e.* torture, inhuman or degrading treatment/punishment) has been made is to be welcomed as there is no reason for limiting it to complaints of torture. It is also important that arguable claims of inhuman or degrading treatment/punishment inflicted by state agents be thoroughly investigated in order to punish the perpetrators and deter others from engaging in similar misbehaviour.

Subsequently a unanimous Grand Chamber of the full-time Court also endorsed a similar broadening of this investigation obligation in *Ilhan v Turkey*.[44] The Court held that states were under a duty to undertake effective investigations, '[w]here an individual has an arguable claim that he has been tortured or subjected to serious ill-treatment by the State . . .'[45] In this case the Court had already found Turkey liable for torture due to the serious head injuries inflicted during the arrest of the applicant's brother and the delay of thirty-six hours before he received medical treatment. Therefore, the victim had an arguable claim for the purposes of Article 13. The Court found significant defects in the Turkish investigations, including significant discrepancies in the gendarmes reports of the arrest and the prosecutor's failure to interview key witnesses.

> 103. For these reasons, no effective criminal investigation can be considered to have been conducted in accordance with Article 13. The Court finds therefore that no effecive remedy has been provided in respect of Abdullatif Ilhan's injuries and thereby access to any other available remedies, including a claim for compensation, has also been denied.
>
> Consequently, there has been a violation of Article 13 of the Convention.

Another Grand Chamber has indicated that states may not always be obliged to conduct Article 13 investigations where the allegation is that public bodies have failed to protect persons from infringements of their basic Convention rights by other private persons. The four teenage applicants in *Z. and Others v*

---

[43] 1998-VIII.
[44] Judgment of 27 June 2000.
[45] *Ibid* para 97.

The United Kingdom,[46] complained, *inter alia*, that the responsible local authority had failed to take adequate protective measures, over several years, in respect of serious abuse and neglect by their parents. The Grand Chamber stated that:

> 109. The Court has previously held that where a right with as fundamental an importance as the right to life or the prohibition against torture, inhuman and degrading treatment is at stake, Article 13 requires, in addition to the payment of compensation where appropriate, a thorough and effective investigation capable of leading to the identification and punishment of those responsible, including effective access for the complainant to the investigation procedure (see the *Kaya v Turkey* judgment . . .). These cases however concerned alleged killings or infliction of treatment contrary to Article 3 involving potential criminal responsibility on the part of security force officials. Where alleged failure by the authorities to protect persons from the acts of others is concerned, Article 13 may not always require that the authorities undertake the responsibility for investigating the allegations. There should however be available to the victim or the victim's family a mechanism for establishing any liability of State officials or bodies for acts or omissions involving the breach of their rights under the Convention. Furthermore, in the case of a breach of Articles 2 and 3 of the Convention, which rank as the most fundamental provisions of the Convention, compensation for the non-pecuniary damage flowing from the breach should in principle be available as part of the range of redress.

By fifteen votes to two, the Court determined that the applicants did not have such a means of redress available to them and consequently there had been a breach of Article 13. An explanation for this limitation of the investigation duty under Article 13 may be that states' positive obligation, under Article 3, to protect persons from torture, inhuman or degrading treatment inflicted by other private persons encompasses the investigation and prosecution of such perpetrators.[47]

Thirdly, in respect of Article 13 complaints involving allegations of forced disappearances of persons in breach of Article 5, the Court recognised a duty of investigation under the former Article in *Kurt v Turkey*.[48]

> 140. . . . In the view of the Court, where the relatives of a person have an arguable claim that the latter has disappeared at the hands of the authorities, the notion of an effective remedy for the purposes of Article 13 entails, in addition to the payment of compensation where appropriate, a thorough and effective investigation capable of leading to the identification and punishment of those responsible and including effective access for the relatives to the investigatory procedure (see, *mutatis mutandis*, the . . . *Aksoy*, *Aydin* and *Kaya* judgments . . .). Seen in these terms, the requirements of Article 13 are broader than a Contracting State's obligation under Article 5 to conduct an effective investigation into the disappearance of a person who has been shown to be under their control and for whose welfare they are accordingly responsible.

---

[46] Judgment of 10 May 2001.
[47] See, *A v UK* above ch 3.
[48] 1998-III 1187.

By seven votes to two the Court determined that there had been a breach of this duty as there had been no 'meaningful' investigation by the public prosecutor into the applicant's petitions that the whereabouts of her son was unknown since he was last seen (five years ago) surrounded by security personnel.

In later cases[49] the Court has applied the above definition of the effective investigation obligation to find breaches of Article 13 in the context of disappeared persons. Judge Golcuklu, sitting as an *ad hoc* judge in Turkish cases determined by the full time Court, regularly dissented on the ground that when the Court has already found a violation of a duty of effective investigation under other Articles (*e.g.* Article 2) no separate issue arises under Article 13. For instance in *Akdeniz and Others v Turkey*,[50] the Court concluded, *inter alia*, that there had been breaches of Articles 2, 5 and 13 due to the lack of effective investigations into the forced disappearances of the applicants' eleven relatives. In his dissenting opinion Judge Golcuklu cited the Court's judgments in *Kelly and Others* and the related Northern Irish cases[51] to support the view that once a breach of a Convention investigation obligation has been found there is no requirement to consider the issue again under Article 13.

In conclusion we can note that the Court has developed an expanding range of investigation obligations under Article 13. The justifications for recognising these duties are the importance of the substantive rights involved (*e.g.* the right to life in *Kaya* and the prohibition of torture in *Aksoy*), together with the vulnerability of the alleged victims *vis-à-vis* state agents. However, the Court has been opaque in referring, in *Yasa*, to the 'stricter' investigation duty under this Article compared with the inquiry obligation under Article 2. The Court did not explain in what ways the former duty was more demanding of states. Indeed, as we have already considered,[52] the institutional and procedural requirements for inquiries under Article 2 are stringent. Also the Court has on a number of occasions (*e.g.* in *Velikova* and *Yasa*) referred back to its earlier findings of breaches of the investigation duty under Article 2 to support its determinations that the similar duty under Article 13 has been violated in the same case. Another ambiguity in the Article 13 cases relates to the circumstances where the Court is willing to examine whether there has been an effective investigation under both substantive Articles (*i.e.* Articles 2, 3 or 5) and Article 13. Judge Golcuklu has regularly dissented on the ground that once the Court has found a breach of the investigation obligation under the former Articles that excludes the need to reconsider the issue under Article 13. Furthermore, the Chamber determining the Northern Irish cases (*Kelly et al.*) ruled that no separate issue arose under Article 13. What appears to be decisive for the Court, although it is not always clearly stated, is whether the lack of an effective investigation undermined the possibility of the complainant invoking any other

---

[49] For example, *Tas v Turkey* (14 November 2000) and *Sarli v Turkey* (22 May 2001).
[50] Judgment of 31 May 2001.
[51] Examined above n 37.
[52] Above ch 2.

domestic remedy (*e.g.* to claim compensation for the killing or serious mal-treatment of his/her relative by state personnel).[53] Where an effective investigation is the crucial foundation for other remedies then the Court is likely to examine the issue under Article 13, in addition to applying the analogous inquiry obligations under the substantive Articles, (as in *Akdeniz*).

General conclusions

Recent times have witnessed a significant expansion in the range of positive obligations recognised by the Court under Article 13. During the last three years of the original Court's existence the judges initiated the development of effective investigation obligations under Article 13 in respect of alleged breaches of Articles 2, 3 and 5 (*e.g.* in *Kaya*,[54] *Aksoy*[55] and *Kurt*[56]). A process which has been continued, not always in a fully clear manner, by the full-time Court (*e.g.* in *Kelly and Others*[57]). The latter Court has also articulated (in *Kudla*[58]) the new obligation upon states to provide an effective domestic remedy to deal with complaints of alleged unreasonable delays in civil and criminal proceedings. Furthermore, in contemporary times the Court has become more rigorous in its scrutiny of the effectiveness of domestic remedies in areas of national security decision-making (*e.g.* in *Smith and Grady*[59]). Therefore, Article 13 is an increasingly important source of institutional positive obligations.

---

[53] The Court explicitly linked the two in *Anguelova v Bulgaria* (13 June 2002) para 162.
[54] Above n 29.
[55] Above n 39.
[56] Above n 48.
[57] Above n 37.
[58] Above n 2.
[59] Above n 15.

9

Conclusions

⟶◦⟵

As we saw in *Plattform*[1] the Court has not articulated a general theory regarding positive obligations under the Convention. However, where the Court has developed implied positive obligations across a number of substantive Articles a common justification for this judicial creativity has been to ensure that the relevant rights are 'practical and effective' in their exercise. Examples of this explanation being proffered include the creation of the obligation upon states, under Article 2, to conduct effective investigations into deaths caused by public officials and private persons so as to deter unlawful killings (*Ilhan*)[2]; the obligation for states to enact criminal law prohibitions against the sexual abuse of mentally handicapped persons in order to effectively deter such abuse and respect their private lives under Article 8 (*X. & Y. v Netherlands*)[3]; the obligation upon states to protect media organisations and their personnel from acts of violence designed to inhibit freedom of expression guaranteed by Article 10 (*Ozgur Gundem*)[4] and the obligation for states to deploy appropriate police resources to protect lawful demonstrators' right to freedom of peaceful assembly, under Article 11, from violent opponents (*Plattform*).[5] In these diverse situations the Court concluded that various forms of positive action (encompassing procedural/institutional duties to undertake rigorous investigations, obligations to amend domestic laws and the deployment of police and security personnel) were required of states to ensure that specific Convention rights were effectively safeguarded. This approach by the Court demonstrates that it expects states to be active in the guaranteeing of Convention rights. Passive non-interference by governmental authorities with persons' Convention rights is not sufficient to ensure that many of those rights are fully and effectively respected. Hence, Professor Merills' linking of the principle of effectiveness with the development of positive obligations has been confirmed by the subsequent jurisprudence.[6]

We must also appreciate, though it is not always clearly stated in the case law, that the needs of the Court have been another factor motivating the

---

[1] *Plattform "Arzte fur das Leben" v Austria* A.139 (1988) above ch 7 n 24.
[2] *Ilhan v Turkey* (27 June 2000), above ch 2 n 43.
[3] A.91 (1985), above ch 6 n 2.
[4] Judgment of 16 March 2000, above ch 7 n 18.
[5] Above n 1.
[6] Above ch 1 n 24.

development of positive obligations. For example, the Report of the Evaluation Group[7] indicated that the Court's desire to minimise the use of time-consuming and expensive fact-finding missions to examine specific complaints had been achieved, in part, by imposing positive obligations to conduct effective investigations into killings/ill-treatment/disappearances on states. Likewise, the full-time Court's establishment of an obligation upon states to provide an effective domestic remedy to deal with complaints of unreasonable delays in civil and criminal proceedings (*Kudla*)[8] was partly inspired by the wish to reduce the overwhelming number of cases being lodged at Strasbourg alleging a breach of the reasonable time guarantee enshrined in Article 6(1).

The dominant group of positive obligations expressly imposed upon states, by the text of the Convention, encountered in this study were concerned with different stages of the criminal justice system.[9] They required, *inter alia*, arrested person to be informed of the reasons for their arrest (Article 5(2)), detained suspects to be brought promptly before a judge to determine whether they should be granted bail or held on remand (Article 5(3)), charged persons to be provided with detailed information concerning the accusations against them (Article 6(3)(a)), impecunious defendants to be provided with free legal assistance when they were facing serious charges (Article 6(3)(c)), the provision of free interpretation services where defendants could not understand the language of the domestic court (Article 6(3)(e)) and the determination of charges by a fair trial within a reasonable time resulting in a public judgment (Article 6(1)). As with implied positive obligations, the Court's jurisprudence regarding express obligations demonstrates substantial creativity. Examples include the expansion of the obligation under Article 5(2) to provide an explanation of the grounds of detention to persons being held under civil law powers (*e.g.* psychiatric patients in *Van de Leer*);[10] the articulation of an obligation under Article 5(4) for judicial bodies to conduct regular reviews of the need for the continued detention of persons, such as psychiatric patients or prisoners subject to indeterminate sentences, whose personalities are liable to change over time (*Winterwerp*);[11] and the requirement that states consider requests for the provision of free legal assistance in respect of crucial pre-trial proceedings (*Berlinski*).[12]

If we look beyond the Court's jurisprudence we can find a more theoretical explanation for states' positive obligations regarding Convention rights in the writings of Professor Shue.[13] He has sought to rebut the traditional distinction

---

[7] Above ch 2 n 44.

[8] *Kudla v Poland* (26 October 2000), above ch 8 n 21.

[9] Above chs 4–5. More generally see, A Ashworth, *Serious Crime, Human Rights and Criminal Procedure* (London, Sweet & Maxwell, 2002).

[10] *Van der Leer v Netherlands* A.170 (1990), above ch 4 n 15.

[11] *Winterwerp v Netherlands* A.33 (1979), above ch 4 n 30.

[12] *Berlinski v Poland* (20 June 2002), above ch 5 n 68.

[13] I am indebted to my colleague Professor David Harris for drawing my attention to this literature.

between positive rights and negative rights based upon the former imposing positive duties and the latter negative duties.

> . . . [T]here are distinctions, but they are not distinctions between rights. The useful distinctions are among duties, and there are no one-to-one pairings between kinds of rights and kinds of duties. The complete fulfilment of each kind of right involves the performance of multiple kinds of duties. . . . I would like to tender a very simple tri-partite typology of duties. For all its own simplicity, it goes beyond the usual assumption that for every right there is a single correlative duty, and suggests instead that for every basic right-and many other rights as well—there are three types of duties, all of which must be performed if the basic right is to be fully honoured but not all of which must necessarily be performed by the same individuals or institutions. . . .
>
> So I want to suggest that with every basic right, three types of duties correlate:
>
> i. Duties to *avoid* depriving.
> ii. Duties to *protect* from deprivation.
> iii. Duties to *aid* the deprived.
>
> This may be easier to see in the case of the more familiar basic right, the right to phys-ical security (the right not to be tortured, executed, raped, assaulted, etc.). For every person's right to physical security, there are three correlative duties:
>
> I. Duties not to eliminate a person's security- duties to *avoid* depriving.
> II. Duties to protect people against deprivation of security by other people duties to *protect* from deprivation.
> III. Duties to provide for the security of those unable to provide for their own duties to *aid* the deprived. . . .
>
> If this suggestion is correct, the common notion that *rights* can be divided into rights to forbearance (so-called negative rights), as if some rights have correlative duties only to avoid depriving, and rights to aid (so-called positive rights), as if some rights have correlative duties only to aid, is thoroughly misguided. This misdirected simplification is virtually ubiquitous amongst contemporary North American theorists and is, I think, all the more pernicious for the degree of unquestioning acceptance it has now attained. It is duties, not rights, that can be divided amongst avoidance and aid, and protection. **And—this is what matters—every basic right entails duties of all three types.** [emphasis added] . . .
>
> It is impossible for any basic right—however 'negative' it has come to seem to be fully guaranteed unless all three types of duties are fulfilled. The very most 'nega-tive'—seeming right to liberty, for example, requires positive action by society to protect it and positive action by society to restore it when avoidance and protection both fail.[14]

Subsequently Professor Shue has endorsed the reclassification of the duty 'to avoid depriving' persons of their basic rights as the duty to 'respect' those rights.

> To 'respect' someone's right is precisely to take some trouble to see to it that one does not deprive the person of what he or she has a right to. Hence the 'duty to respect' rights is an accurate, and certainly more elegant, name for what I called the duty

---

[14] H Shue, *Basic Rights: Subsistence, Affluence, and US Foreign Policy,* (Princeton, NJ, Princeton University Press, 1980) reprinted in Second Edition (1996) 52–53.

to avoid deprivation; I am quite content, then, with the trio of respect, protect, and aid.[15]

In the second edition of his book Professor Shue repeated his original contention that all basic rights involve both negative and positive duties.

> . . . [W]hile some duties are at the negative end of the spectrum and others are at the positive (and many are in between), no right can, if one looks at social reality, be secured by the fulfilment of only one duty, or only one kind of duty. If one looks concretely at specific rights and the particular arrangements that it takes to defend or fulfil them, it always turns out in concrete cases to involve a mixed bag of actions and omissions . . . what one cannot find in practice is a right that is fully honoured, or merely even adequately protected, only by negative duties or only by positive duties. It is impossible, therefore, meaningfully and exhaustively to split all rights into two kinds based upon the nature of their implementing duties, because the duties are always a mixture of positive and negative ones.[16]

However, he warned against becoming obsessed with seeking to define conceptually the precise number of different classes of duties embodied in basic rights.

> Thus there is no ultimate significant question of the form, how many kinds of duties are involved in honouring rights? Three? Four? A dozen? Waldron[17] is closer to the mark in saying 'successive waves of duty' How many waves? Lots- more sometimes than others.
>   The 'very simple tripartite of duties,' then, was not supposed to become a new frozen abstraction to occupy the same rigid conceptual space previously held by 'negative rights' and 'positive rights.' The critical point was: do not let any theorist tell you that the concrete reality of rights enforcement is so simple that all the implementation of any right can usefully be summed up as either positive or negative. The constructive point was: look at what it actually takes to enable people to be secure against the standard, predictable threats to their rights- focus on the duties required to implement the right.[18]

From the above philosophical analysis of Professor Shue we learn that basic rights, as guaranteed in the Convention, require those subject to their corresponding duties to undertake a number of different types of obligations. Whilst the specific balance between negative and positive obligations will vary according to the particular right at issue, all basic rights involve some positive obligations. Hence as member states are the principal duty bearers under the Convention it is logically inevitable that they will be under correlative positive obligations. Consequently, even apparently 'negative rights', such as the prohibition of torture contained in Article 3, have been found in our study of the Court's jurisprudence to embody significant positive obligations (*e.g.* to take

---

[15] H Shue, 'The Interdependence of Duties' in P Alston and K Tomasevski (eds) *The Right to Food* (Dordrecht, Martinus Nijhoff, 1984) 84–85.

[16] H Shue, *Basic Rights,* 2nd edn (Princeton, NJ, Princeton University Press, 1996), "Afterword" 155.

[17] J Waldron, *Liberal Rights: Collected Papers, 1981–1991* (Cambridge, CUP, 1993).

[18] Above n 16 p 160.

vulnerable children into public care to protect them from abuse by their parents,[19] a duty clearly falling within Shue's second category of protection). Furthermore, Shue's analysis of rights and duties explains why we have discovered positive obligations within Articles that confer rights (*e.g.* Article 2, the right to life, which requires *inter alia*, the deployment of police/security officers to protect individuals from real and immediate threats to their lives posed by others),[20] prohibit specified forms of behaviour (*e.g.* Article 3, prohibition of torture, inhuman or degrading treatment/punishment)[21] and confer freedoms (*e.g.* Article 11, freedom of peaceful assembly and freedom of association, which obliges states *inter alia* to protect the rights of trade union members to use their unions to represent them).[22]

Thus, the Convention's positive obligations can be explained theoretically by Shue's analysis of the forms of duties arising under basic rights. And, from a more pragmatic stance, they can be justified through a combination of express requirements laid down by the text of the Convention together with the creation of implied obligations where the needs of individuals and/or the Court require affirmative action by states to guarantee the effectiveness of Convention rights.

Our detailed examination, in Chapters Two to Eight, of the key positive obligations developed by the Court under the major substantive Articles will hopefully constitute a useful (but inevitably partial) response to the calls of both Professor Shue and Professors Steiner/Alston[23] for others to concentrate upon elaborating the duties embodied in basic human rights. Within those chapters we can discern some broad groupings of positive obligations that have been recognised across a number of different Articles. One of the most prevalent types of positive obligation is the duty upon states to take reasonable measures to protect individuals from infringement of their Convention rights by other private persons. At its most basic level this positive obligation may be satisfied by the respondent state having adequate domestic legal provisions criminalizing the conduct which threatens another's Convention rights. We have, nevertheless, encountered several cases where states have been found to have breached this duty. These include the failure of English law to protect a child against severe physical punishment administered by a stepfather (thereby breaching Article 3)[24] and the absence of appropriate provisions in Dutch criminal law to safeguard a mentally handicapped young person from serious sexual abuse by an adult (resulting in a breach of Article 8).[25] A more onerous form of this positive obligation demands that states deploy personnel to provide physical measures of security for potential victims known to be facing immediate threats of violence. Breaches of this duty have occurred under Article 2 (*e.g.* where no

---

[19] As required in *Z v UK* (10 May 2001), above ch 3 n 2.
[20] As in *Mahmut Kaya v Turkey* (28 March 2000), above ch 2 n 13.
[21] For example, as in above n 19.
[22] See *Wilson v UK* (2 July 2002), above ch 7 n 34.
[23] Above ch 1 n 23.
[24] *A v UK* 1998-VI, above ch 3 n 1.
[25] *X & Y v Netherlands*, above n 3.

protection was given to a trade union activist who had informed the authorities that he had received threatening phone calls)[26] and Article 10 (where the authorities had received repeated requests for protection from journalists/publishers of a newspaper that had been subject to numerous violent attacks).[27]

Another broad collection of positive obligations is concerned with the manner in which states treat persons detained under the authority of their criminal justice systems. Failure to provide adequate medical treatment to such detainees can breach both Article 2[28] and Article 3.[29] Also, holding detainees in poor conditions (*e.g.* where there is gross overcrowding and/or insanitary conditions) will violate Article 3.[30] As we have already noted earlier in this chapter,[31] under Article 5 there are a number of express positive obligations owed to detainees. These duties have also been supplemented by the vital implied positive obligations upon states to account for detainees and take effective measures to safeguard against their disappearance whilst in custody.[32] Many of the above positive obligations have the common feature that they are designed to protect detainees from abuse of their Convention rights by public officials (*e.g.* police officers should not be dilatory in seeking appropriate medical care for seriously injured detainees[33] and detainees suspected of having committed criminal offences should be brought promptly before a judge in order to determine the legality of their detention).[34]

The groups of positive obligations concerned with protecting persons from violations of their Convention rights by others and the treatment of detainees can both be classified as falling within Professor Shue's general duty to protect. They also contribute to the basic protective role of states identified by several writers considered in Chapter One.[35]

Another significant group of positive obligations is concerned with the duty upon states to conduct effective investigations into credible claims that serious violations of Convention rights have occurred. As we have found, the Court has developed an extensive body of case law elaborating when such investigations must take place and the requirements of these inquiries. The most comprehensive jurisprudence concerns Article 2 and requires effective investigations where states know of killings[36] or where they receive an arguable claim that a detainee has disappeared in life-threatening circumstances.[37] Key institutional and procedural features of effective investigations have been articulated by the Court;

---

[26] *Akkoc v Turkey* (10 October 2000), above ch 2 n 17.
[27] *Ozgur Gundem* above n 4.
[28] For example, *Anguelova v Bulgaria* (13 June 2002), above ch 2 n 29.
[29] For example, *Keenan v UK* (3 April 2001), above ch 3 n 28.
[30] For example, *Kalashnikov v Russia* (15 July 2002), above ch 3 n 17.
[31] Above n 9.
[32] See *Kurt v Turkey* 1998-III 1187, above ch 4 n 1.
[33] For example, as occurred in *Anguelova* above n 28.
[34] See *Brogan v UK* A.145-B (1988), above ch 4 n 19.
[35] Clapham *et al* see ch 1 n 31.
[36] See *Ergi v Turkey* 1998-IV, above ch 2 n 39.
[37] See *Cyprus v Turkey* (10 May 2001), above ch 2 n 40.

including the independence of the investigators, the capacity of the investigation to identify those responsible for unlawful killings, the need for promptness in the conduct of the investigation and public scrutiny of the investigation.[38] The duty to conduct investigations under Article 3 is more circumscribed and arises when there is an arguable claim that a person has been seriously ill-treated by state agents.[39] Furthermore, the Court has not been entirely consistent in applying this obligation.[40] The Court needs to address this problem and adopt a policy of requiring effective investigations under Article 3 when states have received credible complaints that persons have been subject to ill-treatment (violating the substantive prohibitions of Article 3) by state agents. The danger that state agents might be tempted to ill-treat individuals is not insignificant in many member states, as the case law on Article 3 unfortunately demonstrates,[41] consequently a robust application of the effective investigation duty will provide additional discouragement for this form of abuse. Requiring such investigations under Article 3, rather than under Article 13, will reflect the seriousness with which the Court characterises this type of ill-treatment. The Court has developed a separate positive obligation under Article 5 requiring states to conduct effective investigations where they have been presented with an arguable claim that a person in custody has disappeared.[42] The remaining investigation obligations arise under Article 13. We have seen how these duties have considerable overlap with the analogous investigation obligations under the substantive Articles.[43] The decisive issue for the Court appears to be whether the absence of an effective investigation has undermined the adequacy of other domestic remedies—where this has occurred a breach of Article 13 will also be found.[44]

The above obligations of investigation can be characterised as forms of the duty of aid described by Professor Shue. This is because the complainants allege that they, or members of their families, have suffered serious violations of Convention rights (such as being killed, tortured or disappeared from custody) and there have been no effective investigations designed to secure redress for violations that are found to have occurred (*e.g.* by facilitating the prosecution of those guilty of murder and the paying of compensation where the government is liable for the actions/omissions of its agents).

From our examination of the jurisprudence it is possible to identify a number of eras in the Court's development of positive obligations. The earliest case law regarding these obligations was generally concerned with interpreting and applying express positive obligations. Examples include the institutional and procedural requirements of the obligation to provide detainees with access to speedy judicial proceedings to determine the lawfulness of their detention

---

[38] See *Kelly v UK* (4 May 2001), above ch 2 n 48.
[39] See *Assenov v Bulgaria* 1998-VIII, above ch 3 n 33.
[40] See *Ilhan v Turkey* (27 June 2000), above ch 3 n 39.
[41] For example, *Selmouni v France* 1999-V 149.
[42] See *Akdeniz v Turkey* (31 May 2001), above ch 4 n 14.
[43] See the section 'Obligations of Effective Investigations' above ch 8.
[44] See *Ergi v Turkey* 1998-IV, above ch 8 n 30.

(Article 5(4)),[45] the nature of the duty to provide free interpretation assistance for defendants facing criminal charges (Article 6(3)(e))[46] and the substance of the obligation to provide free legal assistance for impecunious defendants facing criminal charges (Article 6(3)(c)).[47] It is understandable that complainants would initially focus upon those positive obligations which are overtly included in the text of the Convention.

The next significant phase began in the late 1970s and continued until the early 1990s. During this period the Court elaborated a diverse range of positive obligations derived from the requirement of 'respect' found in Article 8(1). These obligations extended from the duty to provide legal recognition of the family relationship between parent(s) and illegitimate children[48] to the obligation to protect persons' homes and family lives from serious environmental pollution.[49] Once the Court had determined that the notion of 'respect' contained positive elements,[50] the breadth of the rights protected by Article 8 (private and family life, home and correspondence) ensured that complainants could assert related positive obligations in many different contexts.

The final era in the original Court's development of positive obligations began in the mid 1990s and ended when the Court was dissolved (October 1998). During this time the Court rapidly articulated several key positive obligations under Article 2, including the duty to undertake effective investigations into killings[51] and the obligation to provide protection to persons whose lives are known to be at immediate risk from the criminal acts of others.[52] By the end of this period analogous investigation obligations had been developed under Articles 3[53] and 5.[54] The burgeoning case load of complainants alleging significant violations of fundamental Convention rights (including the right to life, prohibition of torture and the right to liberty) by the Turkish security forces provided the jurisprudential context in which a number of these positive obligations were developed.

The full-time Court has expanded the situations in which positive obligations developed by its predecessor must be undertaken and elaborated the measures that states are required to take in respect of many of these obligations. For example, under Article 2, the contemporary Court has refined the fundamental components of effective investigations.[55] It has also found breaches of the pro-

---

[45] See *De Wilde v Belgium* A.12 (1971), above ch 4 n 29 and *Winterwerp v Netherlands* A.33 (1979), above n 11.

[46] See *Luedicke v Germany* A.29 (1978), above ch 5 n 74.

[47] See *Artico v Italy* A.37 (1980), ch 5 n 57.

[48] For example, *Marckx v Belgium* A.31 (1979), above ch 6 n 36.

[49] For example, *Powell & Rayner v UK* A.172 (1990), above ch 6 n 96.

[50] Above n 48.

[51] First stated in *McCann v UK* A.324 (1995), above ch 2 n 37.

[52] See *Osman v UK* 1998-VIII, above ch 2 n 12.

[53] See *Assenov v Bulgaria* above n 39.

[54] See *Kurt v Turkey* 1998-III, above ch 4 n 8.

[55] See *Kelly* above n 38.

tective policing obligation[56] and broadened its ambit to encompass the public authorities having responsibilities for a prisoner's welfare.[57] Failures to provide adequate medical care for seriously injured detainees have been found to violate the nascent obligation to supply medical services.[58] Under Article 3, the obligation to protect vulnerable persons has been enhanced to mandate the deployment of state officials, such as social workers,[59] in addition to the basic duty of ensuring that domestic law contains adequate protection for such persons. The full-time Court has become increasingly willing to find that poor conditions of detention violate Article 3,[60] as does the failure to provide appropriate medical care for detainees.[61] Legal recognition of post-operative transsexuals' new gender must now be accorded by states in order the satisfy the positive obligation to respect such persons' private lives under Article 8.[62]

In addition to furthering the evolution of existing positive obligation the full-time Court has also created several important new positive obligations. These include the duty upon states, under Article 10, to take operational measures (such as deploying police and/or military personnel) to protect media organisations and their employees/distributors from acts of violence intended to undermine the freedom of expression of the targeted organisation/persons;[63] the obligation upon states, derived from Article 13, to provide an effective domestic remedial mechanism for dealing with arguable complaints that persons have been subject to unreasonable delays by the national courts in the determination of their civil rights/obligations or criminal charges against them[64] and the duty upon states to avoid discriminating against persons in the enjoyment of their Convention rights (prohibited by Article 14) by ensuring that they treat persons differently when they are in diverse circumstances.[65] These emerging positive obligations demonstrate that the full-time Court is continuing its predecessor's practice of developing the spectrum of such obligations according to the legitimate needs of both complainants and itself assessed against the background of contemporary European societies. In other words, this is an aspect of the dynamic interpretation of the Convention identified by Professor Feldman.[66]

Our study has revealed the growing importance of positive obligations in the jurisprudence of the Court. This protean element of the case law is to be welcomed as member states in the Twenty-First Century should be expected to undertake positive measures to safeguard and enhance the basic rights

[56] For example in *Mahmut Kaya* above n 20.
[57] See *Edwards v UK* (14 March 2002), above ch 2 n 20.
[58] For example in *Anguelova* above n 28.
[59] See *Z* above n 19.
[60] For example in *Dougoz v Greece* (6 March 2001), above ch 3 n 11.
[61] For example in *Keenan* above n 29.
[62] See *Christine Goodwin v UK* (11 July 2002), above ch 6 n 15.
[63] See *Ozgur Gundem* above n 4.
[64] See *Kudla* above n 8.
[65] See *Thlimmenos v Greece* (6 April 2000), above ch 7 n 41.
[66] Above ch 1 n 47.

embodied in the Convention. It is not sufficient for states to simply abstain from interfering with those rights. Of course, there are financial costs incurred by states in complying with their positive obligations, for example the £19 million expenditure on sound insulation for 16,000 homes near Heathrow airport designed to reduce the worst effects of noise pollution from aircraft which enabled the British authorities to demonstrate that they had complied (in the 1980s) with their Convention duties to respect residents' family lives and homes.[67] As economic prosperity, hopefully, increases in member states, especially for the newer members (the planned admission to the European Union in 2004 of Cyprus, the Czech Republic, Estonia, Hungary, Latvia, Lithuania, Malta, Poland, the Slovak Republic and Slovenia[68] can be expected to provide significant impetus to the further economic development of these states), the Court should feel less inhibited in expanding the current outer limits of positive obligations. Those obligations awaiting maturation include the provision of health care services (under Article 2),[69] the provision of legal aid for civil proceedings (under Article 6(1)),[70] the provision of social and recreational facilities for disabled persons (under Article 8(1)),[71] the provision of housing for those unable to secure their own accommodation (under Article 8(1)),[72] facilitating the maintenance of traditional lifestyles by minorities (under Article 8(1))[73] and the provision/dissemination of information by public authorities (under Articles 8(1) and 10(1)).[74]

Although, as we have discussed in the earlier Chapters and above, the Court still has work to do in refining existing positive obligations and nurturing inchoate ones we must not underestimate the practical benefits for the 800 million persons living under the protective jurisdiction of the Convention that have been achieved by the Court's creative approach to these obligations.[75] Also, from a jurisprudential perspective, the Court's case law regarding positive obligations[76] has contributed to the partial erosion of the generational gap

---

[67] See *Powell & Rayner* above n 49.

[68] Agreed at the European Union's Copenhagen summit in December 2002. Accession negotiations are continuing with Romania and Bulgaria. Turkey applied for membership in 1987 but formal negotiations will not begin until at least 2005, pending, inter alia, improvements in the human rights record of the Turkish authorities Croatia formally applied for membership in February 2003. Further details on the enlargement of the European Union can be found at: http://europa.eu.int/comm/enlargement

[69] See *Cyprus v Turkey* (10 May 2001), above ch 2 n 32.

[70] See *McVicar v UK* (7 May 2002), above ch 5 n 9.

[71] See *Botta v Italy* 1998-I 412, above ch 6 n 29.

[72] See *Marzari v Italy* (4 May 1999), above ch 6 n 35.

[73] See *Chapman v UK* (18 January 2001), above ch 6 n 86.

[74] See *Guerra v Italy* 1998-I 210, above ch 7 n 12.

[75] Extending from recognising the right of persons detained under mental health powers to be informed promptly of the reasons for their detention (see *Van der Leer* above n 10) to requiring states to create effective mechanisms for determining paternity disputes (see *Mikulic v Croatia* (7 February 2002), above ch 6 n 27).

[76] For example, by obliging states to protect persons' homes from serious environmental pollution, above n 49.

between Convention rights and later generations of international human rights.[77] These are estimable achievements.

[77] As we already observed in *Airey v Ireland* A.32 (1979), above ch 5 n 4, the Court stated that:

Whilst the Convention sets forth what are essentially civil and political rights, many of them have implications of a social or economic nature. The Court therefore considers, like the Commission, that the mere fact that an interpretation of the Convention may extend into the sphere of social and economic rights should not be a decisive factor against such an interpretation; there is no water-tight division separating that sphere from the field covered by the Convention. (para 26).

Index